Locked Doors

Locked Doors

The Seizure of Jewish Property in Arab Countries

ITAMAR LEVIN

Translated by Rachel Neiman

Foreword by
Abraham Hirchson and Israel Singer

Westport, Connecticut
London

Library of Congress Cataloging-in-Publication Data

Levin, Itamar.
    Locked doors : the seizure of Jewish property in Arab countries / Itamar Levin ;
    translated by Rachel Neiman   ;   foreword by Abraham Hirchson and Israel Singer.
        p. cm.
    Includes bibliographical references and index.
    ISBN 0–275–97134–1 (alk. paper)
        1. Jewish property—Arab countries—History—20th century.   2. Arab-Israeli conflict—
    Confiscations and Contributions—History—20th century.   I. Title.
    DS135.A68L48   2001
    323.1'1924056'09045—dc21   00–052458

British Library Cataloguing in Publication Data is available.

Library of Congress Catalog Card Number: 00–052458
ISBN: 0–275–97134–1

First published in 2001

Praeger Publishers, 88 Post Road West, Westport, CT 06881
An imprint of Greenwood Publishing Group, Inc.
www.praeger.com

Printed in the United States of America

The paper used in this book complies with the
Permanent Paper Standard issued by the National
Information Standards Organization (Z39.48–1984).

10 9 8 7 6 5 4 3 2 1

And Esther obtained favour in the sight
of all those who looked upon her.
(Esther 2,15)

In loving memory of my mother,
Esther Levin

Contents

Foreword

A sad-eyed girl peers out at us from the center of a photograph, preserved in the Central Zionist Archives in Jerusalem. In her hand, she carries a large suitcase tied with rope. Her expression is one of fright and pain. Only moments earlier, this anonymous child disembarked a ship in the port city of Piraeus with her family. This was no pleasure cruise, however, but a cruel, traumatic expulsion from their home in Egypt. The child's only crime was that she was born Jewish.

Only a few years earlier, six million people paid the heaviest price imaginable for the same crime—that of being Jewish. A mere decade had passed since the world learned of the horrors of Auschwitz and Treblinka, and now the Jewish communities of the Arab world were being cut down. The Jews were ousted from their workplaces, banished from their homes, and stripped of their clothes. In many cases, these incidents were reminiscent of the persecution and suffering experienced in Europe under the Nazis.

But there was one significant difference between the Jewish Holocaust in Europe and the tragedy of Middle East Jewry: the State of Israel. When the Jews of Iraq, Egypt and Syria could no longer continue to live in the lands of their birth, their Israeli brothers welcomed them with open arms. There were enormous problems of absorption and acclimatization, and many mistakes were made, but their lives were saved. In time, they and their sons became leading Israeli citizens.

Although fifty years have passed, those who were wounded spiritually and materially have yet to heal. The Middle East tragedy was not limited to one people, as suffering knows no boundaries. But as the long-awaited peace between Israel and its neighbors draws near, so does the need increase for the public agenda to include the understandable and indisputable demand for compensation of purloined Jewish property, partial and late though it may be.

In this book, Itamar Levin, the pioneering investigator of the Holocaust victims' property affair, turns his efforts to the equally righteous battle for the return of property belonging to Jews from the Arab world. In precise detail, Levin presents the pageant of torture, robbery, and murder that befell two generations of our brethren. Reading these pages, we suffer along with them, but the pain also strengthens our resolve to right the injustices done.

Thanks to this book, the information is now available and cannot be ignored. The Knesset Parliamentary Inquiry Committee for the Location and Restitution of Assets of Holocaust Victims and the World Jewish Congress will not allow this account to remain open. Recognizing the sins of the past, and atoning for them in the present, are steps that must be taken on the way to reconciliation and peace.

Abraham Hirchson, MK
Chairman, Parliamentary Inquiry Committee for the Location and
Restitution of Property of Holocaust Victims
President, "March of the Living" Project

Dr. Israel Singer
Secretary General of the World Jewish Congress
Chairman, World Jewish Restitution Organization

Abraham Hirchson

Israel Singer (photograph by Ariel Jerosolimsky)

Introduction

Over the past fifty years, hundreds of thousands of Jews have emigrated from Arab countries. Today, what remains in these countries are but pitiful remnants of once magnificent Jewish communities that still flourished even one or two generations ago. If these immigrants have a common legacy, it is the loss of income, property, and savings. A Jew emigrating legally from Iraq in 1950, a Jew expelled from Egypt in 1957, and a Jew escaping Syria in 1991—all tell similar stories of leaving behind houses, furniture, books, Judaica, clothes, and businesses. The images in photographs also repeat themselves: frightened, exhausted families disembarking from ships or planes, each family member holding, at most, a single suitcase.

The overwhelming majority came to Israel. Since the establishment of the State, 600,000 out of 800,000 Jews leaving Arab countries entered Israel as new immigrants. For many years in its early years, a good number of them were forced to live in almost inhumane conditions due to the dire economic straits the new State found itself in. At best, the roof over their heads was made of tin; at worst it was a canvas tent. The sun beat down in summer, while in winter, rain flooded their beds. If they found a source of income, it was hard physical labor to which they were unused. Their suffering gave rise to the feelings of resentment, which in turn resulted in the difficult social problems that still hinder Israeli society today.

A significant part—perhaps even all—of these problems could have been prevented had these new immigrants been able to bring their property with them. Let there be no misunderstanding: As in every society, the social structure of the Jewish communities in Arab countries was a pyramid, with the lower classes at the base and a small moneyed elite at the top. But to the newly established State of Israel, where 600,000 residents had to absorb an equal number of new immigrants within a few short years, every Egyptian piastre, Iraqi dinar, and Syrian pound was important. Nevertheless, the Arab states prevented these Jewish emigrants from taking that which was right-fully theirs.

The Arab states' policy toward the Jews was influenced by two factors: anti-Semitism and pragmatism. Noted Middle Eastern scholar Professor Bernard Lewis devotes his book, *Semites and Anti-Semites*,[1] to dispelling the notion of Arab anti-Semitism, as if Arabs are not and cannot be anti-Semites because they themselves are Semites. But the word *anti-Semite* has one single, special meaning: one who hates Jews because they are Jews, justifying this hatred on a so-called objective level, even on a so-called scientific level. Over several decades, we have witnessed the Arab countries carry out some of the world's most horrific forms of anti-Semitism: Holocaust denial, dissemination of "The Protocols of the Elders of Zion," and publication of cartoons perfectly suited to the Nazi press. These actions should not be mistaken for anti-Zionism or for being anti-Israel. The fact is that, in present-day Egypt, over two decades after the signing of a peace treaty with Israel, one can purchase anti-Semitic literature freely, and the press depicts Zionism as a continuation of Nazism. The social and economic persecution of the Jews on the part of the Arab states, as the following pages will show, are very reminiscent of Nazi actions toward the Jews during the Holocaust, with the exception, of course, of systematic slaughter.

The Arab states' pragmatic approach toward the Jews in their midst, unlike their anti-Semitism, is indeed tied to the Arab-Israeli conflict. Various governments in various Arab countries have persecuted the Jews since the UN Partition Plan was announced in November 1947. In general, persecution escalated in a direct correlation to border tensions between a particular Arab country and Israel. Defeat in a war against Israel almost always meant a rise in anti-Jewish sentiment, while restrictions on emigration in general, and to Israel in particular, were perceived as a way of stemming Israel's population growth.

Why then, in the end, have all the Arab states allowed their Jewish citizens to emigrate? In some cases, a government decided that the damage incurred by emigration was less than that inflicted by a minority whose loyalty was ever-waning. In other instances, the Arab countries gave in to pressure from the international community. There were cases in which Jewish expulsion was a by-product of developments unrelated to Israel. And there were those cases in which the Arab leaders were convinced that a wave of mass immigration would serve to weaken Israel, as it lacked the resources to absorb new residents in such large numbers.

All these events and circumstances have one thing in common: The Jews were permitted to take with them not much more than a few dollars in cash, some personal effects, and a little jewelry. These elements, therefore, converged: Anti-Semitism was a motivating force in preventing the Jews from emigrating; this was coupled with the desire to stop Israel from benefiting from the new immigrants' property. At the same time, the Arab leaders themselves wanted the benefit, either personal or public, of the Jewish property left behind.

No objective outsider would deny that these acts constitute a violation of the most basic human legal right, which determines that a person is entitled to keep the fruits of his or her legally earned labor. Can the Arab states claim that they, too, have acted according to law in seizing or confiscating property belonging to their citizens, a right known and recognized by international law? This contention is unacceptable. An opinion, handed down recently in a lawsuit currently pending in the New York courts regarding the property of an Egyptian-Jewish family, stated unequivocally that the treatment of Jews in that country was categorized as persecution on racial and religious grounds and, thus, forbidden by international law.[2] In Syria and Iraq—two other countries this book will deal with at length—the measures taken to confiscate property were far more extreme, leaving no doubt as to their illegality. In 1987, former U.S. Supreme Court justice Arthur Goldberg reached a similar conclusion in an opinion in which he wrote that the measures taken regarding Jewish property in Arab countries were, without exception, violating international law.[3]

Another possible claim is that actions taken by the Arab countries against the Jews in general, and their property in particular, were nothing more than a means of taking compensation for Israel's acts against the Palestinians, specifically confiscation of Palestinian property and transfer of ownership to the State of Israel. But historical fact refutes this claim for the simple reason that the Arab states threatened to expel the Jews well before a single Arab refugee ever left Palestine.[4] Moreover, the Palestinian refugee problem was created mainly by circumstances surrounding Israel's wars; Israel's Jewish leaders generally requested that Arab citizens remain in their homes. By contrast, the Jews in Arab lands were forced to emigrate due to systematic persecution, and in some cases they were simply expelled from the lands of their birth. And so, we are left with no legal, moral, or historical justification, only hatred, on one hand, and the desire for political or material gain on the other. These are the only reasons the Arab countries had for persecuting their Jews, expelling them, and stealing all that they owned.

The timing of this book is no accident. At the time this is being written, in April 2001, there is a good probability that the Palestinian authority, as they resume within the framework of negotiations with Israel for a permanent settlement, will demand compensation for properties confiscated from Palestinian refugees. This book presents decision makers and public opinion shapers with information on Israel's counterdemands, as regards property belonging to Jews from the Arab states. As early as 1951, Israel stated that at such time when Palestinian claims were discussed, it would demand parallel talks regarding Jewish claims. This statement has never been retracted. This book is intended as a basis for discussion on the question of whether to maintain the aforementioned policy and, if so, which claims deserve to be put forth.

I would like to stress two important points. The first is that this book does not deal with Palestinian refugee property issues for the simple reason that its sole subject is the fate of Jewish property. And second, this book does not express an opinion as to what the State of Israel's policy should be; it would be arrogant of me to make suggestions. That does not mean I will not express my opinion. Quite the contrary. Regarding the central question, my opinion is clear and unequivocal: The Arab countries stole Jewish property, cruelly, illegally, and unjustifiably. I do not pretend to be objective on this issue, and whoever takes this as a point against me, well, that is their right.

This book deals with only four of the Arab states: Iraq, Egypt, Syria, and Lebanon. My choice was the result of two considerations. First, these are (or were, in the case of Egypt) Israel's major opponents, but enemies with whom there exists the possibility of negotiation, including negotiating the fate of confiscated Jewish property. Second, these countries once had great Jewish communities, some very established and wealthy; many were forced to leave their homes against their will and were unable to take their property with them. The Jewish communities of North Africa, by comparison, left in an organized fashion and were able to take their property out unrestricted.

Research and writing of this book began as part of my work at Israel's daily financial newspaper *Globes*, where, for the past several years, I have dealt with the fate of property belonging to victims of the Holocaust. For giving me the opportunity to deal with the theft of Jewish property in the Arab world, I must thank *Globes* editor-in-chief Haggai Golan, *Kessef* weekly supplement editors Zvika Zoref and Amir Ziv, and *Globes This Week* editor Ronit Shave. *Globes* staff writer Dalia Tal extended a helping hand in interviewing a series of Jewish immigrants and, in doing so, contributed significantly to the human aspect of this story. Additional assistance came from my colleagues Ran Dagoni in Washington and Amira Liss in London, along with Egyptian journalist Samir Raafat. Special thanks are due to all those who gave willingly of their time in order to share their stories and the information at their disposal. Some have asked to remain anonymous, primarily for reasons of personal safety, and those requests have, of course, been honored.

The staffs of five archives assisted me in locating the documents and photographs that are the foundation for this book. I would like to thank Gilad Livneh, Ronit Cohen, and Galia Bar-On at the Israel State Archives in Jerusalem; Batya Leshem and Reuven Koffler at the Central Zionist Archives in Jerusalem; Sarah Kadosh at the Joint Distribution Committee Archive; the staff of IDF soldiers and archivists at the Hagana Archives in Tel Aviv; and the staff at the Public Records Office in London. Without their professionalism and assistance, this research could not have been accomplished.

Rachel Neiman was not only an excellent and efficient translator, but a friend whose useful advice contributed greatly to this joint effort. Working again with the professional staff of Greenwood Publishing Group, especially with Jim Sabin and Betty Pessagno, was a pleasure as always.

My wife Irit and our sons Ariel and Aviad were, for a number of months, forced to settle for a weekend husband and father, as my evenings—after a full day's work—were devoted to writing this book. Not only did these three not complain, each one in his or her own way helped me with support, encouragement, or a smile. Without them, this project could not have been completed.

Chapter 1

"Precisely as in Nazi Germany"

The Jews of Iraq, from the Golden Age to Persecution, after the Establishment of the State of Israel

They were nights that the Jews of Baghdad would never forget. Whenever a car would pass by a Jewish home, most of the family inside would wake up in fright. Some fell to their knees, praying the car would not stop; stopping meant brutal searches, random arrests, torture, and even death. A year earlier, in 1969, nine Jews were hanged in downtown Baghdad, falsely accused of spying for Israel. The Jews of Baghdad did not dare weep in public, for fear it would implicate them. "We were traveling to the university, and the driver, who didn't know we were Jews, began telling us, with great pleasure, what a wonderful show it was. One of us started crying, but we slapped her to make her stop immediately. We were scared," relates one woman, who was a young student in Baghdad at that time.

In 1970, the daughter of one of Iraq's richest Jewish families fled the country. This family was so wealthy that, between 1928 and 1930, King Faisal rented their luxurious Baghdad house until construction of his palace was completed. Today, Sadaam Hussein's presidential compound stands on land that once belonged to that same Jewish family. But years of persecution, confiscation, and theft left the family almost penniless. The only thing they could do was write up a detailed claim for their house and properties, worth tens of millions of dollars, and file it with the government of Israel. And they are still afraid. "Don't even hint at our name," says one daughter, who has lived safely in Canada for thirty years. True, no family members remain in Iraq. True, the chances of receiving something in return for their vast wealth are slight. But the trauma of 1970 still exacts its price.[1]

FROM ABRAHAM THE PATRIARCH TO
THE BRITISH MANDATE

The Jewish community in Iraq is one of the world's oldest Diaspora communities. The roots of Judaism itself run deep in this land situated between the Tigris and Euphrates Rivers, all the way back to Abraham the Patriarch. The Jewish community was established after the fall of the First Temple, in 586 B.C.E., when King Nebuchadnezzar transferred all residents of Judaea to this land, then called Babylon. After the Roman total conquest of the Land of Israel, in the first and second centuries, Babylon became the primary spiritual center for the Jewish people, as evinced by the Babylonian Talmud, Judaism's most important tractate after the Bible.

Under Muslim rule, following the conquest of the region in the seventh century, Jews played major roles in trade and government, and reached high positions in the courts of the caliphs. At the same time, in accordance with Muslim law, they were required to pay special taxes, were restricted in business activities, and occasionally fell prey to anti-Jewish harassment. Over the centuries, regional control was transferred from the Muslims to the Persians, then to the Ottomans (who were based in Turkey), and the Jews became subject to the whims of the current ruler. Overall, Baghdad's Jewish community continued to be prosperous, dealing mainly in business, craftsmanship, and free trades.[2]

In the mid-nineteenth century, most Iraqi Jews dealt in trade, peddling, and light industry. After the Suez Canal opened, in November 1869, Iraq became a major trade center in the Middle East, with Jews playing an important role in international trade. They superseded the local Muslim and Christian traders; even the European traders who had settled in Iraq found it difficult to compete with the Jews. These developments improved conditions significantly for the Jews of Baghdad and Basra. On the other hand, conditions worsened for the Jews of Kurdistan and Mosul, who suffered as trade was rerouted from the Aleppo to the Suez route.[3]

Dr. Nissim Kazzaz cites sources mentioning Jewish control of Iraq's economy at the beginning of the twentieth century. For example, upon its founding in 1910, one-half the members of the Baghdad Chamber of Commerce steering committee were Jews. In his memoirs, Yehekzel al-Cabbir relates that, while there were successful Arab companies dealing in international trade, "generally, the broker, banker and even the buyer were Jews. The Arab merchant whose affairs were managed by Jews took pride in his staff."[4]

During the British Mandate period (1917–1932), conditions for Jews improved markedly. The British replaced the Turkish bureaucracy and its clerks first with Christians and then Jews, considered "the only progressive element in the country." Lacking any Muslim or Christian alternatives, the British placed more and more Jews in positions of power, including several government ministries. Yehezkel Sasson was minister of the Treasury for the first half of the 1920s; he enacted fiscal reform and scored several important successes in the battle over royalties against the Turkish Oil Company. David Samara was vice president of the High Court of Justice. Sallim Tarazi was named general manager of the Postal and Telegraph Authority. Moshe Shohat was accountant-general to the Postal Authority, Ezra Lewaya was assistant to the comptroller-general, and Ibrahim al-Cabbir was accountant-general to the Treasury; prior to independence, he headed the complicated process of creating Iraq's monetary system.

At the same time, the number of Jews in international trade continued to rise. They benefited from their knowledge of foreign languages, loyalty to the British, and close ties to relatives and friends outside Iraq. Many Jews profited from having obtained exclusive import rights to products supplied to the scores of British and Indian troops stationed in Iraq; these merchants naturally employed other Jews in their burgeoning businesses. As the Jewish educational system expanded, and the number of Jewish academics increased, so too did the number of Jews working in free trades. The number of Jews working in agriculture declined, due to an internal migration from country to city and emigration to the Land of Israel.[5]

THE FIRST YEARS OF INDEPENDENCE:
SEEDS OF DISASTER

Iraq gained its independence in 1932. Great Britain ceased control of internal affairs and instead maintained a military presence intended to preserve its strategic and economic strongholds, primarily airports and oilfields. The following nine years were witness to political instability, primarily on ethnic grounds. In 1933, the Iraqi military slaughtered the Assyrian minority in northern Iraq; in the southern and central regions there were occasional riots on the part of the large Shi'ite minority (most Iraqi Muslims are Sunni). King Faisal lost control of the situation. Things worsened considerably after his mentally unstable son Ghazi rose to power after his father's death in September 1933.

In April 1939, King Ghazi was killed in a car accident, and actual government control was transferred to State Regent Abd al-Ila'a, uncle of the boy-king Faisal II. Political unrest continued to rise, reaching its zenith against the backdrop of World War II and Great Britain's decline as a world power. Four colonels, known as the Golden Square, ruled the country from behind the scenes, while their political appointee, Rachid Ali al-Khilani, headed the government. Rachid Ali, an open admirer of Germany's Nazi government, resigned in 1941 but returned to power three months later during the Golden Square's military coup. He continued to rule as a political puppet but served only one month before being toppled by the British Army. He fled to Germany and served as a propagandist during the Nazi regime. From that point, and until the end of the war, Iraq sided with the Allied Forces under the leadership of a series of pro-British leaders headed by Nuri Sa'id, one of Iraq's outstanding political figures in the 1940s and 1950s.[6]

During the first years of Iraqi independence, the Jews' economic situation was even better than before, but the seeds of disaster for future decades were being sown as well. In years prior to the outbreak of World War II, over half of Iraq's importers and exporters were Jewish, holding 95% of import activity. Jews held only 10% of exports, which were controlled by British merchants. In the years before the war, of the 18 to 19 board members of the Baghdad Chamber of Commerce, between 9 and 11 were Jews. The number of Jewish chamber members was increasing each year. Also increasing were the number of prominent members who were Jews; this ranking was determined by volume of property ownership.

In 1938–1939, among Baghdad's twenty-five richest merchants, ten were Jews. These were members of the Ades family, who dealt in trade, automotive vehicles, and insurance; tea traders David and Shaul Rajwan; David Sasson of a British family of Iraqi origin dealing in trade and construction; the Eastern Bank that was owned by Jews; travel and shipping agent Haim Netanel; banker Abudi Kaduri Zilka; car dealers Kaduri and Ezra Meir Lawy; the French Jews controlling the Orozodi Bank trade company; tea traders, the Shemesh brothers; and money-changer Zion Shlomo Abudi. Shafiq Ades (whose tragic story will be told later on) was ranked the wealthiest merchant in Iraq's capital city that year.

But concurrent to this economic prosperity was a burgeoning hatred for successful, rich Jews. This sentiment already existed in the early 1920s, when Jews, having gained senior positions in the British colonial government, were perceived by the Muslims as poachers being granted privileges they did not rightfully deserve. With no other choice, the Muslim population was forced to accept the reality of an ever-increasing number of Jews working in public institutions, but along with this acceptance, Kazzaz emphasizes, were feelings of bitterness and envy. These emotions began to come out after independence and emerged full force during World War II.

The first action against Jews in the economy was due to the fact that, while many Muslim graduates of secondary school and higher education could not find work, the number of Jewish clerks continued to increase. In 1932, there were 800 Jews employed by the civil service, 800 employed as railway clerks, 100 employed by foreign-owned companies and 66 employed as bank clerks. In an attempt to lower unemployment levels artificially, Iraq's government inflated the civil service workforce, employing hundreds of unnecessary clerks. But the global economic crisis of 1930 hit Iraq as well, forcing the government both to lay off workers and cut the salaries of those remaining. Resentment within the ranks of the unemployed quickly gave rise to a wave of anti-Jewish sentiment.

At the same time, pro-Nazi propaganda in Iraq was on an upswing, spearheaded by Dr. Fritz Groba, Germany's consul general to Baghdad, who had been appointed to the post in October 1932, three months before Adolf Hitler came to power. Groba bought a daily paper, *al-Allem al-Arabi*, and began publishing an Arabic-language version of *Mein Kampf*.

The first practical expression of the rising tide of anti-Judaism and anti-Semitism came in September 1934, when dozens of Jewish government clerks working for the ministries of finance and transportation were fired. The order was given by government minister Arshad al-Amri, known as a virulent anti-Semite, who had been named to his post only two months earlier. The Jews reacted to the firings with a three-day general strike that crippled the economy; it ended only after al-Amri announced there would be no further lay-offs. The next step was taken in 1935, when the Ministry of Education limited, albeit unofficially, the number of Jews allowed to register for public high schools and other institutions of higher education.

In February 1936, around 300 Jewish government clerks were fired, mainly from senior positions. A few months later, it was determined that Jews in government would be promoted only by permission of the minister, and that hiring of new Jewish workers should be discouraged, as much as possible. Lurking in the background was overt incitement on the part of the Iraqi press, which called on all businessowners not to employ Jews. These cries went unanswered on a practical level, as most private businesses had no alternative but to employ Jews. The political opposition in those years also refrained from harming Jews in the private sector, knowing that measures against them meant damaging Iraq's economy.[7]

Despite economic measures against the Jews, the government continued to protect their way of life. Professor Moshe Gat notes that the nationalist movements operating in Iraq in the 1930s were a minority and that the government opposed their statements and actions. The Jewish community leadership, headed by Rabbi Sasson Kaduri, declared their opposition to Zionism, assuming that this move was enough to ensure the future of Iraq's Jewish community.

But in June 1941, the notion of Jewish coexistence in Iraqi society exploded. Decades later, Nezima Mu'allem-Cohen recalled: "All night long, we heard gunfire and shouting, all night long. It went quiet before dawn. That morning, my father went to the synagogue. He did not pray. When he got back, he told Mother what happened: Jewish houses were burned, daughters raped, homes looted. One synagogue was burned down. As Father was talking, they burst into our house, broke down the two doors, entered shouting, waving sticks; Father took us to the stairway leading to the roof. We started to climb, one after another, my mother after us, my father bringing up the rear. Suddenly, my mother heard a shot. She turned, and saw my father, dead. A policeman came. Mother started to cry, telling him,

'They killed my husband.' He said: 'How do you want to die?' and bashed her head in with his gun."[8]

This was Baghdad's Farhud, a pogrom in which 180 Jews were killed. It happened at a time when the city was leaderless; Rachid Ali had already fled, but the British forces had not yet entered. The Farhud was planned in advance; many of its executors were nationalist, pro-Nazi soldiers and officers who burned synagogues and desecrated Torah scrolls. According to official records, 240 Jews were wounded, 586 Jewish-owned businesses were looted, and 99 Jewish houses were destroyed. Unofficial sources put the figures at 700 wounded, with total property damages of $3 million.

Anzo Sirenni, who arrived in Baghdad in April 1942 as an emissary for the Mossad le-Aliya Bet (the prestate organization in charge of Jewish immigration to Palestine), reported in February 1943—almost two years after the Farhud—that, "The riots against the Jews left a severe impression. Those two days in June 1941 shattered [the Jews'] dreams of assimilation into the Arab world, and their heartfelt belief that there was a chance of living a normal life in the Iraqi Diaspora. Their desire to escape escalated. Had all avenues not been blocked, had one passageway opened, all the Jews of Iraq would have rushed through, even those who once believed and had, over the years, declared their loyalty to Iraq."

These feelings, however, diminished within a few years time, replaced again by the illusion that the Jews of Iraq could assimilate into the mainstream. Jewish community leaders did not see Zionism as a solution; they were still convinced that identification with the Zionist enterprise in the Land of Israel would serve only to heighten the threat to their community. In their opinion, the Farhud was the result of a unique set of circumstances; therefore, the community should be rehabilitated as quickly as possible, avoiding any measures that might interfere with the desired result. These leaders noted the fact that, with Abd al-Ila'a's return to power and the installation of a stable, pro-British government, order had been restored. The government established a committee to investigate the events and even offered compensation—mostly symbolic—of 20,000 dinars (one dinar was equal to one pound sterling).

Economic recovery was the main factor at work in repressing the events of the Farhud, Gat adds. After war was declared between Germany and the Soviet Union—a scant three weeks after the Farhud—the Allied presence in Iraq increased. Escalating military activity created a general prosperity that, in particular, benefited the Jews, who dominated foreign trade. At the same time, employment quotas were lifted and Jews could once again work in civil service. Jews became wealthy, moved to modern homes, and expanded their educational institutions. Only a few young Jews, understanding that the situation was temporary, became Zionist activists and set up an underground. In the years to come, this core group would save Iraqi Jewry.[9]

THE JEWS OF IRAQ AND THE ESTABLISHMENT OF THE STATE OF ISRAEL

On the eve of the establishment of the State of Israel, there were 130,000 Jews in Iraq, most dealing in trade, industry, craftsmanship, and services. An employment breakdown by Dr. Tikvah Darvish puts 36.3% in trade; industry and craftsmanship, 26.1%; services, 23.4%; transport and communications, 4.5%; finance and insurance, 3.8%; agriculture, 2.3%; construction, 2%; electricity and water, 1.3%; mining and quarrying, 0.3%. Of those employed in industry, 95% worked in light industry: food, tobacco, clothing and footwear, textiles, and jewelry. Outstanding in the service sector was the large number of Jewish government and municipal clerks (63.5% of all sector employees), with others in free trades and personal services (health, educational, cultural, and religious). Darvish estimates that, prior to mass immigration to the State of Israel, almost 60% of Jewish males were employed, as compared with 57% of non-Jews. Among women, the number of Jews in the workforce was 6%, as compared with 4% among non-Jews.[10]

An undated, unsigned memo from the period of struggle for Israel's Independence, preserved in the Hagannah Archives in Tel Aviv, records the Jews' share in the Iraqi economy. According to the memo, during World War II, the share of import held by Jews reached 80%, their share in export was 5%, and they held 10% of all government and Allied Force contracts submitted to local suppliers. Matters changed considerably after the war; the Jews' share in imports fell to 50%, in exports to 5%, and contracts to local suppliers also fell to 5%. Even if the document does not say so, this change should be viewed as part of Iraq's economic development, when Muslims entered these sectors in greater numbers. Overall economic growth may have enabled the Jews to maintain a relatively strong economic standing, even if, in terms of real numbers, their share in these sectors declined. With the establishment of the State of Israel in May 1948, however, Jews' share in exports dropped to 20%, in imports to 2%, and no government contracts were forthcoming. This situation was the result of intentional economic persecution, to be discussed later.[11]

During that same period, the U.S. Embassy in Baghdad estimated there were 135,000 Jewish residents of Baghdad. The Chambers of Commerce listed 2,430 companies, of which 826 (34%) were Jewish-owned. The Chamber's vice chairman and five out of sixteen board members were Jewish. The Embassy cites assessments, placing Jewish export ownership at 45%, as compared with 30% of Muslims, 15% foreign nationals and 10% Iraqi Christian. The Embassy also mentions the city's Jewish doctors, pharmacists, lawyers, and engineers, along with Jews employed in the civil service.[12] And what of the communities outside Baghdad? Employment figures for Jews in the southern city of Amara break down as follows: poor, unskilled, and continually unemployed, 5%; lower middle class (including peddlers selling foods, baked goods, and so forth), 15%; middle class (including vendors, craftsmen, industrialists, musicians, and entertainers), 60%; upper middle class (including free tradesmen, educators, clerks), 15%; 15% of Jews were wealthy, including traders, bankers, and money changers.

Among Amara's Jews were a few uniquely skilled professionals: an itinerant shoeshine man, a cheese seller, a cinema ticket vendor, a consultant to newlyweds, a faith healer, a *kebab* maker, a *henna* (or engagement) ceremony drummer, a healer using glass cups, a kindergarten escort, an seamstress specializing in gold thread embroidery, and a home remedy expert. These professions were passed down from generation to generation, family businesses that spanned the centuries. Among tailors, for example, it was traditional for fathers to go from village to village, selling their wares, while the rest of the family worked in production.[13]

At the other end of Iraq, in the city of Mosul, Jews were primarily traders, vendors, silver- and goldsmiths, money changers, shoemakers, peddlers, housepainters, clerks, and teachers. Here, too, professions were handed down from father to son, with entire families identified over generations with their professions. Many of Mosul's Jewish traders were wholesalers; others dealt in textiles, haberdashery, pharmaceuticals, and foodstuffs. Other Jews were peddlers, wandering among the regional villages and bedouin camps.

Among Mosul's important Jewish traders were the Akrawi family, who dealt in textiles; gold dealer Salman Hamou; livestock importer David Shalem, whose dealings extended to the Far East; and exporter Ya'akov Kafchun. Many other Jews were traders on a smaller scale; these included grocery and produce shops, candy stores, and even some who sold bootleg *arak* liquor.

The Jews of Mosul specialized in pharmaceuticals, spices, and perfumes, including home remedies for headache, skin conditions, and childhood diseases. Several became international traders, whose business extended to the Land of Israel and Europe; the head of the community, Suleiman Barazani, was a well-known pharmacist. Two other professions, essentially monopolized by Jews, were silver- and gold-smithing, and tailoring (women comprised an unusually large part of this profession). Another leading profession among the Jews of Mosul was shoe-making: cobbling new shoes, repairing worn shoes, sewing rubber boots for farmers, and shoe-shining. Some Jewish peddlers were also smugglers, a high-risk occupation that often cost them their lives. Other Jewish professions included house-painting, watch-making, photography, and processing the entrails of sheep and cows.

THE VALUE OF JEWISH PROPERTY IN IRAQ

What was the value of property belonging to Iraq's Jews on the eve of the establishment of the State of Israel? There are conflicting answers with a great many gaps in information. The reason for this is clear: All cases cite

First immigrants from Iraq to Israel, March 1950 (Central Zionist Archives)

estimates only, as no official census was ever taken. The closest thing to an official census is a registry of land belonging to the Jews of Baghdad, done in 1951 under the auspices of Mordechai Ben-Porat, the Mossad le-Aliya Bet emissary in Baghdad. The project was carried out by engineers Salim Khahtan and Naji Efraim Shashoua, and was submitted by Ben-Porat to Mossad le-Aliya Bet headquarters in Tel Aviv. Ben-Porat still keeps a copy of the report, which he refuses to make public "so as not to show our hand before the time is right," as he believes the information should be used in future negotiations over the repatriation of Iraq's Jews.[14] There has been one attempt at such negotiations, initiated in 1999 by the leaders of Great Britain's Iraqi-Jewish community; they appealed to the Embassy of Iraq in London, asking whether Iraq would be willing to negotiate compensation. Iraq answered in the positive, even saying it would be willing to host a British delegation. For reasons that are unclear, the initiative was not carried out.[15]

This being the case, the only thing left is to cite those disclosed sources containing numerical assessments. In September 1948, the Middle Eastern

Division of Israel's Ministry of Foreign Affairs submitted estimates placing the value of property belonging to Jews leaving Iraq at £10 million, of which £1 million belonged to Jews emigrating to Israel. Another memo, apparently issued in late 1948 or early 1949, set the total property value at £55 million.[16]

In October 1949, Minister of Minority Affairs Behor Shitrit assessed the value of Iraqi Jewish property as at least 156 million Israeli pounds (IL), according to the following breakdown: 15,000 families with an averaged capital of IL 2,000 each; 9,000 families with IL 750 each; 4,000 families with IL 7,500 each; 300 families with IL 75,000 each; 100 families with IL 150,000 each; and the fifty wealthiest families with IL 300,000 each; land value was set at IL 5 million and community property was valued at IL 2 million.[17]

The following month, two different estimates were made regarding the amount of Jewish property in Iraq. In an internal document, Israel's government set the property value between £50 and 150 million,[18] while a letter to the *New York Times* from Moshe Keren, of the Israeli Embassy in Washington D.C., claims that property values were $250 million, "the prize spurring on the government of Iraq, which is currently in very dire financial straits." Given the dollar-pound sterling rate of exchange at that time, it appears that Keren averaged out the range stated in the internal document; the figure he mentions equals £90 million. This figure may also rely on estimates made at that time by Iraqi Jewish community leader Yosef al-Cabbir who mentioned the £90 million figure. Also at that time, Ezra Danin of Israel's Ministry of Foreign Affairs claimed the figure was £60 million.[19]

In the early 1950s, at the height of immigration to Israel from Iraq, attempts were again made to estimate property values. An internal Mossad le-Aliya Bet memo from January 1951 sets property values between 150 and 200 million dinar, equal in value to the same sum in pounds sterling, or $450 and 600 million.[20] But a claim on property lost between November 1949 and August 1952, filed by 2,150 Iraqi immigrants to Israel, named a value of $35,814,576. It is difficult to extrapolate the total property value based on this sum, as only 6% of Iraq families emigrating to Israel filed such claims; the economic status of those who did not is also unclear.[21] Taking the declared property figure as a sample, however, it represents an overall value of $560 million in 1950's dollar terms, or more than $4 billion in present-day terms. Lacking any more accurate figures, this sample could be regarded as the most reliable information at our disposal, at present.

POLICIES OF REPRESSION AND OFFICIALLY SANCTIONED DISCRIMINATION

"Although the government did protect the lives of the Jews, at this stage it embarked on a policy of repression and discrimination against them." In this statement, Moshe Gat succinctly sums up Iraqi Jewish history from the

UN Partition Resolution in November 1947 and onward. In his book, Gat goes on to explain the opposing forces that determined Baghdad's policies, primarily an ever-worsening internal situation: deep economic crisis, rising inflation, drought and food shortages, and struggles between the nationalist and Communist factions as they campaigned for the upcoming elections of July 1948. The government feared that actions against the Jews would escalate into general antiestablishment violence; by the same token, it feared that overt protection of the Jews, at a time when their brothers were "stealing" Arab land in Israel, would arouse outrage within the nationalist parties.

"In general and in principle, the government was not interested in harming the Jews," Gat concludes. "It could be said that the existence of Jews on Iraqi soil became an internal problem as far as the government was concerned, a problem whose solution was not yet clear. At this time, the government should have adopted policies to prevent extremist groups from inciting anti-Jewish riots, on one hand, and on the other, protecting the lives of the Jewish community as a whole. The policy upon which the government did decide, on its own volition, was one of repression and regulated discrimination, all the while keeping a firm grasp on the reins of power."[22]

A Mossad le-Aliya Bet document from September 1948 describes in great detail the edicts placed on the Jews of Iraq following the UN Partition Resolution. Immediately after the UN resolution, Jews were forbidden to leave the country, barring extraordinary circumstances such as life-threatening illness. Even then, they were allowed to exit only after making a security deposit (initially 2,000 dinar, then 3,000 dinar), "which did not include the bribes required by various clerks in different departments." After the State of Israel was declared, on May 14, 1948, Jews were forbidden entirely from leaving the country unless granted special government permission. Those who had exited the country and had not returned by the end of October 1948 lost their property. In March 1949, the Jewish community was ordered by the authorities to report on who had left the country since 1933 and not returned, so that their properties could be easily confiscated.

On May 15, 1948, the date the British Mandate expired and the Arab states invaded Israel, military rule was declared in Iraq and the green light given to overt persecution of the Jews. The police searched thousands of Jewish homes, "at all hours of the day and night, and in the most brutal fashion. If the owners did not open the doors fast enough, they were broken down. Dishes were broken during the searches, closets broken, bed linens ruined. Jewelry and valuables were stolen either on the sly, or openly, but no one dared complain. In isolated cases, this was enough but in most cases household members were taken to the police station for additional interrogation. There, they squeezed more money out of them."

The policy of overt persecution encouraged ordinary Iraqis not to repay debts owed to Jews, while others extorted money from their neighbors with threats of informing on them to the authorities. "Even the most pure of heart could fall afoul of these scoundrels, and all are forced to pay bribes and protection fees," the Mossad le-Aliya Bet reported.

Within the framework of military rule, four military courts were established; their main business was passing judgement on Jews—who could be present or not—regarding various and unusual accusations, most of which were false. "The judges shower the accused with waves of insults and abuse; the accused must stand quietly and not answer. If he speaks, it must be politely otherwise his punishment will be more severe or, as has already been the case, the judge will lean over and give the accused a few slaps across the face or bestow several kicks." Most Jews were found guilty, some were sentenced to death (as in the Ades case, to come) or long-term imprisonment, along with heavy fines. If the accused did not have enough cash to pay the fine, his property was confiscated.

The author of the previously quoted document goes on to describe the economic edicts that were the main tool of the military regime: "One guiding principle of the economic persecution policy against the Jews is to drain them of their money and transfer it to the government treasury. This is done via military court-ordered fines, taxes, and levies on government services, donations to refugees, and the like—all in addition to blackmail and hush money. This positive, good-neighbor policy, that brings in cash to the national treasury, also has the desired negative effect of depriving the Jews of their income."

The economic measures were varied. The regime took advantage of income tax laws that allowed it to put new levies into effect, retroactive to the past five years. It then demanded huge sums from Jewish merchants on profits ostensibly earned in years gone by. The Jews of Iraq were forbidden to sell or rent real estate worth more than 1,500 dinar unless they could prove—naturally, this involved a bribe—that they had no intention of transferring the money to Israel. Those Jews allowed to exit Iraq legally were forbidden from buying foreign currency; they were therefore forced to turn to the black market and, if caught, accused of smuggling funds to Israel. In August 1948, the foreign currency exchange licenses of Jewish-owned banks Zilka Credit and Edward Abudi were revoked; the reason given was that the banks were assisting Israel and smuggling capital to evade the Iraqi authorities. Understandably, the activities of both banks were severely damaged.

Hundreds of Jews suffered from the wave of civil service layoffs that began on May 15.

At first, people were fired individually and for different reasons: unacceptable behavior, disloyalty, inefficiency, sabotage and the like. Sometimes, the layoff came in the form of an extended vacation—even up to five years. In October 1948, an order was given to fire all Jewish clerks and other employees in government departments on the grounds of "government security" . . . this damaged the lives of hundreds of Jewish government clerks, many of whom were

senior employees in important positions, who had served the country faithfully and well for many years. The reasons given for firing could also serve as
the basis of a court accusation, after which the convicted individual was thrown
into prison, or fined heavily.

The government also appealed to foreign-owned companies, asking then to
fire their Jewish clerks. If they refused, they were asked not to hire any new
Jewish clerks. According to one estimate, the number of Jews fired at this time
reached 1,500. They were followed by the police, who were given special orders not to let these people engage in any other forms of work. The Jewish
institutions were also instructed not to employ them. In a country in the throes
of a severe economic crisis, their suffering were doubled and redoubled; they
have reached a point where they have almost nothing, they live in poverty on
savings, on money earned from selling pots and pans, or even charity.

The management of the Baghdad railway, for instance, fired 315 Jews at once
on September 1.

Another cruel blow was visited on Jews in foreign trade when, in September 1948, they were forbidden completely from import activity and partially
from export activity. Their licenses were given over to Muslims, but as the
new traders knew nothing about international trade, "the licenses were offered back to the Jewish traders, for a fee." The government noted what was
going on and ordered license applicants to state the full names of managers
in their employ, to ensure they were not Jews. The author, an official at the
Mossad, continues: "Needless to say, government contracts that in the past
were given to Jews are once again denied them, completely." In addition,
the Iraqi press called on all citizens to do their weekly shopping on Saturdays when Jewish-owned stores were closed.

Day-to-day Jewish life was disrupted. They were denied access to government services such as hospitals, clinics, infant care centers, convalescent
homes; Jews had already been banned from public schools when a 5% quota
was set, even before May 14, 1948. Jewish neighborhoods did not have street
cleaning, roadwork, or maintenance. The Jewish community was asked to
provide these public services to its members, but the severe damage done
to Jewish incomes naturally affected the budgets of community and charitable institutions at the very moment when they were most needed. The final blow came when Jewish newspapers were shut down, either by direct order or because the staff was imprisoned.[23]

PERSECUTING THE RICH AND THE CHILDREN TOO

A review written by Israel's Ministry of Foreign Affairs in 1948 showed
that most of Iraq's political parties—divided on every other issue—were
united in their hatred for the Jews. By late December 1947, the political
parties had already turned to the government ministries, banks, companies,
and other economic entities, demanding that they fire all Jewish employees.

At the same time, a "propaganda campaign for contributions benefiting the Arabs of Palestine" was launched in Baghdad. "Naturally, most of the contributors were Jews. Half a million dinar was extorted in this fashion." The regime also decided to confiscate Jewish houses and public institutions, such as synagogues, schools, and clubs, in order to house refugees from Palestine.[24]

One case touched the hearts of all those who witnessed it. Doctors had recommended sending a six-month old Jewish infant, suffering from swollen glands, to the United States or England for treatment. After the parents paid £2,000, the government decided to grant one passport, to the infant alone. "The mother took her child to the airport and, with heavy heart, handed her baby over to the pilot, begging him to put the child in the hands of a charitable organization like the Red Cross that would care for the baby and make sure he was cured. This incident broke the heart of every Muslim present in the airport; some even cried. This mother gave her child over to the world in order that he be cared for, and she paid for it."

By contrast, Baghdad refused to grant passage to a well-known merchant suffering from cancer. All the local doctors recommended that he be treated in the United States or England. He requested a passport, but received it only when his condition became critical, and after paying £6,000 for passports for his wife and himself. The man set out for the United States. Ten days after arriving at his destination, he passed away. The attending physician confirmed that, had the man reached the hospital earlier, he might have been able to at least extend his life.[25]

Shafiq Ades paid with his life for being a wealthy Jew. Ades was an assimilated Jew, completely disinterested in Zionism and well connected personally to the authorities in his hometown of Basra. He was a major contributor to the Palestinian cause and, as previously mentioned, was the wealthiest member of the Baghdad Chamber of Commerce on the eve of World War II. Ades's main line of business was representing the U.S. car manufacturer Ford. He was arrested in 1948, accused of buying tanks, trucks and other equipment from the British military stationed in Basra, and sending it to Israel via Italy. The prosecution failed to prove Ades's guilt, but the court ignored this fact and the fact that Ades's share in military surplus transactions was only 10%. His business associates were all Muslim, including prominent public figures, but their names were never mentioned during the trial. No witnesses were called to testify.

Within three days after the trial commenced, a month after his arrest, Ades was convicted, sentenced to be hanged, and fined 5 million dinar. State Regent Abd al-Ila'a—Ades's frequent houseguest—approved the sentencing. Ades was hanged publicly in Basra on September 23 and his corpse left on the gallows for five hours. For the Muslims, it was a day of celebration. For the Jews it was a severe shock; they felt that if this could happen to a man like Ades, clearly there was no hope of ever assimilating into Iraqi society, and no Jew could ever feel safe.[26]

Indeed, other wealthy Jews were also brought to trial during the second half of 1948. Among them were Moshe Shohat, deputy manager of the Iraqi Railways who, like Ades, was accused of smuggling military equipment abroad; millionaire Salman Zilka, part-owner of a family-run bank, accused of smuggling funds to Tel Aviv; millionaire Haim Netanel, owner of a Baghdad shipping company was apparently accused (the document is unclear) of smuggling Jews into Israel; while millionaire Stanley Shashoua stood trial for having letters from Israel in his possession. The documents do not detail what each man's fate was, but had they been punished severely it would have been indicated in the documentation. The total volume of collected fines, according to Egyptian newspaper *al-Ahram*, which could never be accused of being overly sympathetic to the Jews, amounted to 20 million dinar, or $80 million. Property belonging to the Jewish prisoners was impounded "temporarily" to ensure fines would be paid but was never returned, even in those rare cases where the prisoners were finally released.[27]

During the Ades trail, on September 17, 1948, Iraq's Jewish community prepared a memorandum intended for Count Folke Bernadotte, UN negotiator to the Middle East, who was to visit Baghdad. The memo was never submitted, as Bernadotte was assassinated in Jerusalem before reaching Iraq, but a copy has been preserved. It is a testament to the bravery demonstrated by this persecuted community. The authors did not hold back from claiming that the regime's actions resembled Hitler's: "One after another, they get rid of the Jews, strip them of their property by way of bribes or fines, then throw them into the pit until they rot or die." Indeed, economic dispossession is the first stage in the Nazi plan for the physical destruction of European Jewry; the comparison is therefore apt. The memo goes on to say that one candidate in the June 1948 parliamentary election campaign delivered the following one-sentence speech: "Heil Hitler, choose me, I am an enemy of the Jews."

The memorandum called on Bernadotte to ignore Baghdad's official statements, not allow himself to be duped, and to disbelieve statements made under duress by Iraqi Jews, where they might say the situation was fine. The unnamed authors asked Bernadotte to seek out the truth by finding the man in the street and looking into his eyes. The memo enumerated the repressive measures taken against the Jews, including preventing them from leaving the country, false accusations, searches, confiscation of property, firings, and more and more calls to censure the Jews ("Precisely as in Nazi Germany") in order to block their sources of income.[28]

THE ECONOMIC MOTIVE FOR JEWISH PERSECUTION

Even in those days, outside observers noted that an economic motive—greed for Jewish possessions—played an important role in their persecution. In January 1948, a member of the Mossad le-Aliya Bet wrote: "This government, which sees the Jews and their goods as its own property, and has already made it difficult for the Jews to leave Iraq, intends to make sure Jews be unable to transfer their money outside of Iraq. [The government] therefore passed a law several months ago forbidding cash transfers from Iraq to anywhere else. Jews now living in Israel with assets in Iraq, who wish to transfer them, pay 5–7% of the total amount in return for these special, tiresome services."[29] Other sources do not mention this adjustment on assets transferred out of Iraq but the idea that the government of Iraq wished to retain possession of Jewish property, is a logical one.

The World Jewish Congress (WJC) reached a similar conclusion in October 1948, in a memorandum circulated among UN members. The WJC requested that recipients put persecution of Jews in Arab countries (mainly Iraq and Egypt) on the agenda of the UN General Assembly. The WJC review of events in Iraq opened with this statement: "The Government of Iraq has embarked upon, and is in the process of, executing a policy designed systematically to destroy the economic existence of the Jewish population, and to obtain possession of Jewish property through confiscation, and for State purposes."[30]

Iraq's Jewish community itself claimed that their persecution was, in part, motivated by economics. A letter sent by "The Jews of Iraq" to the U.S. ambassador to Baghdad in 1949, reads: "Due to its cash deficit, incurred during the war against the State of Israel, the government of Iraq planned to bring a number of wealthy Jewish merchants before the military courts, firstly, in order to levy heavy fines on them, and secondly, as a kick in the head, the first step in stripping them of their social and economic standing." The authors drew parallels between this trend and the Ades trial, as well as fines levied on Haywa Jedda and Ya'akov Haskel of $4 million each, fines of $40,000 to $120,000 levied on other wealthy Jews, and fines of $2,000 to $10,000 issued to hundreds of Jewish merchants.[31]

With the hindsight of decades, Dr. Esther Meir concludes that there was an economic motive to Iraqi government policy. She notes that Jewish persecution in the second half of 1948 is very reminiscent of the dark days of the 1941 Farhud. Meir lists a number of reasons, chiefly the Arab defeat in general and Iraq's loss in the war against Israel in specific, anti-Jewish sentiment resulting from Iraqi nationalism, efforts to quell the Zionist underground movement already active in Iraq, and the aimlessness of the ruling class and power struggles within the regime.

Regarding the economic motive, second on the list of reasons for Jewish persecution, Meir writes: "Economic motives also played an important part in this situation, primarily in making the Jews a scapegoat for the economic crisis; extorting money to fill the empty State coffers by way of 'donations', high taxes, fines, exorbitant taxes and the like. Decisions forbidding Jews from selling real estate and revoking the Jewish-owned banks licenses to foreign currency transaction, were made out of similar economic considerations; they prevented Jewish capital from leaving the country. Even if these measures were perceived by the Jews as persecution for persecutions sake alone, the economic aspect cannot be ignored."[32] Also in this category is government-sponsored extortion, such as the 113,000 dinar 'donation' benefiting Israel's Palestinian population, presented by the heads of the Jewish community to Iraq's prime minister in 1948.[33]

At that time, there were several prominent Iraqi leaders who had personal financial motives for persecuting Jews. In July 1948, the British ambassador to Iraq reported to the Foreign Office in London that, "according to reliable sources, Iraq's Minister of the Interior has amassed great sums of money, first by accusing and then by blocking lawsuits filed by well-to-do Jews."[34] Eyewitness accounts report significant sums of money given over to hundreds, even thousands of Iraqi clerks on every bureaucratic level, in return for exit passes or as protection against false accusation, harassment, and arrest.

PERSECUTION IN 1949 AND THE OCTOBER CRISIS

The wave of Jewish persecution continued into 1949 and focused mainly on individual attacks followed by random arrests. At this point, there were not many clerks left to fire or businesses to shut down. A review by Israel's Ministry of Foreign Affairs in April 1949 listed, for the first four months of that year, 103 Jews sentenced to death or imprisonment. A portion of the judgments were made in absentia (these included all death sentences) on charges that included "dissemination of libelous information," possession of a Jewish New Year's card imprinted with the Star of David, "sabotage of a telegraph machine and delay of telegraphic messages," "making statements endangering public security," "Zionist propaganda," and intention to emigrate from Iraq. Most were sentenced to pay thousands of dinar in fines; in those cases where the accused no longer lived in Iraq, their property was impounded in lieu of payment.[35]

Avraham Shashoua remembers what happened to his uncle, Abudi Kattab. "One day in mid-1949, a soldier came into Abudi's shop and bought some teacups. As Abudi was wrapping the cups, the soldier demanded the saucers and spoons that, to his mind, were included in the price. The whole deal amounted to pennies, but a dispute ensued and within a short time Abudi found himself before an emergency court session, charged with selling tea, not teacups, at a time when tea was a food staple with an official, standard price. Abudi was accused falsely of selling tea at inflated prices and sentenced to four months in prison. By the time we heard the news, he was already in jail; that's where my aunt and I went to see him. That day, in return for the appropriate bribe, we were allowed to visit and bring him food. And we continued to visit and bring him food; each visit meant another bribe for the prison guards."

When Kattab was released from prison, he discovered that he would have to reapply for his shopkeepers' license, which would be granted—naturally—only in return for a handsome fee. Then came "the third blow, a draft notice for compulsory military service." Years earlier, Kattab paid the official fee required of every Iraqi Jew in return for a draft deferment. He was already 40 years old and the father of six but the regime claimed the prison term nullified his deferment. In December 1949, on furlough, Kattab asked Shashoua, who was involved in the underground emigration to Israel movement, to help him leave the country. After many adventures, he succeeded in reaching Israel.[36]

In late October 1949, matters reached a boiling point and the leadership of the Jewish community decided to protest the government publicly. The underlying reason for this unusual act was an announcement made by the State of Israel Government Press Office (GPO) on the twenty-third of that month; this was the first time Israel had intervened directly on behalf of the Jewish community in Iraq. The GPO attributed renewed persecution to attempted escape efforts made by Iraqi Jews and went on to say:

> In the middle of the Day of Atonement, on October 7, police burst into the synagogue in the city of Amara, south of Baghdad, and arrested ten worshippers, including the head of the Jewish community. The prisoners were not informed of the charges against them. Three days later, fifty Jews were arrested in Baghdad and their houses searched. The next, we learned they were tortured cruelly, so that they would admit affiliations to the Zionist movement and the migration organization. On October 12, searches were again carried out in Baghdad, this time in dozens of houses, and again there were arrests. These new prisoners were also tortured. Since then, [the pattern of] searches and arrests, imprisonment and torture, has escalated at a ever-increasing pace. Schools have also been searched; teachers and students taken into police custody . . . torture is carried out using the best Nazi methods. There are reports of the most brutal physical torture, life-threatening crimes against the victims bodies. Among the torture victims are young women.

What Israel did not publicize was the fact that, one day after the Day of Atonement, fifty members of the Zionist underground were arrested in Baghdad. The police had been close to eliminating the underground entirely. In the Baghdad Jewish community historiography, these events became known as the "October Crisis." Israel's statement was issued not only as an attempt to protect the Jews of Iraq, but also to save Israeli emissaries and the hard work invested over many years in organizing the underground and its escape routes. Israel's minister of foreign affairs, Moshe Sharett, also appealed to the four world powers—the United States, the USSR, Great Britain, and France—apprising them of the gravity of the situation.[37]

The Jewish community itself could not help but protest. On October 24, several of its leaders met with the deputy Prime Minister and acting Minister of the Interior Omar Nadhami. They demanded that Jews be allowed to exit the country, sell real estate, attend institutions of higher education, and that the policy of layoffs on ethnic grounds be terminated. Nadhami's answer was that government policy was not directed against the Jewish community but against the Zionist movement in Iraq.[38]

On October 28, the head of the Jewish community, Sasson Kaduri, joined the protest, after not having participated in the previous meeting. The next chapter deals more fully with the dramatic events of the weeks that followed, but here are some selected quotes from Kaduri's memorandum to the government of Iraq relating to the economic persecution of his community:

> The mass layoff of Jewish clerks in government offices and institutions leaves hundreds of people without a source of income. This could have been alleviated had alternate workplaces, outside the government, been arranged. But the economic situation had already affected most of those laid off, and many families are still in deep distress. By the same token, policies adopted by the Ministries of Food and Import, regarding Jewish merchants, resulted in a complete paralysis of their businesses, with worrisome effects both to their individual standards of living, and to the economic situation on a national scale. This policy has raised the number of unemployed and needy in our community.
>
> Another factor has exacerbated the situation: limitations of the sale, purchase and mortgage of real estate by Jews. Services have suffered greatly because of this [policy] which has affected the national economic situation. In turn, export and trade activity has shut down and opportunities for income taken from many people. At the same time, economic distress with the Jewish community has risen and young people despair of finding any type of work. The gates to official institutions of learning, colleges and scientific delegations are closed before Jewish students; this is a cause for great concern regarding future education. . . . The feeling among Jews, regarding the exaggerated financial estimates of their properties, is that this is being done to charge them with a high property tax; the same is true of income tax and revised estimates regarding previous [tax] years."[39]

Kaduri was an anti-Zionist who always tried his hardest to please the regime. Taking this fact into account, along with the persecution and fear engulfing the community, makes clear how bad the situation must have been for Kaduri to dare write such things.

Chapter 2

"They Wallow about in a Desperate State"

The Jews of Iraq Lose Their Citizenship and Property

Unrestricted immigration for all Jews is one of the founding principles of the State of Israel. For many years, this principle was a point of conflict between the Jews and the British mandatory government, a conflict that often turned bloody and was a central reason for London's decision to withdraw the mandate. Israel's Declaration of Independence states unequivocally that "The State of Israel will be open to Jewish immigration and the ingathering of the exiles."

Very quickly, however, the difficulty in implementing this principle became apparent. The small, young country was fighting for its life, almost without resources of its own. The most important thing was to ensure Israel's existence. At the same time, hundreds of thousands of Jews from every part of the world were knocking at the door. On the day of its establishment, there were 650,000 Jews living in the State of Israel. Within two and a half years, by the end of 1951, the population had more than doubled with the arrival of 700,000 immigrants of all cultures, levels of education, age, and economic status. The situation was exacerbated in light of the fact that many immigrants were aged, infirm, children, disabled, mentally ill, or from other groups in need of welfare from the moment they arrived. As previously mentioned, resources were lacking to provide every immigrant with the minimum support needed for absorption and basic livelihood, not to mention employment and long-term housing.

Given these conditions, the Jewish Agency and Israel's government had no alternative but to set monthly immigration quotas for the various Diaspora communities. The government accepted the criteria set in January 1950 by the head of the Jewish Agency's Immigration Division, Yitzhak Refael, dividing the Diaspora into five groups, ranked (in descending order) according to the immediacy of their immigration to Israel: (1) rescue from immediate danger—Jews in Arab states: Iraq, Egypt, Syria and Bahrain; (2) states with high probability of border closure—Eastern Europe; (3) rescue from economic, social, cultural deterioration—North Africa, Iran; (4) diversity of human capital—Educated, economically stable immigrants who will contribute to the State and society; and (5) prosperous states—A cadre of immigrants to come after mass immigration is complete.[1]

INDIVIDUAL DISCRIMINATION TURNS TO MASS FLIGHT

As mentioned above, the Jewish community of Iraq was seen as being in mortal danger, and emigration to Israel was given top priority. Things in Iraq, however, were not so simple, neither relations between the community and the government nor inter-Jewish relations. Up until April 1948, emigration

Immigrants from Iraq arrive at Lod airport near Tel Aviv, January 1951 (Central Zionist Archives)

Inspection of Iraqi immigrants' belongings at Lod airport near Tel Aviv, March 1950 (Central Zionist Archives)

to the Land of Israel from Iraq was clandestine, conducted by a 1,500-person strong Zionist underground that, since 1942, was operated by Hagana emissaries. In August and September 1947, the Zionist underground flew 100 Jews to the Land of Israel; this activity expanded in the following months.

It must be emphasized, however, that on the eve of the founding of the State of Israel, the Zionist underground was, in Moshe Gat's words, "outside the [Iraqi] Jewish community's sprit and structure. The community leadership continued managing Jewish life, and excluded the underground completely. Not only have these leaders not considered cooperation or identification with the underground's goals, they feared even knowing about it. They were convinced that the underground's existence not only jeopardizes the community and its position, but its very existence." Despite the traumatic Farhud, the conservative leadership believed it "could return to the concept of Jewish by religion and Iraqi by nationality. The Iraqi regime has stated repeatedly that it makes a clear separation between Judasim and Zionism; that Jews will be granted full rights, like any Iraqi citizen."[2]

As mentioned in the previous chapter, Israel's War of Independence created a fundamental change. After encountering physical, social, and cultural
prejudice and persecution, the Jewish community understood it would be
almost impossible to integrate or ignore their religion. The government protected their lives but did not do much more than that. Quite the opposite:
This was the same regime that stole their property, plundered their homes,
suppressed their rights, imprisoned their sons, and executed several of their
notable personages.

Right before the establishment of the State of Israel, hundreds of Iraqi
Jews escaped to the Land of Israel via three westward routes: two going
through Syria and one through Trans-Jordan (today known as the Kingdom
of Jordan). But when fighting broke out in Israel, these routes became too
dangerous and almost impossible to use. They were replaced by a longer but
safer route, via Iran. As opposed to what came before, this route enabled
large groups, in the dozens, to escape from Iraq. The starting point was the
southern port city of Basra, where the Jews gathered and crossed the Shat
al-Arab to the Iranian shore. Iran rejected Iraq's requests to prevent Jews
from entering, or arrest and return those Jews already there. Therefore,
Baghdad had no choice but to try, from its side, to stop the Jews from
fleeing.[3]

This effort peaked in October 1949, when Iraqi police arrested five
members of the Zionist underground in Baghdad. A short time afterwards
dozens of underground activists were arrested, along with local Jews with
no connection whatsoever to the underground. After severe torture, some
of the captives were forced to give details that led to additional arrests; the
underground was close to being obliterated. Members who were not arrested
went into hiding, and underground activity all but ceased. This difficult crisis,
as mentioned in the last chapter, forced Israel to give a public and official
statement supporting the Jews of Iraq, something it had avoided up until
then, so as not to further endanger the community's standing.

UPHEAVALS WITHIN THE BAGHDAD COMMUNITY
LEADERSHIP

Looking back it is clear, as Gat proves, that Iraq's actions were not geared
against the Jews but against an underground movement that was operating
against state law. The regime had even made an official announcement to
the community, saying that the police target was the underground and that
innocent Jews would not be harmed.

The Jewish community leadership, which was very conservative and
traditional, got the message. This was exactly what the Zionist underground
feared. The heads of the underground movement pressured community
leaders to declare a day of fasting, prayer, and work stoppage, in solidarity

with the prisoners. The community leaders, headed by Sasson Kaduri, refused, convinced it would be best if the underground would give up its arms, and its members leave the country. This internal conflict continued, pressure from the underground on the community leadership mounted, and tens of thousands of Jews were gripped by fear. In the end, this combination of factors brought Kaduri around; he agreed to a fast day on October 25.

The underground leadership was not satisfied, and decided to stage a demonstration against the government and the Jewish community leadership as one on October 23. The protesters, mainly relatives of the captives led by young underground members, attacked Kaduri physically, dragged him from his office, and forced him to join the protest. The following day, several community leaders—excluding Kaduri—filed the memo cited in the previous chapter with the government of Iraq. Four days later, Kaduri filed his own memo, also quoted previously.

That same day, Kaduri resigned as head of the Jewish community. The Iraqi government refused to accept his resignation, but the underground was determined to oust him. After heavy pressure from within the ranks, Kaduri reiterated his resignation and stepped down on December 19. His place was filled by Yehezkel Shemtov, a wealthy Jew with close government connections, yet respected by the underground where his son was active. Shemtov became, in effect, the underground representative to the Iraqi government. At the same time, police actions against the underground ceased; apparently it was realized their success was limited and, additionally, there was international pressure.[4]

THE CITIZENSHIP DEPRIVATION LAW AND ITS BACKGROUND

No Jew who lived in Iraq in 1950 will ever forget the Purim holiday that fell on March 3 that year. Says Iraqi-born, former Israel Knesset speaker and government minister Shlomo Hillel:

The Jews of Iraq have always loved this holiday, perhaps because of a geographic proximity to the land where the miracle of Purim took place. It was a great celebration, with costumes, story telling and merry-making . . . but this time it was as if lottery was redrawn, as if all hope was lost, and the sword pressed against their throats again. On March 2, when the Jews congregated in their synagogues to read the Book of Esther, they were informed that Minister of the Interior Sallah Jabar had filed a proposal for legislation with the Iraqi Parliament. The proposed law would allow Jews to leave Iraq, so long as they left permanently, and renounced their citizenship. The Parliament had begun discussing the proposal. The Book of Esther gained new meaning for all those who read it that night. When the cantor wailed 'The Jews had light, and gladness, and joy, and honor. And in every province, and in every city, wherever the king's commandment and his decree came, the Jews had joy and

gladness, a feast and a holiday,' time lost all meaning; it was as if Baghdad was
the ancient Persian capital city of Shushan, where the Jews suddenly awoke
after months of confinement, torture, and terror, to light, gladness, joy, and
honor.[5]

At that time, Hillel was at home in Israel, after months of caring for Iraqi
immigrants who had arrived via Iran. It was there that Hillel received a mis-
sive sent by the head of the Mossad le-Aliya Bet, Moshe Carmil, a copy of
Mordechai Ben-Porat's famous telegram. As Ben-Porat tells it:

On March 3, 1950, I was summoned to our wireless radio station. Itzhak Sa'ig
and Shimshon Hubeiba were in the final stages of turning off the instruments
[for the night]. I asked them to wait, took out a piece of paper and, by
lamplight, began reading the following telegram:
   We are entitled to break down and cry, when we see the fruits of our labor

Mordechai Ben-Porat, former chief Aliya emissary
to Iraq and co-founder of the World Organization
of Jews from Arab Countries (WOJAC) (photograph by Yossi Zeliger)

and the labor of those who came before us. Salvation is finally at hand for this miserable Jewish community. The government has decided, in a majority vote, to allow the Jews to leave. Minister of the Interior Sallah Jabar filed the Citizenship Deprivation Law, according to which:

1. The Cabinet has the right to revoke the citizenship of any Jew wishing to leave Iraq on his own volition, after having signed certain forms;
2. An Iraqi Jew exiting Iraq illegally will lose his citizenship;
3. An Iraqi Jew who has left Iraq illegally for a period of two months or longer will lose his citizenship;
4. The Minister of the Interior will banish any Jew who has lost his Iraqi citizenship;
5. This law will remain in effect for a one-year period; its implementation may be terminated by royal order;
6. The law will go into effect from the day of publication in the official state newspapers;
7. The Minister of the Interior is responsible for enacting the law.[6]

What made the government of Iraq enact the Citizenship Deprivation Law? Apparently, the reasons given at that time were accurate. On March 10, a Mossad le-Aliya Bet memo gave "possible reasons leading to the Iraqi government taking this step":

A. Illegal emigration. At first pitiful, it has grown exponentially in recent months. As government pressures increase, so do the escape attempts. In January and February of this year, 2,000 persons have managed to cross over to Iran. Police actions have failed. The government most certainly assumes those people are smuggling large sums of money, over which it has no control. It is faced with a choice, to either invest all resources in border patrols (again, chances for success are slight), or to at least grant itself the option of inspecting both the exits, and those exiting. This way, it ensures that exits will be orderly, and legal.

B. The Persian [Iranian] government's announcement that it would provide shelter to Iraqi refugees. Since May 1949, the government of Persia has taken every opportunity to pressure the government of Iran into returning these refugees. During a visit [to Iran] by Crown Prince Abdallah of Iraq, this topic headed the list of Iraq's demands. Persia subsequently issued a statement, significant in that it encouraged illegal emigration and increased its proportions. Persia's statement effectively obligated Iraq to a political response. Iraq was, once again, faced with a choice: conflict with Persia or accept the inevitable.

C. International public opinion. In the global arena, Iraq has more than once been put in an uncomfortable position. This was particularly true last fall [October 1949] when, in a police action, Iraq attempted to crush the underground and Zionist movements, and faced harsh criticism from every nation, international and economic organization.

D. Jews are an unwanted element.

1. Doubtlessly, Iraq reached the conclusion that it is better to rid itself of a disloyal Jewish element. They may have been directed towards this end by the British. It is clear to Iraq that within Jewish community there is a strong, organized Zionist movement and leadership. Attempts to break it failed completely but gained international attention. Iraq may also have estimated (or over-estimated) the Zionist's military might, primarily the potential resources required to develop and maintain an army of this size.

2. It is known that Iraq believes (baselessly, of course) that the Jews are an active element in the Communist Party, as members and leaders. They may have concluded that anti-Communist activity (now ongoing in eastern Iraq) would be aided most efficiently by getting rid of "Communist germs."

E. Burdening Israel. It is believed the Iraqis think that if they send tens of thousands of people to State of Israel, now in financial and economic difficulty, they will accelerate its collapse. (Although it is hard to believe Iraq does not know Israel is basing its future solely on the absorption of additional manpower, and that despite hard times, Israel is absorbing, of its own free will, tens of thousands of new immigrants. Also, Israel is trying constantly to increase immigration from Iraq, albeit via alternate routes and illegally, and despite the additional cost to Israel's government.)[7]

F. Economic considerations.

1. Assessments are that Iraq suffers from spiraling inflation, and that the government has concluded that allowing Jews to leave will result immediately in lower values for land, real estate, merchandise (Jewish) and property overall. The buying power of Iraqi currency will then increase, and the economy will balance out.

2. Beyond a shadow of a doubt, every action is motivated by the desire to seize the bulk of Jewish property. Granting exit visas to Jews enables the government to confiscate their property openly, and leaves them with no form of recourse.

Perhaps some, or even all of these considerations led the government of Iraq to this decision. In any case, it is incomprehensible that the opposition faction and the press accepted this measure fairly readily, and ignored the fact that Iraq—the leader in "Second Round" proponents [a renewed attack against Israel]—is sending tens of thousands of people to Israel, and is therefore reinforcing our military might. There are rumors that each person will be permitted to take out 200 pounds in cash (in addition to household effects and property). This generosity is hard to understand, as the end result will be large sums of money taken out of the country. (If 50,000 people take out 200 pounds each, that is already 10 million pounds.)[8]

Esther Meir concludes, with historical perspective, that the main reasons for enacting the Citizenship Deprivation Law are those cited in the Mossad le-Aliya Bet document, that is: inability to stem illegal emigration, desire to control the export of property and foreign currency,[9] removal of an insubordinate social element, and eradication of the Zionist underground.

Baghdad assumed that, at most, several thousand youths, unemployed, and poor persons would leave. It was also hoped that, in the wake of their departure, there would be improvement in the local population's attitude toward the Jewish community, in Iraq's international position, and the country's socioeconomic recovery.

Both Meir and Gat emphasize economics as a central motivating force. Meir writes: "Despite the waves of layoffs and economic sanctions, Jews still held key positions in Iraq's economy, particularly in finance. They reduced economic activity out of fear for their financial future and physical safety, limited credit extensions, and sold property so as to have liquid cash assets in hand, in case of emergency. This only exacerbated Iraq's market slowdown and economic hardship. The government of Iraq was aware that as long as the Jewish business community felt insecure, the economy would not improve."

Gat sees things from the other side, that is: the danger inherent in unmonitored emigration. "Jews were deeply involved in Iraq's economy. The Iraqi leadership recognized the fact that mass emigration by Jews, who held high positions in the financial and business circles, might affect the economy seriously, which was, in any case, in upheaval after the end of World War II, and further affected the regime's tenuous position. . . . As the Iraqi government saw it, the poor would comprise most, or all, of those wishing to leave. Therefore, most upper-class Jews, those dealing in trade and finance, would stay. Following this logic, the government of Iraq believed it could bring life back to normal, get out of market recession, gain economic improvement, and rid itself of the social unrest that plagued it so."[10] Given these considerations, it is easy to understand why Baghdad was so surprised at the number of emigrants and the amount of property they were taking with them—and why, one year later, the government decided to freeze all assets belonging to the Jews of Iraq. This matter will be discussed more fully as our story continues.

THE PROPERTY'S FATE: INITIAL RESCUE ATTEMPTS

Israel's immigration emissaries dealt intensively with the problem of property from the moment the Citizenship Deprivation Law was passed. Next to the problem of organizing the mass immigration to Israel, this was a burning issue that required immediate attention, for obvious reasons. The immigration campaign, called "Operation Ezra and Nehemia," is too long and complicated a story to tell here. Suffice it to say that after months of difficult negotiations with the government of Iraq, it was agreed that the Jews would be flown to Cyprus via Near East Air and from there to Israel. There were also occasional direct flights, without the Iraqis' knowledge. In all, 120,070 Jews immigrated to Israel from Iraq; 31,627 in 1950, 88,161 in 1951, and 282 in 1952.[11]

As early as March 10, the day after the Citizenship Deprivation Law was officially announced, the Mossad le-Aliya Bet reported:

> The information we have on the government of Iraq's intended actions regarding the matter of property belonging to emigrants, is still unclear. Initial reports are that the government will allow Jews to take out 200 pounds in cash, plus travel expenses, household effects and movable goods.
>
> We fear this report is too optimistic, but in any case, we have a wide field of operation both within the law, and outside. We have reports that the government of Iraq has repealed the law forbidding Jews from selling property (real estate). This act in itself, coupled with the announcement that Jews are allowed to leave Iraq, has lowered Jewish property values considerably. Certainly, if 15,000 households try selling off their property within one year, they will not profit from the sales. Staggering the sale of property should be considered. A suggestion has been made to establish a company (American?) or bank responsible for gradual property sales, made over a longer period of time.
>
> Jews may be offered possible cash transactions, smuggling gold, diamonds and the like. We must organize and supervise this matter. If Jews are allowed to take some property in the form of objects or merchandise, once again, it is our job to guide them, supervise purchases, and organize shipments.
>
> The government of Israel must formulate a position regarding the possible exchange of property for that belonging to Arab refugees. One problem is the possibility that Jewish property values will decline, making it impossible to factor it into Israel's debt to Arab refugees. Another possibility that certain refugee elements [i.e.: Palestinians] now in Iraq, may be interested in exchanging property in Israel for Jewish property in Iraq. What is our position on these matters, and how can we oversee them? It has been suggested that property sales and transfers might be expedited via Turkey, by setting up a Turkish-Iraqi company responsible for the complex problems of property exchange, purchase, sale and transfer to Israel.[12]

Israel's government was not insensitive to the problem of what would happen to Jewish property. It was certainly aware that Iraq's Jewish community was the richest in the Arab world; their property could aid the absorption process at a time when Israel was wrestling with supremely difficult economic issues. As early as March 1950, Israel began looking into the possibility of establishing a Iraqi-Turkish-American holding and liquidation company, but the attempt failed when it became clear Baghdad was completely unwilling to allow Jews to exit with their property.

In April 1950, then Israeli minister to Washington, Teddy Kollek, met with Phillip Erlich, legal counsel to the Bank of America, on the matter of Iraqi Jewish property. At that meeting, Kollek assessed the entire value of Jewish property in the hundreds of millions of U.S. dollars. Property belonging to those expected to immigrate to Israel (at a time when no one predicted that almost an entire community would leave) was valued in the tens of millions, including houses, shops, and merchandise. The idea was to set up a Bank of

America subsidiary that would receive property belonging to Iraqi Jews, sell it over time, and transfer the money to Israel in the form of cash or export goods. Kollek suggested a small percentage of the property be transferred initially, to enable the new immigrants a respectable absorption, and expressed confidence that, in the end, Baghdad would agree to transfer at least a portion of property to Israel.

Erlich requested official approval of the plan by Minister of Foreign Affairs Moshe Sharett and Minister of Finance Eliezer Kaplan, and the two agreed immediately. Erlich wanted to ensure the bank would receive a reasonable profit on the proposed company's activity but, after seven months of research, concluded that problems were vast and a fast solution was impossible. Bank of America withdrew its participation, and the plan was shelved.[13]

Y. Bihhem, an emissary sent to Teheran by Kaplan to examine the possibility of rescuing Iraqi Jewish property reported, on his return to Israel in April of 1950: "The situation is dominated completely by chaos, as it is impossible to legally transfer funds out of Iraq. We are partially to blame for the situation; if we could not hope for an official arrangement with Iraq and Iran, we could have created legal channels for bringing money into Israel. Needless to say, these channels would have helped not only new immigrants [but others, too]." Bihhem suggested appointing a Baghdad representative of the State of Israel, or the Joint Distribution Committee, responsible for collecting dinar from potential immigrants to Israel, and in return issuing checks in Israeli pounds at a 1:1 exchange rate. The Iraqi dinar would be sold for British pound sterling in Teheran, then be transferred to Israel's banks accounts. According to Bihhem's calculations, Israel would lose 6.5% to 7% on this activity, which it could withstand.[14] The proposal was never carried out, perhaps because at that same time a far more compelling offer was under consideration: exchanging Jewish property in Iraq for Palestinian property in Israel.

THE PROPERTY'S FATE: THE EXCHANGE PLAN

The suggestion was raised by Ezra Danin, advisor to the Middle East division at the Ministry of Foreign Affairs and formerly of the Hagannah information service, where he was a leading authority on Arab affairs. Danin's opinion was that there many Arabs residents of Israel who were not expected to stay but refrained from selling off their properties in Israel because if they did so, they would not be able to take the profits out of the country. Therefore, Danin suggested exchanging their properties in Israel with those of the Jews in Iraq at 1947 values. Danin's proposal dazzled the Ministry of Foreign Affairs and the prime minister's office, not only because it offered a possible solution to the problem of Iraqi Jewish property, but because—and this may have been the primary reason—it might encourage Arab emigration from Israel.

In a June 1950 memo to Minister of Finance Kaplan, after making an initial examination of the matter, Danin wrote:

> There is nothing preventing the Jews of Iraq from selling property and transferring ownership to an Iraqi citizen, Jewish or Arab. Foreign nationals are not allowed to register property [in their own names] but [Arab] refugees of means coming from Israel to Iraq will be able to receive Iraqi citizenship. . . . The Jews of Babylon are in a rush to leave for Israel. Upon departure, [Iraq] demands excessively large taxes. They are not allowed to take valuable property with them. Because of their hasty departure . . . vast amounts of property, in the form of real estate, is dumped on the market. In many cases, properties are 95% below their pre-War of Independence value. Property values for Arabs have also dropped, due to excess supply, but are not under pressure to emigrate, and will cope with these difficulties until property prices stabilize after the Jewish emigration storm has passed. It should be noted that many property owners within the regime would like see an end to this trend so that property prices will rise; they will therefore assist in advancing the proposed exchange plan.
>
> Movable goods are almost worthless. Values have dropped for shops, factories, cinemas, stock companies, etc. The value of Jewish-owned gold and precious stones has also dropped, due to heavy supply; the Arabs are sure prices will decline further when out of necessity, Jews will be forced to sell for even less. The value of Jewish property is estimated at £60 million in real estate, and £5 million in gold and precious stones. In addition, there are businesses and factories not included in these estimates.

Zalman Liff, advisor on land matters to the prime minister's office, supported the idea of an exchange plan. Just one day after Danin submitted his memo, Liff wrote to Prime Minister David Ben-Gurion and Ministers Sharett and Kaplan saying: "An initial examination shows many possibilities for property exchange and, in doing so, rescuing millions in real estate and property, along with encouraging the emigration of a certain segment of the Arab population from Israel that cannot acclimatize itself to the new economic situation, and therefore does not view Israel as its permanent place of residence for all time."

The following statement by Liff, it must be said, was completely divorced from reality and could only be written by someone who knew nothing about the Iraqi Jews' situation. "As a first step, I would suggest instructing our representatives in Persia to tell groups within the Jewish community of Iraq to stop selling property at wholesale, discounted prices and hint that there is a chance they may divest their properties under much better conditions, on an exchange basis. At the same time, we must prepare the tools needed to care for every aspect of the problem; we may need to establish a special company, under government supervision, for the multifaceted handling of this problem. This type of company could operate as a trustee benefiting new immigrants with property, or on a commercial, entrepreneurial basis." Given the panicky mood gripping scores of Jews hurrying to leave Iraq, there was no chance they would agree to sit and wait until something happened with the exchange plan—an idea still in its infancy.

In July, Kaplan authorized Liff to start examining the matter. A number of meetings were held with the representatives of a number of Arab families in Israel (mostly Christian), who agreed in principle to the idea. Concurrent to the "drawn-out, tiresome negotiations," as Danin termed them in December 1950, three Israeli representatives were ready to be sent to Iraq—naturally, in the guise of citizens from other countries—to present the proposed plan to the Jewish community. Due to a delay in receiving visas from Iraq, Danin instead sent a detailed letter to a Mr. Bilbul in Baghdad, but this too was delayed. Only after several attempts, over several months, did the letter reach its destination.

Meanwhile, however, Nuri Sa'id had returned to head the government of Iraq. He was not only anti-Jewish, but "more than others, greatly appreciated the economic significance of an Iraq without Jews," as Danin put it. Additionally, in the seven months during which Danin had begun handling the matter, a number of important changes had taken place. In a memo from early 1957, he wrote to Ben-Gurion, Sharett, and Kaplan:

A. The value of Jewish property in Iraq, which was devalued completely, has risen significantly [and therefore more Palestinian property must be given in exchange].

B. Apparently, the government of Iraq does not make it very difficult for Jews to sell their property to Arabs. By charging a very high retroactive income tax it plunders what it can.

C. Reports of hard living conditions in Israel, and difficulties encountered by new immigrants regarding the investment and transfer of funds to Israel, has frightened many off. Whether or not they are right, the fact is that they have found ways of smuggling out their remaining property, investing it in different places around the world. This refers as well to gold, jewelry and diamonds. Thus, the exchange plan, too, was set aside.[15]

LOSS OF PROPERTY, THREATS, AND DEATH

In contrast to the last lines of Danin's statement, in reality, the government of Iraq made it very difficult for Jews to take property out of the country. Every emigrant over the age of ten was allowed to take out 20 dinar, those aged ten to twenty were allowed 30 dinar, ages twenty and up—50 dinar, worth about $200; at that time, the average senior civil servant salary was 30 dinar, monthly. Emigrants were allowed to take three summer outfits, three winter suits, one pair of shoes, a blanket, six pairs of underwear, socks and sheets, one wedding ring, wristwatch and a thin bracelet. Emigrants were compelled to sell their remaining property at a minimum, often at 10% of its real value. Courtyards of Jewish homes and coffeehouse sidewalks became open markets, with Jewish-owned items selling for 5% of their real value. Some opposition parties called on Muslims not to buy Jewish goods out of this simple consideration: Should one pay for something today when it could be gotten for free tomorrow? In public, of course, the reasons given were more high-minded, like the following ad, which appeared in Baghdad newspaper *al-Hasson* in April 1950:

> To every citizen loyal to his country, people and nation; to every student, soldier, merchant, teacher and worker. This appeal is to you: Boycott the purchase of used items belonging to Jews, and publicly oppose its sale. The money you pay for rags will return in the form of bullets, lodged in the hearts of your sons and brothers. Moreover, buying from Jews destroys the market and upsets the economy. Boycott them. The boycott has several advantages: We will reduce the enemy's military stronghold, save money, and help our economy that has been damaged by Jewish speculation. Boycott them and fear God. God will be with you, so long as you believe in him.

And on March 30, the anti-Jewish newspaper *al-Yakza* published a Muslim religious-legal ruling forbidding the purchase of Jewish property.

There were two main ways for Jews to smuggle cash out of the country: hiring professional smugglers and money changers operating out of Iran and Beirut, or using Israel's immigration emissaries. Whoever used money changers ran the risk of losing all or some of his money; this did occur in several cases. Moreover, some Jews were unwilling to transfer even 50 dinar to Israel as the exchange rate set by the government was too low for their liking and preferred smuggling their money to other destinations. Israel's emissaries, for their part, used the money received from immigrants to cover ongoing expenses; a portion was transferred to Iran so that Zion Cohen, the Mossad le-Aliya Bet emissary there, could bribe the appropriate clerks and bring Jews in. The Mossad le-Aliya Bet staff then messaged Israel: So-and-so is due such-and-such amount of dinar, please pay him in Israeli pounds upon his arrival. Despite all these maneuvers, Ben-Porat estimates that in the year between the passage of the Citizenship Deprivation Law and the time Jewish assets were frozen, new immigrants from Iraq lost 90% of the value of their property.[16]

The immediate effects of this situation on the new immigrants were severe. Ronny Barnett, the man in charge of the airlift campaign, reported in September 1950: "Several thousand have arrived (more accurately put: were expelled) from rural towns, penniless and lacking in everything. They wallow about in a desperate state. . . . At first they consume the money obtained, somehow, to pay for the flight. After that, they become a burden on the community. I assume you know that there have been fifty cases of infanticide." Jewish residents of rural towns were forced to flee their homes under duress; their neighbors threatened their lives, and demanded their property—all with the support of the Iraqi police. They fled to Baghdad only to live in horrid, crowded conditions in synagogues, schools, and other locations.

Hygiene, says Gat, was substandard; not surprisingly, there were instances of illness, death, and violence, including attacks against the emissaries. This situation resulted directly in increased pressure from the government of Iraq to expel the Jews as quickly as possible. This served only to increase their distress, required them to sell more goods at a pittance; the cycle continued.[17]

Their troubles did not end when they finally got to the airport, as another round of humiliation and seizure of property at the hands of customs agents awaited them. Ben-Porat wrote: "The tax officials would cut their suitcases to search for documents or other contraband material. Khaki garments and other forbidden items were pulled out of suitcases and thrown into a pile for return to the synagogue [Mas'uda Shemtov, location of the immigration camp]. The immigrants' relatives would come to collect the forbidden items. These were kept in a special room [in the synagogue] where there was a table upon which rested a Torah scroll. Anyone coming to claim an item had to swear [on the Torah] it belonged to one of their relatives." To cut down the amount of searches, immigration emissaries would bribe the customs agents: Every official received 60 dinar a month, or four times their official salary. The new head of the Customs Authority, on receiving the position at the height of "Operation Ezra and Nehemia," demanded and received 500 dinar a month, or twenty times his monthly salary.[18]

THE NEW IMMIGRANTS' DISTRESS

The most tangible, often heart-rendering expressions of pain on loss of property may be found in a series of reports now preserved in several archives. There are affidavits to customs authority headquarters in Tel Aviv, sent by Yerahmiel Asa, a senior immigration emissary to Baghdad, requesting the release of the few jewels that the new immigrants had succeeded in bringing in. Salim Sadka, head of a family of four, had a "gold necklace with pendant, gold bracelet, pearl bracelet, watch with a gold chain, and his name made out of gold," and twenty Turkish pounds [apparently these coins were used as jewelry]. Ya'akov Samara al-Nabi and his wife were lucky: They managed to take out a "bracelet studded with British sovereigns, a gold necklace with pendent, twelve gold bracelets, a gold brooch, two intertwined gold bracelets, ten coins, gold earrings with Ottoman (Turkish) sovereigns." Meir Ezra David, his wife and five children brought with them twelve gold children's bracelets, eight gold ladies bracelets, two ladies pocket watches, two children's ankle bracelets with bells, and two without bells, and several more bracelets, chains, earrings, and rings.[19] Bear in mind that jewelry is not only merchandise, it has also—sometimes mainly—great sentimental value. Nevertheless, the Jews of Iraq were forced to leave most of these things behind.

A letter, sent by the Mossad le-Aliya Bet in Teheran to Israel's Customs Authority at Lod Airport, reveals something about the manner in which the jewelry made its way to Israel. "A few months ago, an Egyptian Jew named

Abdallah Masri deposited with us . . . the enclosed bracelets. He told us that at Kassar Shirin, the border crossing between Iraq and Iran, they had been confiscated from a Jew by the name of Eliahu Mu'allem, who said they were the property of [a woman named] Salha Nissim. Masri also told us that after much hardship he managed to release the bracelets and brought them to us in Teheran so that we might remit them to Salha Nissim, who recently emigrated to Israel. For our part, we waited for a convenient, safe opportunity to send them, as the tax authority here is very problematic as regards gold and jewelry." Accompanying the letter were twenty gold bracelets and a request to pass them onto the owner, "Aziza Mizrahi, Me'ah Shearim Street, after the Berman bakery, Chabad courtyard. For Salha Nissim, northwest Lod B."[20]

Other touching pieces of evidence are the requests filed by immigrants with the Israeli authorities and the Jewish Agency. In December 1954, Y.S.[21] reported on the property he had left behind upon immigrating to Israel in early 1951. The form was filled out during a comprehensive effort made by Israel's government to record claims made by immigrants from Arab countries (to be discussed more fully in Chapter 4). Y. S. claimed he was owed 263,900 dinar (I£ 1,319), the premium paid annually to German insurance company Allianz via the Ottoman Bank branch in Baghdad; the insurance policy had been confiscated by the Iraqi regime. The man also claimed 75 dinar (I£ 375) on a retirement fund after having been employed for thirteen years by the Iraqi railway. Most importantly, Y. S. was seeking compensation for the confiscation of merchandise from a shop owned by him and his partner Ibrahim Mu'allem, located in Baghdad's Suq al-Deri open market, valued at 2,838,900 dinar (I£ 12,500). In real terms, the value of Y. S.'s claim totals $76,000.[22]

As early as 1950, Yael Markuzo appealed to the Jewish Agency's Near Eastern Jewry Division, reporting on considerable amounts of family property remaining in Iraq. Her brother, Abdallah Zakaria, and sister, Menna Zakaria, had also immigrated to Israel, but due to ill health were hospitalized permanently in Jerusalem. Abdallah left behind 12,248,336 dinar (almost $300,000 in real terms) in Iraq, while Menna had left behind a deposit of 5,308,218 ($127,000). The two were entitled to government pensions of 57 dinar per month; these had been terminated in February 1948, "due to the situation," in other words: escalating Jewish persecution. In the fall of 1947, Yael's mother, Mas'uda Zion Suiri, paid the government of Iraq the 2,000 dinar levied on every Jew exiting the country. As she never returned, the money, naturally, remained in the hands of the authorities.

But these cash amounts were peripheral relative to the family fortune. Markuzo reported, in great detail, on valuable real estate in Baghdad belonging to her family, including the exact place where the record of ownership would be found in the land registry books. There was a building with four ground floor shops and a second storey, on al-Rashid Street; a building in the Bab al-Ara neighborhood; two stores on Suk al-Bazazin Street in the same neighborhood; a house on al-Srir Street; a two storey building in the al-Sannak neighborhood; and a large tract of land in the Bab al-Shaih neighborhood with stores, restaurants, and more.[23]

Others made heartfelt appeals to anyone they thought could help them. Yehezkel Shemesh did so in a letter, sent in August 1951, to Knesset Speaker Joseph Sprinzak. Shemesh said he had managed the telegraph and post office in the city of Hila from 1927 to 1948. "On August 8, 1948, during [Israel's] War of Independence, I was arrested by Iraqi authorities, accused of sending Morse code signals via radio to the government of Israel. On these grounds, I was imprisoned and brought before a military court," Shemesh said. "The trial lasted about a year and a half. In the end, the military court dismissed the charges, due to lack of evidence." After his release, Shemesh requested and received a meager monthly pension of 10.5 dinar. He had no other sources of income and almost no property left to sell, as his family had lived off it during his incarceration.

In November 1950, Shemesh renounced his citizenship, and his pension payments stopped immediately. He immigrated to Israel in February 1951, and two months later got a job with the Israel postal authority in Jerusalem. Shemesh was asking that the government of Israel pay the difference between his pension plans, given Minister of Foreign Affairs Sharett's statement on offsetting Jewish and Arab claims (a subject to be discussed at length in the next chapter).

It is very likely that Shemesh knew Menashe Fannani, who also worked at the post office in Jerusalem, and turned to Sharett in June 1951 with a similar request. Fannani had been in charge of the Basra telegraph office from 1920 until August 1948, when he was imprisoned suddenly and exiled to the village of Tikrit [Saddam Hussein's birthplace], where he remained under arrest until January 1950. His family was forced to sell their belongings in order to survive while he was in prison; after his release, Fannani received only a meager, partial pension of 12.750 dinar per month. In Israel since October 1950, Fannani was now asking Sharett to secure his monthly 12.750 dinar pension payments, which had been appropriated by the Iraqi government.

However, Shamai Cahana of the Ministry of Foreign Affairs' Middle East Division explained in his response, Sharett had not committed to compensating the Iraqi Jews immediately. "It was said only that the value of Jewish property confiscated by Iraq will be taken into account when the time comes to discuss reparation. This time has not yet come, and there is no telling when it will come, and the entire thing is still a matter for the future," he added.[24]

HARD TIMES FOR IRAQ DUE TO
JEWISH EMIGRATION

Mass emigration caused problems not only for the emissaries and their handlers, but for the Iraqi government as well. As noted previously, Iraq had predicted that, at most, a few thousands poor Jews would leave, while those with means would stay. This assumption was one of the main motivations for the Citizenship Deprivation Law, for example, the poor Jews would go, the rich would stay with a renewed sense of security, and the wheels of economic progress would begin moving again. But within a few months, this assumption blew up in the regime's surprised face when it was presented with forecasts of 8 million dinar being taken out of the country by Jews, or 17% of Iraq's national budget for that year.[25]

Even before the Citizenship Deprivation Law was passed, the most extreme of Iraqi nationalists understood the cause that they advocated—eliminating the Jews from the economy and positions of power—worked against national interests. In April 1949, the anti-Jewish newspaper *al-Yakza* claimed state policies on import, export, and banking were controlled by Jews and complained that on Saturdays, the streets of Baghdad looked like those of Tel Aviv. The paper called for the establishment of companies that would compete with Jews in all areas of activity. In November 1949, the same paper wrote: "If we were to examine the percentage of Jewish clerks in various government ministries, the results would be depressing . . . and we would see the gravity of the situation that awaits us, as taxes, trains, finance and so on and so forth, are managed mainly by Jews."[26]

A far more objective opinion was expressed by the U.S. Embassy in Baghdad, in March 1949, in estimating the grave economic damage that would befall Iraq should the Jews leave. The American report forecast that six main areas would be harmed: export, import, marketing of imported goods, small business financing, real estate, and the loss of Jewish clerks in the private sector. The report summed up: "These factors taken together will have a negative effect not only on the economy, but on Iraq's stability and security."

Even after March 1950, the nationalist front feared economic collapse. As early as March 12, *al-Yakza* editor Salman al-Safwani expressed his concern for the future of Iraq's Postal and Telegraph Authorty, Office of the Comptroller General, Department of Irrigation and others, all of which employed many Jews. Al-Safwani called on the government to learn a lesson from what had happened to the Railway Authority—where many Jews had been fired in the 1940s—and begin training employees to take the place of the departing Jews. Two months later, the same editor wrote that, because of the government's inability to train non-Jewish workers, it was now compelled to import manpower from Pakistan.[27]

Fears quickly became reality. By late March 1950, the British Embassy in Baghdad had already reported that Jewish-owned companies were cutting back or ceasing activity; Jews were selling real estate, causing prices to drop and construction to shut down. The sale of other property was forcing prices down and hurting other businesses who could not turn over their inventory. As mentioned, this situation was more or less what the government had hoped for—in order to reduce inflation—but not so much or so quickly. The government itself created some of these problems beforehand, having instituted a banking inspection law in mid-January. This law limited activity for banks and money changers, most of whom were Jews, contributed to a lack of liquid assets, reduced credit, and caused many Jewish businessmen to go bankrupt. In turn, these persons sold property in order make a living, and in doing so, fueled the crisis. When Jews began withdrawing funds from bank accounts, the major money changers were drawn into deep financial difficulties.

In the second half of March, the Mossad le-Aliya Bet emissaries reported: "The Jews buy practically nothing. Their lively lifestyle and markets have gone quiet. . . . Their situation, of course, affects the non-Jewish residents." A month later, Iraq's government issued an order closing the banks for one week. The official reason given was to prepare annual reports, "but the real reason was the banks' concern for capital being withdrawn by Jews about to leave the country," concluded the research division of Israel's Ministry of Foreign Affairs. Ben-Porat says the immediate effect of this action was to induce panic among the Jews, many of whom went bankrupt.

And so, an endless loop was created: more and more Jews affected by the economic crisis began fearing for their future and closing their businesses, exacerbating and increasing the scope of the problem. The trade attaché at the British Embassy in Baghdad observed these events with a keen eye and forecast their future impact correctly: He described the Jewish middle class, established old merchant families, saying they did not wish to leave Iraq, but "recent events have caused them to doubt whether life in Iraq can possibly continue for them." Economic insecurity played a central role in turning Jewish emigration from Iraq into a mass movement; the ramifications resulted in a government seizure of Jewish property.[28]

Most serious of all was the damage done to Iraq's banking system. A British report from 1954 stated: "Jewish emigration from Iraq has hurt banking severely. Two major commercial banks and most money changers have ceased activity, or granting small amounts of credit, causing interest rates to rise inordinately, which has harmed business . . . the possibility of making a profit has encouraged new money changers to take the place of those exiting. A great deal of experience and acumen in the field of banking has been lost, and although the situation has been repaired in part, activity in these businesses is not what it was before."[29]

In February 1951, right before end of the one year period allocated to Jewish emigration under the Citizenship Deprivation Law, Israel's Ministry of Foreign Affairs requested that the Mossad le-Aliya Bet answer a long list of questions regarding immigration from Iraq. The Mossad le-Aliya Bet believed Iraq's government and press were in favor of the Jews leaving quickly as possible, but cited the difficulties that this mass immigration would bring:

> At first, the man in the street was excited at the thought of Jews leaving, and thought this was the moment when he would be free of Jews, a much-hated element. But with the passage of time, the Arab shopkeeper in a Jewish neighborhood has come to see the damage caused him, as a result of a decline in the number of Jews. Even Arab customers miss the good service given them by Jewish shopkeepers; now that they are gone, customers must turn to Arab shopkeepers, with all their faults. Many of the average Arabs have tried convincing their Jewish friends to stay, tried to prove that the period of persecution was temporary, a result of the British influence on the government, and that the Arabs are not to blame for these persecutions.
>
> The economic field was sustained and directed mainly by Jewish money, and when the government cut down on the number of import permits granted to Jews, this field suffered greatly; the Shi'ites and Sunnis filling the void in the economy left by the Jews are not as experienced in import, or state economic policy, as were the Jews. We have seen, as of three months ago, a market literally drained of the most basic staples to the point where the press has begun writing articles demanding that the government rescue its citizenry from starvation and lack of clothing. In the end, the government established a private company to import goods. It has assisted this company, and funded it with government capital.
>
> Many government departments—particularly railways, post and telegraph—have suffered when the Jewish technical manager, or accounts manager, in charge of things for many years, from before the national regime [i.e.: during the British Mandate], surprised the government by resigning, and having their citizenship revoked. Some departments requested injunctions to restrict Jewish clerks from leaving, and successfully stopped a large number of people for a period of time. . . .
>
> As you know, the banks here are run mainly by Jews. Bank managers are now going through a difficult administrative period, as Jews leave their posts. The banks have cut down on the number of customers; they have unsuccessfully tried using Arab clerks, the children of government ministers, and others from the wealthy classes as bank clerks, and have had to get rid of them within a few days. A month ago, the bank managers came before the Minister of the Interior, asking for more time to find replacements by delaying the departure of Jewish bank clerks. They will apparently have to bring in British citizens to replace the Jews."

The emissaries believed it would take a year before the damage caused by Jewish emigration could be assessed. They claimed—with unbelievable arrogance—that while the leaders of the Iraqi regime expressed doubts concerning heavy damage to the country, they "did not think things through, as material gain dominates their every thought and deed. They are like 'the blind man with a cane who does not see the wall until he walks into it.'"[30] Two weeks after this statement, it became clear that the government did see what was happening, and took action in a way that stunned the Jewish community, Israel, and its emissaries.

Chapter 3

"It Caused a Panic"
Freezing Property Owned by the Jews of Iraq

It was the Sabbath day. That morning, the streets of Baghdad were abuzz with the rumor: The Iraqi Parliament was to convene. On a Saturday? At 3:00 in the afternoon? Why? What was happening? The answer came within a few hours: The government had frozen all assets belonging to Jews. It was March 10, 1951.

Latif H. (who has requested his full name not be published), was 18 years old at the time. His father ran a textile shop in the Suq Menahem Daniel open market, named for a prosperous Jew who was a member of Iraq's senate in the 1950s. It was there, Latif recalls, "I would walk on Saturdays [when] everything was closed. The houses in the Jewish section were twice the price of those in the Muslim area, because the Jews were rich and could afford them." In the 1940s, his family had purchased a half-acre property in Baghdad al-Jadida (New Baghdad). Latif pulls out an envelope and removes a meticulously folded document: A copy of the Land Registry document, listing his father as the most recent owner of the property.

When the State of Israel was established, suddenly there was electricity in the air. I began feeling that because I was a Jew I should go indoors. My father felt a change in his business: His neighbors began stealing his customers in a disgusting fashion. They called him "Jew" as he walked down the street. My father would always say: Whatever you see, don't talk, stay quiet. He always told me not to talk back, because he was afraid my temper would flare up, and a fight would break out. The Jews became second-class citizens, though not officially. But in fact, you couldn't stand up for your rights and express an opinion—and that's worse than being second class; that's fear.

Recalling the property freeze, Latif strikes his forehead, saying: "It caused a panic, created insanity. Whoever had cash brought it to someone who hadn't waived their citizenship, for them to hide. My father had eleven employees, all relatives of ours, who had signed documents requesting to leave the country. He came to me and said, 'Latif, leave school and come to the office, I have no one there.' At night I studied, and during the day I was with him. Those same people would come by, say 'Hello, Latif,' throw a wad of cash on the table, say 'That's 200,' and run off, because they were afraid we wouldn't want to take it."

Did they get receipts? Latif almost laughs. "No receipts and no nothing. It was a lot of money, off the books, intended as a temporary deposit. We returned it all to them via Beirut, through all sort of channels, after they got out of Iraq." You returned it all? This time Latif laughs out loud. "If there had been anyone who thought they hadn't got it back, I wouldn't be alive now. That you see me alive before you is a sign that there is nothing like that."

Latif again turns serious as he explains what the freeze on property meant. "People in the prime of life suddenly couldn't work because they [the government] closed their shops and offices. Many Jews in Baghdad were merchandise buyers working out of town—suddenly their offices were closed, so they began sending us textile shipments without notification; we were [then] to tell their customers to come to us."

In September 1953, Latif left Iraq by himself, after being accepted to the American University in Beirut, and institutions of higher learning in England and the United States. "I preferred Beirut, so I could stay in contact with my parents back in Iraq," he explains. "When the Jews left, they sold their possessions for pennies. A rug worth 2,000 to 3,000 dinar sold for 20 to 30 dinar. In 1960, my father decided to leave as well. He said 'Enough, there's nothing more to be done here.' His children had all gone—three were in Israel, and I was in Beirut. He moved to Beirut, retired, and lived off his savings. They sold our house, which was worth 30,000 dinar, for 1,500 dinar. My father never talked about what was left behind. It was over and done with. The man had gotten out healthy and in one piece—that was enough."[1]

THE SURPRISINGLY SUDDEN DECISION TO FREEZE PROPERTY

What Latif describes so richly was also outlined in a dry and factual telegram sent by Mossad le-Aliya Bet emissaries to Israel on March 10, 1951:

A. A secret, extraordinary meeting was called this morning by the Parliament.

B. At the meeting, a law was passed, controlling and managing properties confiscated from Jews who have recanted their citizenship.

C. The word property refers to real estate belonging to persons who have renounced citizenship or possessed in the form of a guarantee, lease, deposit or any other means. Similarly, this refers to [profits on] the sale of property, deposits, guarantee, lease and all other associated rights, in addition to debts owed, cash, shares and manifest import [import licenses] and deeds.

D. Property belonging to persons who have renounced their citizenship under the Citizenship Deprivation Law will be frozen, and they are forbidden from using any of these means from the day this law is enacted. A custodial office to manage this property will be established, administered by a Custodian-General, to be appointed by decision of the Cabinet. Costs incurred by this office will be covered out of the property.

E. Rules and regulations in the spirit of this law will be set primarily by the Custodian-General's authority, regarding property management, seizure and sale, and also under the authority of others connected to renounced citizenship, including various government ministries and banks.

F. Those breaking the law will be subject to a two-year jail term or a 4,000 dinar fine, the maximum allowed by law. Complaints against the Custodian-General may be submitted, within one month, to the Minister of the Interior who has the authority to pass final decisions [on this matter].

G. During the debate over the law, there were extremist delegates who demanded seizure of communal property, as well as property owned by remaining individuals. There were some who demanded the ouster of Jewish representatives [to Parliament] so long as the majority of Jews were without citizenship.

H. Banks have been instructed by management to stop all payment to Jews until rules and regulations are issued.

The Jews were stunned, but they were not the only ones. The government ministers themselves learned of the proposal only a few hours before being summoned hastily to approve it. On the day Parliament convened, Baghdad's phone system was disconnected, to prevent details of the law from leaking out. The Citizenship Deprivation Law had expired two days earlier; the government revoked the citizenship of those Jews who had requested it, even though deprivation had not been put into effect—a fact that might have indicated something unexpected was going to happen. There was something in the air, and rumors that Jewish property might be confiscated. Despite all this, Gat says, the new law caught the Jews by surprise.

The government of Iraq took great care in announcing not a confiscation or nationalization of property, but only a freeze. The reason: According to international law, confiscation or nationalization obliged Baghdad to compensate property owners—out of the question, as far as the regime was concerned, in this case. One noted Israeli law professor says there is no doubt that, in actual fact, this was confiscation deserving of compensation. He adds: "We may go as far as accusing the Iraqi government of deceitfulness. It froze property one year after inviting Jews to give up their citizenship and register for emigration, and then took the property. If the Jews had known what was going to happen, they might not have registered. This is a clear case of deceit."

IMPLEMENTATION OF THE LAW AND THE VOLUME OF FROZEN PROPERTIES

Iraq's Minister of Finance immediately ordered a bank closure—first one day, then two additional days—to prevent Jews from making transactions in the period between legislation and enactment, when the freeze would go into effect. Jewish merchants came to work to find their shops closed, their warehouses locked and sealed. Merchandise left outside shops and warehouses fell prey to watchmen and porters, who freely took whatever they could. Out of desperation and fear, many Jews agreed to sell their property at any price offered. Trucks carrying Jewish emigrants to the airport were pelted with stones. Postal clerks refused to serve Jewish customers.

By government order, banks and commercial companies fired all Jews without citizenship. As a result, some banks could not operate and were in danger of closing. "Jews walking down the street are attacked by regular police, secret police and just people, who take everything they have in hand, or in pocket," Mossad le-Aliya Bet emissaries wrote on March 12. "The police are liable, at any moment, to enter houses in search of silver and gold. The market has shut down completely. Today, the banks issued detailed lists of sums of money belonging to Jews."

The next day, the Mossad le-Aliya Bet emissaries reported: "After a police closure of all shops, the Jews were forced to buy food, including meat, in Arab shops. The police have already begun entering silver and goldsmiths, and homes where they believe merchandise or gold may be found. Today, they impounded all cars belonging to Jews. Many emigrants whose travel fees were deposited with banks, or money changers, now find themselves without a penny, and we have found families without money to live. These Jews are knocking at our gates [of the camp set up the emissaries], requesting to emigrate to Israel without payment. The Jews have never experienced such critical period, [where] with every arrest and search, the police reveal their barbaric true nature. For the general Iraqi population, these are days of great national celebration."[2]

By March 15, S. Cahana of Israel's Foreign Ministry could summarize the latest developments. Among other things, he mentioned the nomination of a Custodian-General of Jewish property, Hamid Rif'at, formerly Director General of the Ministry of the Interior, "considered respectable, in general, and we hope he can be influenced into softening the decree." An enormous infrastructure of dozens of clerks was set up rapidly alongside Rif'at; the budget was no problem, after all, as costs were in any case covered by purloined Jewish property. Rules and regulations resulting from the law stated that the Custodian-General would issue, out of the frozen property, funds for dependents of the property owners, but in practice this was never done, and "many Jews have become needy, and in need of community assistance."

The emigrants, once allowed to take 50 dinar out of the country were, since the freeze, allowed to take out only 5 dinar, and sometimes not even that paltry amount—depending on "the heartstrings of the airport customs official." These officials also handled—or grossly mishandled—searches among the emigrants effects, confiscating property, which up until that point, Jews had been permitted to take out of the country. In the city streets, Jews fell victim to policemen who confiscated packages, often for themselves. "The Jews of Iraq are stunned and fear riots. In the meantime, many Jews have been arrested, accused of breaking the new law," Cahana reported, adding:

> The law hurts any candidate for emigration who has not yet exited Iraq, in particular about 30,000 who have signed up over the past two months [requesting their citizenship be revoked] but have not yet managed to liquidate their properties, and smuggle the money out to Israel, or keep it in cash. Although for several months rumors abounded among Iraq's Jewish community, we have found that many did take [the word "not" is missing] appropriate measures and continued to keep money in banks, or hesitated from selling property in the hope that prices would rise. Some did withdraw funds, then re-deposited them, having deluded themselves into believing their property was not endangered. In any case, we assume most Jews have managed to covert a certain portion of their property into cash, and have hidden or transferred it outside of Iraq, as a general preventative measure.[3]

On March 22, the government of Iraq widened the scope of the law to encompass property of Jewish citizens of Iraq residing abroad. Those Iraqi passport holders who exited the country legally as of January 1, 1948, and onward, also lost their property. It could be returned, minus the Custodian-General's fee, if they came back to Iraq within two months from a certain date, to be set by the government. In addition, property belonging to Jews who left before 1948 was also frozen, unless they could prove they had reason for living outside the country, as they were dealing in trade. This law damaged several thousand wealthy Iraqi Jews living in the United States, Europe, Iran and Israel.[4]

The Jewish Agency estimated the value of frozen assets at 12 million dinar, of which 6 million dinar was in cash. At that time, one dinar was worth four U.S. dollars, making the property value $48 million, or $290 million in current values. In June 1951, an Israel Ministry of Foreign Affairs memorandum cited estimates valuing frozen assets at 6 million dinar, but noted that "this information is unreliable." The highest estimate, made in April 1951 by new immigrants from Iraq, including a former senior official from a local branch of the Ministry of the Interior quoting the Iraqi press as saying assets were 21 million dinar, of which 4 million dinar were bank deposits.

In current values, this is over $500 million. The same new immigrants also claimed that the actual sum was probably higher. Other new immigrants in that month mentioned 50 million dinar, or $1.2 billion in current values.[5] It should be borne in mind that these figures refer to property that owners were unable to sell prior to leaving Iraq, and that much was sold at a fraction of its real value. In addition, it is unclear whether these estimates—especially regarding real estate—relate to the true property value or income the owners would have received had they been able to sell. Certainly, the value of Jewish property lost to Iraq was in the billions of dollars.

DAYS OF FOREBODING FOR THE JEWS OF IRAQ

The coming days were of fear and foreboding for the Jews of Iraq. Reports filed by emissaries of the Mossad le-Aliya Bet reflected both their desperation and, moreover, that of the local Jews. On March 15, Yerahmiel Asa wrote:

> The situation is unchanged. The market is paralyzed completely. The Division of Public Trade has appealed to the Ministry of Education, demanding they requisition students of economics for work at banks and other companies, in order to bridge the gap left by Jews in these offices. Many [Jewish] families are starving for bread. We fear that emigration to Israel may be damaged by non-payment. Well-to-do families have been left without their emigration fees, now that their assets have been frozen . . . perhaps you can influence British circles in England into putting pressure on [Iraq's] Regent, to repair the situation. The shocking airport searches continue. Government clerks in all ministries continue their negative treatment of Jews. The Postal and Telephone offices refuse to serve Jews. The general public mood is getting to be like [that of] 1948.[6]

The following telegrams were sent in the next days:

> The [foreign-owned] banks received orders from their head offices abroad, forbidding them from transferring frozen assets to the government, keeping it instead. They have been permitted to transfer [to Iraq's government] deposits kept in safety deposit boxes.[7]
>
> [March 19:] The situation remains unchanged. The government formed a committee to visit shops, in the presence of shop-owners, and take inventory. Three lists will be made, one for the shop-owner, two to be submitted to the government. The man in the street's hatred for Jews mounts daily, expressed in many incidents on the streets of Baghdad. In country villages, it is expressed through stealing watches stolen, money and anything else. Jews are afraid of going into the street. Emigration fees from Akra [a city on the Turkish border; the reference is to savings prepared for payment to the Mossad le-Aliya Bet in return for passage to Israel] were taken by the Chief of Police, on the day the Jews set out for the capital, en route to Israel.[8]

[March 20:] In close cooperation with the committee [of the Jewish community] we are trying to obligate the Custodian-General [for Jewish property] to grant further deductions [above and beyond those allowed by the law] regarding payments and business liquidation. We have begun refusing the poor [candidates for emigration] as all their money is frozen and they have no means of payment. . . . Most of those boarding our most recent flights left behind furniture in their houses, and merchandise in their closed shops. We assume this situation will continue as regards the emigrants on upcoming flights. Jews whose property has been frozen have appealed to us, asking if they may present documents in Israel proving ownership of the frozen property. If so, how should these documents be transferred.[9]

[March 20:] According to our people in Babylon, the percentage of well-to-do emigrants is 20%. Only people without means boarded our last three flights. The question has come up, should we slow down the pace, to force the government of Babylon into giving money to the emigrants, to cover their cost.

The reasoning behind the last suggestion was that, since the government of Iraq wished to rid itself of Jews, it might be susceptible to pressure.

On March 22, as mentioned above, the Property Freeze Law was amended to include Jews holding Iraqi passports, who had exited Iraq as of 1948. The following day the Mossad le-Aliya Bet reported to the Ministry of Foreign Affairs that the new law "relates to most of the remaining property belonging to Iraqi Jews who had not renounced their citizenship. This includes the major Jewish merchants who had left Iraq but whose businesses continued to be managed by relatives. . . . Our emissaries believe the law could bring about an 80% freeze on property of Jews who had not renounced their citizenship. This law has so broken the spirits of those Jews who had not renounced their citizenship, that their leadership, headed by Ezra Daniel, met yesterday and decided to request that the government of Iraq now rescind their [own] citizenship as well, of all the Jews who had not renounced their citizenship"[10] [underlined in the original].

TESTIMONIES OF EMIGRANTS IN MARCH AND APRIL 1951

During those weeks, Jewish Agency employees in Israel routinely asked the immigrants arriving from Iraq: Why were Jewish assets frozen? Who is managing the frozen property? What is the Jews' security situation? What is the economic situation of emigration applicants? How can the property be saved? What is the public reaction to the government's action? Is the Jewish community taking measures to counteract the freeze? Are there [any] reports of violence against Jews? Most answers were similar in spirit, if different in style. This is what Basra port clerk Semah Menashe Nawarani and engineer Nazem Yehuda, both of whom arrived in Israel on March 15, had to say:

The number of attacks on the street rises from day to day. Every day you hear rumors of beatings and theft on the street. The mob sees this as an opportunity to steal, claiming it is better that Jewish money be put in its hands, rather than government hands. The situation has created great tension among the Jews; this atmosphere prevents them from leaving the house. In cases where they must leave the house, they empty their pockets of every penny.

Starvation is drawing closer. Yesterday, it was very hard to find a slice of bread for the children. They spend the few pennies they have at home but are not earning anything, and this increases the danger looming overhead. This fear is greatest among the last emigration candidates [those last in line]. The situation improved somewhat when a few greengrocers and butcher shops opened. Whoever has Arab friends or acquaintances, meanwhile, is selling off their household goods at low, low prices, before the government manages to enter their houses and take inventory. Meantime, they are hiding the money until they find a way to transfer it, after things calm down. They believe they may be able to save part of their property, using Jews whose Iraqi citizenship has not yet been rescinded, but for now, nothing of this sort has been attempted, out of fear."

As shown by Latif's story, told earlier in this chapter, this channel was used later on.[11]

A summary report of testimonies delivered by immigrants arriving in Israel on March 20 mentions street attacks and that

dozens of instances of outright robbery, in public, are perpetrated on Jews, on a daily basis, particularly by the police. . . . The Jews try to sell furniture and movable goods to their Arab neighbors at 5% of their true value. This is better than handing their possessions over to the police. At the airport, the customs officials steal the emigrants' few belongings, and happy is the man with only half his things stolen, who gets away without being beaten, cursed, spat on and kicked. Some police get on the plane and strip the emigrants of some of their clothes. The children cry incessantly from thirst but are not given water, and the police make fun of them.[12]

On March 24, civil engineer Anbar Abdallah Habza and customs agent Na'im Yossef Darvish landed in Israel. They testified: "The past few days have been relatively quiet in terms of street attacks. The improvement is because, at first, the Arabs thought the new law [freezing property] meant they could wreak havoc on Jews, permitted them to attack and intimidate, but their dream turned out to be a disappointment. There is only one way to save Jewish property: It must be smuggled out by Jews who are not signed up for emigration to Israel. But the amount that can be saved through this method is negligible, compared to what needs saving."

Regarding the treatment of emigrants at the Baghdad airport, Habza and Darvish said: "The height of cruelty was on the day police began beating the emigrants with clubs. The groans of adults being beaten mingled with the cries of children weeping from hunger and thirst. They are forbidden from bringing any money at all, not to mention the fact that emigrants are robbed, often stripped of the clothes they wear [by customs officials and policemen] who take them for themselves."

Other emigrants related:

> According to one regulation, emigrants were granted the right to sell furniture for income, but this regulation is still but ink on paper. Some Jews sell their possessions on the sly. Whoever has a few pennies, sits and rots in the coffeehouse all day long, and whoever doesn't, wanders the coffeehouses, and begs from door to door. . . . Jews smuggle money to England. The process takes 13% of their money [as a commission] in return for British pounds sterling. The amounts being smuggled out are very marginal, as the matter is just getting started. The other smuggling routes, most if not all, are shut down. Most smuggling activity, at present, is carried out by Jews who have not signed up to emigrate to Israel.[13]

The testimonies of April's immigrants remained harsh. Sallim Nahum Shakuri was an importer of a range of goods, and Yitzhak Sallah Sultan was a senior official at Iraq's Ministry of the Interior, before coming to Israel on April 5. They said:

> Although it was announced that Jews were allowed to sell kitchenware, household furnishings and simple items, this is done only in secret, as the first ones who tried selling were caught by the police, and suffered greatly. Even if Jews do begin selling their things in public, the sales will bring in only a fraction of their expenses. These objects are being sold for cheap, at prices that are hard to believe, for example: a set of the finest table linens for not more than 4 dinar. The situation has forced a good number of Jews into wandering the coffeehouses, begging for alms. . . .
>
> In the past few days, [the regime] has begun taking inventory of shops, in the presence of shop owners. (Inventory of the warehouse belonging to new immigrant A [Shakuri]) took over two days, and the total value of merchandise was 4,000 dinar). They are not given receipts, aside from some given to owners of impounded automobiles, but in most cases these receipts, too, are confiscated by customs. Estimates made by the Iraqi press put the total value of frozen property at 21 million dinar, of which 4 million is cash that was deposited in banks. But the value of frozen property may be set even higher than Iraqi press estimates, particularly after the announcement of a freeze on property belonging to Jews living abroad.[14]

Over the coming years, more new immigrants gave testimony regarding lost property, as part of the overall registration of claims made by immigrants to Israel from Arab countries. Y. K., who came to Israel in August 1951, said he had left behind 7,525 dinar, $180,000 in current values. He owned a two-story house, two shops, three lots in New Baghdad, an oil production factory in Kirkuk, a 1939 Chevrolet, furniture, shop fixtures, gold, and more. Moreover, six Iraqi citizens owed him 3,370 dinar—close to $81,000 in current values.[15]

THE DEBATE IN ISRAEL OVER REACTION TO THE FREEZE

The Property Freeze Law disturbed the government of Israel for two reasons. First, as seen in Chapter 2, in the months preceding, Jerusalem did try to save at least a portion of Iraqi Jewish property, if only out of economic motivations. The law, naturally, was a death blow to those efforts. Second, and most important, the overall impression of the Property Freeze Law, taken together with eye-witness accounts of physical attacks on Jews, and the pogromlike atmosphere on the streets of Iraq, raised serious concerns regarding not just the Jews' property, but their safety and perhaps their lives. The Israeli press reported in detail on what was happening (apparently relying on testimonies given by new immigrants, and leaked intentionally), and mentioned that the government of Iraq wished to imprison Jews in concentration camps—a particularly chilling expression so little time after the Holocaust. This last point apparently relied on Iraqi Prime Minister Sai'd having made such a suggestion during the government debate over the Property Freeze Law, but his position was rejected, according to reports made at that time by Mossad le-Aliya Bet emissaries.

By March 15, the Israeli government was already discussing the issue and looking into different ways to react, as revealed by its protocol, published for the first time in 1997 by Dr. Zaki Shalom. At the meetings outset, Minister of Foreign Affairs Moshe Sharett explained that the law affected only those Jews wishing to leave Iraq, not those remaining. Regarding those already in Israel, it was said they would "undergo a drastic change. To date, they were free to do as they pleased with their property. They could not take money with them, but could sell their property, [albeit] almost for free . . . or leave it unattended, and—in the absence of any other owners—remain the owners, or assign an executor, whether a Jew remaining behind, or a reliable Muslim. Now they have lost that freedom. Their property stays confiscated."

Sharett gave his colleagues a real-life example: "When you have a law like this, clerks begin interpreting it, and sometimes their interpretations are random. When a man exits Iraq with a ring on his finger, the clerk sees that ring as property that should not be transported across the country's borders, and he pulls the ring off the man's finger. But, it is impossible to know if that ring is then submitted to the State-appointed Custodian-General, or dropped into the clerk's pocket. The emigrant can't investigate the matter. They carry out dreadful property searches, break and tear things, all manner of haphazard, chaotic behavior." Sharett was convinced the Iraqis saw the Property Freeze Law as following a precedent set by the Israel, which in 1948 placed controls on property belonging to Arab refugees, "and in doing so, took this property for ourselves."

The ministers now began discussions on what should be done. The first proposal was to request that the United States and Great Britain intervene and try influencing Iraq to change its decision. Sharett expressed doubt as to the idea's effectiveness: "I must say, from my experience, these appeals neither help nor hinder. To date, they have yielded no results, and there was one instance where the U.S. refused to intervene." That was a year earlier, when Israel had asked the United States to pressure Iraq into increasing the amount of money Jews were allowed to take out of the country. Sharett also feared the world powers would say bluntly: You took the Arab's property, Iraq is taking Jewish property—a statement that would legitimize Iraq's actions. Intervention was therefore a losing proposition.

Sharett also had reservations regarding proposed UN intervention, saying it would result in bringing up the Arab contention that Israel was the human rights violator. In any case, he said, Israel's appeals to the UN never went anywhere and that would be the fate of this appeal, too. On the other hand, Minister of the Interior Moshe Shapira was convinced that appealing to the UN would bring world attention to Iraq's actions; Israel's silence could be interpreted as acquiescence to the property freeze; there was a vast difference between Jerusalem's actions and Baghdad's; this was an opportunity to pay back the Arabs for their anti-Israel propaganda. Shapira said: "All the new immigrant's stories are horrifying. They [the Iraqis] search even wounds, pulling off bandages to see if there are diamonds hidden underneath," and claimed that even if an appeal to the UN wouldn't help, it couldn't hurt.

Minister of Police Behor Shitrit suggested confiscating Arab property in Israel and giving it to the new immigrants from Iraq. In his opinion, the new immigrants could claim rightfully that their distress resulted from the establishment of the State of Israel and therefore Israel had the moral obligation to compensate every immigrant from every country. Minister of Transportation David Remez proposed that every immigrant to Israel be given $200 in financial compensation, in lieu of the 50 dinar they were forbidden from taking out of Iraq. "What you suggest," Minister of Finance Kaplan told Remez, "means printing hundreds of millions of pounds, and tossing them into the economy. There is no logic or justification to this. We can only cause harm with this sort of decision." Sharett and Shapira also opposed the Remez proposal, which represented a huge sum of money for a government already bearing the expense of housing and employment of new immigrants.

At the end of the meeting, a compromise proposal was reached, which became the official policy: Israel would announce that the question of frozen Jewish property would be accounted for when discussion of a permanent settlement between it and the Arab countries would be held, and the value of Jewish property would be subtracted from the amount demanded by Palestinian refugees. At the same time, the government decided to appeal to the United States and Great Britain, while a UN appeal was postponed and handed over to the Ministry of Foreign Affairs for a final decision.

SHARETT'S DECLARATION AND A FAILED ATTEMPT AT GAINING INTERNATIONAL SUPPORT

On March 19, Sharett presented the decision to the Knesset, criticized the Iraqi government's measures against that country's Jews, and announced Israel's official policy. This announcement has significance above and beyond the problem of Iraqi Jewish property, as it refers to Jews in Arab countries in general and forms the basis for Israeli policy on the matter to this very day. Sharett said:

> The government of Israel has considered urgently the emerging situation. We see, in this episode of legally enforced theft, a continuation of the insolently oppressive regime that has always existed in Iraq against defenseless, helpless minorities, [A reference to the Assyrian massacre of 1933]. We have decided to appeal, via diplomatic channels, to those world powers having friendly relations with the government of Iraq, apprise them of this serious situation, and its inherent danger. . . .
>
> For our part, however, we do not see any alternative but to draw direct conclusions from the facts before us. By freezing the property of scores of Jews coming to Israel . . . the government of Iraq has opened an account between itself and the State of Israel. There is an account between us and the Arab world, and it is the amount of compensation owed to the Arabs who left the State of Israel's territory and abandoned their property, following the war of aggression of the Arab world against our country. The act perpetrated now by the government of Iraq regarding the property of Jews, who did not break Iraqi law, disturb its status, or undermine its security, [now] forces us to link the two accounts. Therefore, the government [of Israel] has decided to notify the appropriate UN institutions, and I state this in the plural, that the value of Jewish property frozen in Iraq will be taken into account by us, in [calculating] the compensation we undertake to pay those Arabs who abandoned their property in Israel.[16]

Sharett's statement reached the emissaries and Jewish community in Iraq quickly, as it was published in local newspapers *al-Sha'ab* and *al-Zaman*. The following day, the emissaries reported: "Sharett's announcement to the Knesset has had positive repercussions among the Jews, as well as the Arabs. The Jews believe they have someone they can count on. The depression weighing on them has been greatly eased." That easy feeling resulted from the assumption, soon proved mistaken, that the government of Israel was about to pay the Jews of Iraq compensation out of Palestinian property. Many Jews began asking the emissaries what the guidelines were for proving ownership of frozen property after emigration to Israel.[17]

On March 20, Sharett met with U.S. Ambassador to Israel Monnett B. Davis and the head of the British delegation in Tel Aviv, Sir Alexander Helm. Sharett gave both a memo on the property freeze, delineating the measures, and mentioning possible courses of action discussed by the government of Iraq—confiscation of all properties owned by the Jews of Iraq, and imprisonment of future emigrants in concentration camps. Sharett warned that the Jews were panicky and afraid there might be a widespread mob outburst against them if the world powers did not exert their influence on Iraq to moderate its attitude toward the Jews. He notified them of the linkage between the two accounts, made clear that Israel had no alternative, and promised to waive the linkage should Iraq make an acceptable promise to liquidate properties in a way that would give the Jewish owners what they were entitled to. Sharett noted the heavy financial burden on Israel, in light of the fact that the rate of immigration increased, but the new immigrants arrived with next to nothing. Iraq had demanded that any Jew wishing to leave should do so by May 31, but under this policy, 25,000 Jews would remain behind, stripped of citizenship and property. The world powers were asked to take steps to protect the Jews of Iraq, safeguard their continued emigration, and ensure their property.

Organizations and leaders of the Jewish communities in the United States and Great Britain also tried to assist the Jews of Iraq, and tried to convince their governments to help. A delegation representing the Board of Deputies, Agudat Yisrael, and the British Sepharadic and Portuguese Jewish community met with British Minister of State in the Foreign Office of Kenneth Younger. The delegation drew a parallel between Iraqi and Nazi policy and asked that His Majesty's Government influence Baghdad to cease prejudicial policies, ensure Jewish safety, and allow Jews to benefit from their property. In the United States, Congressman Emanuel Celler appealed to Secretary of State Dean Acheson, claimed Iraq's actions might represent a dangerous precedent, and suggested monetary sanctions against Iraq.[18]

The United States and Great Britain rejected the claims made both by Israel and the Jewish organizations. Washington was convinced that, in general, Baghdad's policy could be defined as restrained, as the city had witnessed neither hate crimes, riots, nor a reign of terror. The U.S. Embassy in Baghdad reported there was no material evidence either that the Jews' situation had deteriorated or that their lives were in danger since the property freeze. In their opinion, Israel was stirring up public opinion intentionally to increase fundraising among the American Jews, in preparation for Ben-Gurion's upcoming visit to the United States in early May. The U.S. State Department was also convinced it was illogical to file an appeal with Iraq regarding Jewish property while, concurrently, Israel was taking similar steps regarding Arab property. Thus, Sharett's predictions came to pass although perhaps even he did not foresee the overt indifference, the avoidance of reality displayed by U.S. State Department officials.

Great Britain took a similar stance. The embassy in Baghdad reported incidents of theft perpetrated by police officers. But these incidents stopped after a few days; the mob no longer swarmed over Jewish property, and there was no violence at all against Jews. London went so far as to say that the Iraqi measures should not be seen as separate from Israel's policies, as the freeze of Jewish property was the result of Arab frustration over the Palestinian's suffering. The same Great Britain that rejected Sharett's claim accepted Nuri Sa'id's contention that his government did not intend to keep the Jewish property for itself, but merely wished to hold it until Israel's policy regarding Arab property was clarified.

For years, the British knew about Jewish persecution in Iraq but did nothing. In January 1955, a Foreign Office official sitting in London summed up his country's policy, and wrote persuasively: "Iraqi regulations governing residence abroad by Iraqi Jews were published in *The Times* in this country and have for some years been applied to Iraqi Jews resident in the United Kingdom. H.M.G. have not protested to the Iraqis against this treatment of their nationals." When the Citizenship Deprivation Law was passed, and it was clear that Jewish émigrés to Great Britain might be included, London took an almost unbelievable step: "A note was addressed to the Iraqi Ministry for Foreign Affairs reserving H.M.G.'s right to deport from the United Kingdom any Iraqi national deprived of his nationality under this ordinance." In other words: Jews losing their citizenship would be banished, most likely sent back to Iraq. And when, in March 1951, it was decreed that Jews not returning to Iraq within two months would lose their citizenship, the British Interior Ministry feared "a flood of unwanted Jews," as the British Embassy in Baghdad put it, four years later. The Embassy therefore announced that Jews in this category might be deported from England. At the same time, Britain began "closely inspecting Jewish entry" into its territories.

For a year, from mid-1951 on, Great Britain tried convincing Iraq to mark clearly, on passports held by Jews, the amount of time they were allowed to spend outside their homeland. The British intention was clear: They wanted to know when permits expired, forbidding their holders from staying any longer. London also decided it had no responsibility whatsoever to bring the Iraqi Jewish problem before the UN, and as mentioned previously, did not protest their treatment. Nonetheless, in 1955, when Baghdad asked for active assistance in enforcing anti-Jewish rules—as we shall see in the next chapter— Great Britain refused.[19]

The British remained indifferent even when, in January 1952, the question arose regarding property in the United Kingdom owned by Iraqi Jews who were now new immigrants in Israel. Documents from British Ministry of Foreign Affairs paint a shocking picture: The British government refused to release the assets owned by the new immigrants but held within its territories. By doing so, it essentially had a hand in Iraq's illegal actions, which at the same time, it officially condemned. As mentioned earlier in this chapter, Iraq most likely froze properties without any form of compensation, as required by international law, and acted with intent to deceive Jews. Great Britain, with its important strategic and economic interests in Iraq, sacrificed Jewish property, justice, and law on the altar of self-interest.[20]

The fate of Iraqi Jewish property held in Britain had already been raised in late December by treasury official D. R. Serpell. A reply to his query from the British Foreign Office, sent in late January, shows Serpell had made a novel proposition as to how to release Jewish property: Reassign the bank accounts to Israel instead of Iraq. But the Foreign Office shied away from the very idea itself, as can be read between the lines of the reply sent by J. C. Wardroup: "I am afraid we could not afford to take the risk of being charged with bad faith, as we certainly should if the matter came to the ears of the Iraqis."

The reply received by Serpell was based on an informal conversation held in early January between F. H. Gamble of the British Embassy in Baghdad and another Englishman, named Phillimore, who happened to be the chief cashier at the Iraqi Central Bank. The two agreed that the chances of the Iraqi government responding positively to the request were nil. In his reply to London, Gamble stressed that the Iraqi government enforced property freeze rules stringently and was unwilling to hear even a mention of a possible release of property.

Serpell didn't give up. In early February, he sent a letter to C. E. Lombe of the Bank of England, conceding that he certainly did not want Iraq to accuse Britain of bad faith, but adding: "I understand, however, that some of these funds are not in fact subject to Iraq Exchange Central and indeed are unknown by the Iraqi authorities to exist." If this was indeed the case, Serpell went on, perhaps the Treasury might do something to "redesignate" these funds, meaning: Transfer ownership to Israel. But it soon became clear that there was no way of distinguishing between those accounts that Baghdad knew about and those that it didn't. What remained was a choice between "redesignation" of all bank accounts—a step the Iraqis would learn of very quickly—and doing nothing. The British chose the latter.[21]

Today, the Bank of England says the accounts were already frozen in 1947, under the laws controlling foreign currency, which, at that time, were intended to maintain British pound sterling values. The bank now says it was not responsible for those accounts, as it almost only handled assets belonging to the British government and other banks; it did not handle not commercial accounts, unless questions arose regarding controls of foreign currency.

Andrew Wardlow of the Bank of England press office responded to this writer: "Iraqi sterling had been blocked since 1947, but redesignating these accounts as Israeli would have made them freely transferable. It was, however, very unlikely that Iraq would agree to this. It would still have been possible to redesignate the accounts of whose existence Iraq might be un-aware, but this was thought likely to be counterproductive."

The torment arising from the stance taken by United States and Great Britain poses questions that will not go away. Would they have reacted in this fashion had the frozen property belonged not to Iraq's Jews but to their own citizens? At least, in the case of Great Britain, one need not guess; the proof is in Britain's quick and definite reaction to Egypt's confiscation of civilian property in 1956, as presented in Chapter 6. True, the situation of Jews in 1951 Iraq cannot be compared to that of European Jewry a decade earlier, but this sort of outrageous, selfish indifference gives rise to such associations.

REGISTRATION OF CLAIMS MADE BY IRAQI IMMIGRANTS TO ISRAEL

To implement the policy linking Jewish and Arab property claims, Israel needed to know how much property the Jews of Iraq left behind. To this end, claims were recorded by the Bureau for External Claims, established originally to record property claims made by Holocaust survivors. In November 1949, the Bureau began registering claims made by Jews from Arab countries but received few applicants. Therefore, in July 1950, the Bureau put an ad in the papers calling on all immigrants from Arab countries to document their claims, "[as] the government can protect the rights of all citizens in any negotiations [with Arab countries] only if it has full details on property in its possession. Property owners who do not notify [the authorities] may not benefit from any agreement signed by the government, and the government will have no recourse but to withdraw its support of those [unregistered] claims on property."[22] But response was still slow, partly because the new immigrants were preoccupied by problems of existence in a new country, partly because they were unaware of Israeli government procedures, and partly because the possibility of a peace settlement, in which property claims would be presented, seemed remote.

In June 1952, Moshe Sasson, then an official in the Middle East Division at Israel's Ministry of Foreign Affairs—and much later on Ambassador to Egypt—reported on registration up to that point to the Israeli Custodian-General. Between November 1949 and June 1950, 110 claims were filed by immigrants from Iraqi, including claims on the estimated value of real estate. There were more than 1,500 additional claims whose real estate value was not estimated as yet. In any case, numbers were submitted by the new immigrants themselves, and "we have encountered difficulties in property valuation, as the property owners do not know the value of their property. A significant number of property owners, including major institutions [apparently major business and company owners] have refrained from registering their properties, as they see no immediate benefit to registration. Presumably, should circumstances change, their positions may alter."

In his report, Sasson also included partial data on Iraqi Jewish property, as reported by the Bureau at the end of 1951. There were only 196 registered claims; for some, property values had not been determined. Among them were claims on several dozen houses in Baghdad, ten houses in Basra, over a dozen lots on Baghdad, three factories, bank accounts, shares in the New Baghdad Company, Iraqi government bonds, and two citrus groves. The total monetary value was 1.21 million dinar, of $29 million in current values.[23]

This presents the opportunity to play with statistics. Let us assume these figures represent a sampling of all new immigrants from Iraq (taking into account Sasson's statement that a significant number of wealthy persons had not filed claims at all). There were 130,000 new immigrants to Israel from Iraq. If the average family had between six and seven members, this means about 20,000 households. If each claim represents one household, and almost 200 claims equal almost $30 million, then 20,000 claims are worth 100 times their value, or $3 billion in current values. Even if this figure is not representative, even given a large positive margin of error, the resulting assessment of the value Jewish property in Iraq is still high, certainly in excess of $1 billion.

THE FREEZE'S EFFECT ON THE IRAQI ECONOMY

The property freeze, and the Jewish emigration that increased in its wake, had a negative effect on Iraq's economy, even with the clearly profitable takeover of Jewish property. The immediate result, in the words of Sir John Troutbeck, British Ambassador to Iraq, was that, "the local market was thrown into confusion, particularly since administrative arrangements are not sufficient to cope with the volume of work involved in implementing the laws." Troutbeck stated definitively that confusion in implementing the law would continue for a long time and warned British companies dealing in transfer of funds to carefully examine the documents of their Jewish contacts before making any business deals.

Troutbeck added that the Iraqi banks had lost half their clerks and did not know with whom of their clients they were permitted to work, as they had been instructed to deal only with Jews who had not renounced their citizenship. Many brokers and agents in many areas of trade were Jews; their activities were put on hold. Muslim- and Christian-owned companies with close ties to Jews, or Jewish employees, were completely at a loss and did not know what moves to make. "In general, there is a standstill in the local markets and no transactions are taking place until it is known how frozen Jewish assets will be disposed of." It was clear that many Jewish businesses would close, and others would suffer from mismanagement for a time, but the ambassador's opinion was that the Iraqi market would get back on the right track within a few months.

The situation remained static through April, as reported by Troutbeck.

> The local markets are depressed and no transactions, except for food products, are taking place. There is a shortage of cash and this is causing a number of merchants to cancel credits at the bank opened in earlier years. Consequently, prices of all commodities have fallen. There were, however, some signs that the confusion which has been caused in March by the laws and regulations freezing Jewish assets was diminishing and that the Custodian-General was administering these laws in a reasonable manner. It is rumoured that about 95 per cent of the Jewish firms in Baghdad now intend closing down.[24]

In his annual report to the Minister of Foreign Affairs Anthony Eden, on the events of 1951 in Iraq, Troutbeck devoted part of Section 30 (next to last in his report) to the property freeze and its ramifications. He wrote that the law caused confusion for a number of months and created a situation where persons with little to no experience were put in positions once filled, for many years, by Jews. Things had improved toward the end of the year, but lack of credit was still a problem, due to the exit of Jewish financiers.[25]

One specific problem noted by the British Embassy was the Iraqi government's difficulty in proper account administration. The reason for Britain's attentiveness to this problem was that the Iraqi government employed 200 British nationals, and administrative problems delayed their salary payments. Another possible reason may be, as we will see presently, that Baghdad's only accountancy firm was British.

In December 1952, the British Embassy in Baghdad contacted the Middle East Division of the Ministry of Foreign Affairs in London, reporting that Iraq's Ministry of Finance had fired the last seven Jewish officials in its employ. One of them handled the British clerks' salaries and "although he was anything but efficient, he has at least a knowledge of accountancy procedures." According to the British Embassy, "The Iraqis have now left themselves, in all their departments, with hardly any trained accountants." T.R.D. Belgrave asked the Foreign Ministry in London if a six- to nine-month course in government accountancy might be organized for the Muslim officials who would be replacing the Jews.

The Foreign Ministry supported the request and handed it over to the Treasury's care. After some research, the Middle East Division at the Foreign Ministry reported its conclusions on the matter. Iraqi accountants could be trained two at a time, by the Treasury and the Ministry of Finance. In addition, they could be sent to accounting and auditing courses, run by suitable private institutions. The Middle East Division emphasized that this did not constitute a precedent for training foreign accountants in the United Kingdom but was prepared for once to break with tradition. Additionally, the British government was prepared to host senior Iraqi government accountants for short visits, during which time they would observe British methods of financial administration; and at the same time, to this end, a senior British accountant might be sent to Baghdad. The ministries concluded there was little to be gained from training junior accountants and that it was preferable to focus on increasing professionalism among senior accountants via the two options. Apparently, according to British Foreign Ministry files, the initiative was never carried out.[26]

Doubtless, Jewish emigration severely damaged accountancy procedures for both the Iraqi government and government companies. Morris Kanne, former president of the Israel Institute of Certified Public Accountants, was born in Baghdad in 1928. His father, Joseph, was a clerk for NAAFI (the British army canteen organization) who dealt in checking prices for products on the free market in order to price them properly for the soldiers. Their close connection to the British was a source of fear for the family during the Farhud of June 1941; in addition to the crime of being Jewish, they feared the mob would accuse them of collaboration. The rioters were stopped before they reached Kanne's well-to-do neighborhood, where the family had meanwhile found refuge in the house of a Muslim neighbor. "He invited us over, and said, absolutely, that they could come in and hurt us only over his dead body," Kanne remembers.

When Kanne was seventeen, he too was employed by NAAFI and stationed at the Habania air base on the banks of the Euphrates, east of Baghdad. Morris Kanne was twenty when the State of Israel was established and was already chief clerk of the Habania NAAFI. At that time, his father Joseph worked as a clerk in a large trading firm in Baghdad, owned by the Danhour family. Later, Morris moved over to the British Winnie-Marie accountancy firm in Baghdad, then the only CPA firm in Iraq. "All the senior auditors were Jews; only later were a few Palestinian refugees accepted to work there. Two office managers and another two senior accountants were British; the rest of the senior staff—all Jewish. In all, they employed about 30 Jews," Kanne relates.

The Kanne family registered for emigration to Israel and sold their property before the freeze; they were among the few unscathed by the law. Joseph Kanne sold the two-story family home at an acceptable loss, while movable goods were sold "for almost nothing." He deposited the money not with a bank, but in a life insurance policy issued by an Italian insurance firm. "We were afraid," Morris explains in brief the reason for the unusual deposit, which to a large extent saved the family: After arriving in Israel, the money was returned in full to the family members. On the other hand, Morris Kanne suffered personal ruin. "When the property freeze came [into effect], the government ordered that only half-salaries be paid to non-citizens, just enough for them to live, and the rest went to the government. I was a senior accountant at my office [one degree below partner], one of six or seven seniors, and my salary was the highest—£50 per month. The government took half of that."

But the damage did not last long, as in April 1951, the Kanne family emigrated to Israel. "I came to the airport with my father, mother and sister. You were allowed to take out one suitcase, weighing 20 kilograms, and if you wanted to take out photographs or documents, you needed official permission, which we had. I was dressed in fine European style—suit, tie and hat. The customs officials opened the suitcases, tore out my hat lining to see if we'd hidden anything. But we hadn't, because my father was very careful and didn't want to take chances." Once in Israel, Joseph Kanne first worked in low-paying jobs, then as an accountant and a clerk, before retiring. "He always longed for the good life in Iraq, but slowly he adjusted, and circumstances improved." Did his father ever mention the possibility of returning to Iraq? Kanne answers immediately and emphatically, "Never."[27]

Chapter 4

"Down to Their Last Crust of Bread"

Highs and Lows for the Jews of Iraq, from the 1950s to Saddam Hussein

In June 1955, Israel's Prime Minister and Foreign Minister Moshe Sharett decided on a concerted effort to register Iraqi Jewish claims on property. Sharett nominated a committee, headed by Mercantile Discount Bank general manager Shlomo Noah, who also housed the committee in his bank offices. The committee members were Dr. Ezra Korin, Ya'akov Lev, and Shlomo Darvish, along with two members of Knesset, Benjamin Sasson and Shlomo Hillel. The official announcement defined the committee's role as: "[to] register and examine all manner of claims, and compile material that can help realize them," but also emphasized, "The intent at this stage is only to register claims and compile material as preparation for any action that may be considered in the future."

One informed source is convinced that, with hindsight, the best information on property belonging to immigrants from Arab countries in general, and Iraq in particular, was collected at that time, before "[they were] taken by flights of fancy." Response was still slight, however, and only a few thousand forms were registered, out of the over 25,000 families that had come to Israel from Iraq. To this day, the official claims summary has still not been made public. Mordechai Ben-Porat explains what happened: "The new immigrants were hesitant to register. They said: 'Not only did they bring us here to suffer, they want to take our property too?' Aside from that, they were preoccupied with getting bread for their children, and finding a place to live."

The committee determined, in October 1955, that property registration would deal solely with land: "We therefore agree that the Jews of Babylon will not be asked about the movable goods left by them in their homes, in accordance with the Prime Minister's opinion that this form of registration might conflict with our compensations policy for Arab refugees which concentrates on real estate only. . . . Conversely, a section of registered claims will be devoted to merchandise submitted to the Custodian-General in return for a receipt. This type of property is dissimilar to Arab property abandoned in the State of Israel."

Questionnaires in Hebrew and Arabic were printed up for claims registration, with the clarification across the top that submission did not obligate the committee or the government in any way. Property values were recorded in Iraqi dinar, and claimants were asked to specify the related documents in their possession, though not to attach them at this time. In accordance with the committee's decision, no space was allocated to movable goods, only real estate (according to 1949 values, in order to weigh them against Palestinian claims), bank accounts (current savings, deposits, bank safes, and safety deposit boxes), life insurance, pension and provident funds, stocks and bonds, debts favoring the claimant, bills of lading, claims made by the Iraqi government or semi-official entities, and "property held by the Inheritance Authority." In the margins, claimants were asked to write down the names of two witnesses, now living in Israel, who knew them in Iraq, and in doing so, "cite the names of prominent personages, in society or business."[1]

A RELATIVELY PEACEFUL MID-1950s

At the same time Iraqi Jews in Israel were being asked to register claims on stolen property, their brothers in Iraq were enjoying relative peace and quiet. The number of Jews left in Iraq after "Operation Ezra and Nehemia" is subject to a broad range of estimates, but most sources agree there were about 5,000.[2] R. A. Beaumont of the British Embassy in Baghdad described the Jewish community in July 1955 in a letter sent to Colonel J. Teague, the head of the Passport Control Division at the British Foreign Office in London. According to Beaumont, "The original trauma against the Jewish community was gone. Many of the remaining Jews were professional, respected Iraqi citizens, and the head of the Jewish community confirmed that relations with the government were good. The Iraqi government had eased the original law restricting freedom of movement for Jews, and it was less likely that the citizenship of the remaining Jews would be revoked." At this point in time, Iraqi Jews receiving permission to leave the country could stay abroad twelve months without losing their citizenship, as compared with the 1950 order issued to Jews already residing abroad, to return within two months or lose their citizenship.[3]

At that time, the British Foreign Office was interested in what happened to Jewish property in Iraq. The Embassy reported that property was frozen, not confiscated, and was being held by the local government until either an arrangement was reached with Israel or its value declined to nothing due to surcharges. This point is very important, as the memo makes clear that Iraq was taking the property for itself slowly, under the guise of covering costs incurred by the Custodian-General. The Embassy noted that the Custodian-General levied a 15% charge on property values over the initial two-year period after the law was passed, with 5% per year charged thereafter.[4] A simple calculation proves that all property would be gone within sixteen years—by 1966, for accuracy's sake. Iraq took this property—ready cash and real estate after sale—essentially, to fund the cost of the theft itself. Other examples have already been presented in which Baghdad's actions are reminiscent of Nazi Berlin during the darkest days of human history. So it was in this case: It was Nazi practice to charge out of confiscated Jewish property, for the cost of confiscation, and more gravely, for the cost of destroying the property owners.

In light of this practice, there is small wonder that the value of Jewish property in Iraq was very low that year. A memo sent in April 1955, by Trade Secretary at the British Embassy R. W. Munro, reported the value of Jewish property was no more than 22.1 million dinar, at the highest possible estimate. After talks with Rabbi Sasson Kaduri, several Jewish community leaders, British bank clerks, and U.S. embassy sources, Munro outlined the following, regarding property:

- Bank assets—Between 600,000 dinar and 1.1 million dinar
- Real estate—Bank estimates: 4 to 5 million dinar; Jewish declarations: 12 to 15 million dinar
- Movable goods—Bank estimates: 1 to 2 million dinar; Jewish declarations: 3 to 6 million dinar

Munro added that the Custodian-General was not very efficient. "They never answer letters or enquiries addressed to them by the Embassy, nor do they appear to be administering the properties under their control in a very correct manner." He said, for example, that a few years before, the Custodian-General had sold a business named "Iraqi Bookshop" for only 700 dinar, when the value of merchandise alone was far higher, and the Publisher's Association of Great Britain owed the business £800 on books. There were allegations, Munro continued, that friends of the Custodian-General staff could buy Jewish property at below market value; for this reason, it was impossible to assess property values accurately.[5] Munro—either innocently or with typical British understatement—did not cite the plain facts: The Custodian-General sold off property at almost any price because even one dinar was clear profit on stolen property.

THE JEWS UNDER QASIM—THE SITUATION IMPROVES

A real improvement in Jewish life in Iraq came only after the bloody coup of 1958, when the monarchy was abolished and a group of military officers came to power, headed by former division commander Brigadier Abd al-Karim Qasim. The revolution was the result of increasing public dissatisfaction with the economic situation, Iraq's defeat in the 1948 war against Israel, the regime's identification with the West, and the influence—albeit conflicting—of Arab nationalism as espoused by Egyptian President Ghamal Abd al-Nasser, along with liberal and socialist ideals. On July 14, 1958, the Iraqi Army 20th Division, led by Abd al-Sallam A'ref, captured the central government offices and broadcast facilities in Baghdad. A few hours later, King Faisal II was murdered, along with Regent Abd al-Ila'a. Prime Minister Nuri Sa'id—symbol of westernization on one hand and Jewish persecution on the other—was murdered the following day.

The Jews huddled in their houses on hearing the news of the revolution. As Odil Dallal tells it: "We were at my brother-in-law's house for a week, behind locked doors, looking outside through the windows or from the rooftop. We were afraid to go into the street. We lived near a central street and could hear shouts erupting from the mob like a fiery volcano. . . . We knew the royalty was dead and Iraq was now a republic, but we didn't know what was going on, or what lay in store for us as Jews."

Only after two weeks and more did the Jews dare go outside their homes, to discover that the new regime had not harmed anyone, aside from members of the old regime. However, in those first days after the uprising, anti-Jewish banners were held aloft in rallies supporting the new regime, and when fire broke out in the oil tanks of southern Iraq, rumors broke out as well that Jews had started the blaze.

But these were isolated incidents. In general, says Dr. Nissim Kazzaz, "Abd al-Karim Qasim's four and one-half years of rule was the best period the Jews of Iraq had known since the mass emigration to Israel. The civil rights were returned to them. The State universities, whose gates were closed to Jewish students during the royal regime, now opened wide, and Jews could be accepted to any faculty or discipline taught therein. The limitation requiring Jews exiting the country to return within six months was abolished. During this period, Jews enjoyed relative security and economic prosperity."

Only a month after the revolution, nine Jews suspected of Communist activity were released from Iraq's prisons and deported to Israel, despite their claims that Iraq was their homeland where they wished to remain.[6] Over the coming months, most Jewish prisoners were released from jail and deported to Israel. The peak was January 1960, when Yehuda Tajar was released after being condemned to life imprisonment on charges of spying for Israel. That same month, the regime canceled the amendment passed in March 1951, that rescinded the citizenship of Jews who had exited Iraq legally but had not returned, and took custody of—essentially confiscated—their property. No less important than abolishment of the amendment was the official explanation, which read:

> Iraqi Jews living in Iraq were subject to many difficulties resulting from enacting this ruling against them, and leaving it in place goes against the revolution's goals and interim constitution which demands equal rights and obligations of all Iraqis. This aside, the principle of revoking of Iraqi citizenship goes against the spirit of the constitution [which states that] citizenship is a natural right and should not be revoked just because [citizens] delayed return to Iraq beyond a date written in their passports, as it could be that the delay was due to such unavoidable circumstances as trade or medical treatment. This aside, the aforementioned limitation causes problems in people's travel [plans], as representatives of the country that is their destination often refrain from granting them entry permits or resident status. Therefore, and because the reasons giving rise to enacting the aforementioned law have disappeared, this law is struck [from the records].[7]

It is important to note that, despite the lofty ideals of natural rights of Iraqi citizens and the principle of equality, the original Citizenship Deprivation Law from 1950 was not abolished, nor was the Property Freeze Law that applied to those Jews who remained in Iraq after March 1951.

Given that Iraq's official archives are inaccessible, we can only guess at reasons for this distinction. Perhaps Qasim wanted to reinforce his regime's standing in the eyes of the world, particularly those of Great Britain, a loyal supporter of the royal regime he had overthrown. Britain also had an important Iraqi-Jewish community. A move like this would characterize his regime as a protector of human rights overall, minority rights in particular, and he would get a successful propaganda- and image-building campaign for next to nothing. By contrast, abolishing the laws revoking the citizenship and freezing the property of Jews emigrating to Israel might provoke a wave of protest within Iraq and expose Iraq to compensation claims from Israel and the emigrants. As previously stated, these explanations are speculation only.

Iraqi Jews could now obtain passports and travel outside the country, but they did not use the opportunity to emigrate. Friends and relations they met abroad told them to leave Iraq, and yet, Kazzaz says, "They rejected the notion, believing they were looking towards security, and glorious future beyond that. . . . They lived with the illusion that this situation would be long-lived. Most were dazzled by the marked improvement in conditions for Jews, and some business owners transferred funds from abroad to Iraq, for investment." The feeling didn't go away, even when Baghdad's old Jewish cemetery was seized by government edict, and Jews were forced, despite their obvious pain and protest, to move their ancestors bones to a new cemetery plot. Even though some graves remained—including a mass grave of Farhud victims—and were destroyed by Qasim's bulldozers to clear space for a monument honoring his government, the Jewish community and its leaders continued to sing their praises.[8]

EMIGRATION TO ISRAEL DURING THE QASIM REGIME

Despite their improved status, the Jews of Iraq could still not legally emigrate to Israel. Firstly, there were still bureaucratic limitations on exiting the country: Anyone born after 1910, and defined as "obligated to military service," was required to pay 75 dinar for an exit permit. Additionally, Baghdad Chamber of Commerce members were required to put up a 2,000 to 7,000 dinar guarantee, depending on the applicant's personal wealth and position in the Chamber. At least a portion of Jews received passports granting passage to Lebanon only; once there, for 100 Lebanese pounds, a forger would add in the appropriate lines so that the passport would be valid in a number of other countries, including Turkey. In 1960, 132 Iraqi Jews immigrated to Israel, most via the circuitous Iraq-Lebanon-Turkey-Israel route.

In April and June 1961, Israel's Office of the Prime Minister examined the Iraqi situation of Iraqi Jews and their chances for immigration. An initial report stated that there were 5,000 Jews living in Iraq, almost all in Baghdad, with several hundred in Basra. "We can categorize the situation of Jews in Iraq as good. Traders are working and profiting better than under the previous regime." However, the Basra authorities had confiscated property belonging to the Jewish community, worth 20,000 to 25,000 dinar, claiming "accounts were not in order." The community could not support its poor or its gravediggers and required assistance from the Baghdad Jewish community. Regarding possible emigration to Israel, the April report stated there was interest on the part of two groups:

A. Small businessmen and all kinds of clerks, generally working in private companies, who have been considering emigration for a long time. But, given their good salaries in Iraq and the possibility of putting aside a reasonable amount of savings, they further and further postpone their date of emigration, as they wish to save enough money so that they may live honorably in Israel, after arriving.

B. The very poor. There are about 500 to 600 in Baghdad and about fifty in Basra. They all wish to emigrate but lack the means to do so. Their situation is so [very] bad that on holidays, the Jewish community collects money to buy them food, Kosher goods and *matza* (unleavened bread) for Passover.

"In general, these families have many children and the family heads fear that they will not find much more in Israel." And yet, "The rich people with money and lands fear coming to Israel because, in their words, so long as there is no peace between Israel and the Arabs, they are unwilling to endanger their lives and property. . . . Many say they will be forced to go begging in Israel, and they will have nothing to do there." Israel's security situation was also alarming, and concerns were raised repeatedly that the British were arming the Arabs and therefore, "Israel is in terrible danger. The Jews of Iraq, without exception, love Israel. They do not stop talking about Israel's wonders and progress. But they still harbor doubts regarding the future."

In June, M. Navot accurately summarized the situation in a memo sent to Yehuda Dominitz of the Jewish Agency's Aliya Department:

> The number of Jews remaining in Iraq is 4,000. Most are well-established people of means. They have no particular difficulty in leaving Iraq for business, medical or educational purposes. On the other hand, emigration would involve substantial losses of property, and they are not willing to take this [loss]. In the opinion of the various investigators, the Jews of Iraq do not wish to leave because things are relatively good, including their financial situation. Most of those remaining are older or aged. In our investigations, we did not encounter any cases of Jews in Iraq without means, or Jews interested in emigrating to Israel [a completely inexplicable contradiction to the previous report, also sent by Navot to Dominitz]. To sum up, the fundamental problem is granting the Jews of Iraq economic conditions and assistance in transferring their property, not helping and encouraging those of little means who wish to emigrate but cannot.[9]

QASIM FALLS AND THE JEWISH SITUATION WORSENS

Only two years after these words were written, even those Jews who wished to leave Iraq could not. A short time after the 1958 revolution, there was a division of opinion within the military junta, and Qasim quarreled with almost every important political party. He did not manage to promote the agrarian reform announced on his rise to power, intended to divide wealth in a more equable fashion. The Kurds of northern Iraq, with their ancient aspirations to independence, revolted in September 1961. That same year, Qasim tried to annex Kuwait but was stopped by a pan-Arab force sent to the tiny principality. He also came into conflict with Iraq's national oil company, which was under British ownership, when he demanded that government royalties on oil production be increased significantly. When his demands were not met, Qasim cut down the area licensed to the company by 99%.

On February 8, 1963, Qasim's regime was toppled by a group of officers and pan-Arab Ba'ath party members. Qasim himself was murdered. Over the next nine months, the Ba'ath's civilian leaders tried to rule Iraq but political and administrative inexperience, defeat in battles against the Kurds, hostility from Egyptian President Nasser, and public hatred engendered by the violent regime caused its downfall in November 1963. General Abd al-Sallam A'ref disbanded the government and took over Iraq as dictator. He was killed in a plane crash in April 1966 and power handed over to his elder brother, General Abd al-Rahman A'ref.[10]

How far the Jewish situation in Iraq deteriorated after Qasim's downfall was expressed clearly in July 1964, when new rules and regulations were issued regarding permission to exit the country. Under Qasim, Jews had been allowed to leave unrestrained, more or less, (though not allowed to immigrate to Israel). A'ref restored the rules that limited passage to the sick and Jewish students studying abroad for fixed amounts of time, but this too was under close watch by the Iraqi security forces. Other Jews were unable to get any sort of permission to leave Iraq.

Reports on the situation of Jews in Iraq were sporadic due to the total isolation imposed on the community by the regime. In October 1965, a message "from a reliable source" sent by Dominitz to his superiors at the Jewish Agency read: "Jews are not persecuted by the Iraqis but the authorities do not help the Jews get permits or passports. Under Qasim, things were much better for the Jews." There were occasional reports of anti-Semitism, such as the statement delivered by Iraqi Minister of Health Kamal al-Sarami, who explained that pharmaceutical warehouses were nationalized because Jews created a monopoly in the drug sector. The same sources estimated that there were 3,000 Jews in Iraq.[11]

A few years later, Israel's Ministry of Education claimed that persecution of Iraqi Jews had escalated in June 1967, on the eve of the Six Day War. According to that same publication—bearing in mind that it was released for educational and, perhaps, propaganda purposes—Jews without identity cards were stripped of their property and citizenship. Later, Iraq ruled it would confiscate the property of Jews who could not prove they were Iraqi nationals. Similarly, property belonging to Jews who left the country, and not returned, was also confiscated. However, most of these rulings applied to Jews no longer living in Iraq; only after the Six Day War did active persecution of the local Jewish community begin.[12]

THE SIX DAY WAR AND ITS RAMIFICATIONS

Initial reports after the Six Day War gave the impression that things in Iraq were not so bad, certainly in comparison to the Jewish persecution that followed Israel's 1948 War of Independence. In retrospect, there was a reason for this difference: Iraq did not participate in the 1967 war; it deployed troops to northern Jordan but did not engage in any significant warfare. In July 1967, a report submitted to the Jewish Agency said that during the war, the Iraqi authorities had summoned a few Jews for interrogation, but this was apparently conducted without the use of torture, and all were released within a few days, thanks to a few bribes. The report also mentioned a "new law regarding limitations of the non-sale of real estate, a freeze on property, cash, etc.," but gave no details. The limitations evidently applied only to Jews still remaining in Iraq; as mentioned previously, property belonging to emigrants had essentially already been frozen.

In September 1967, the Middle East Division of Israel's Ministry of Foreign Affairs sent a confidential report about the Jews of Iraq to a group of Israeli diplomatic outposts around the world. The report's source was an Iraqi Jew, deported from the country as a noncitizen, who had managed to gain entry to England. He quoted the Chief Rabbi of the Jewish Community, Sasson Kaduri, who estimated the number of Jews in Iraq at 2,000, and who claimed that until the Six Day War "we enjoyed relative calm, and were able to subsist, undisturbed, whether by trade or clerking. Natural defense mechanisms in the face of possible danger has brought most of the traders among us into partnership with non-Jews, while the clerks among us worked mainly for foreign companies. Treatment of Jews in the street is indifferent, although the authorities have spared no effort in damaging Jewish interests. Any Jew going before a government clerk has been perjured against and humiliated." Given Kaduri's traditional and long-standing pro-Iraqi stance, one must assume the situation was difficult, if he mentioned "relative calm" but also admitted the authorities' acts against the community.

And what happened after the Six Day War? The report continues:

> In late May, with the escalation of tensions in the Middle East, the Jews situation worsened and, in the street, the atmosphere was electric. Along with increased incitement against Israel, there was growing animosity towards Jews which reached its peak after reports of an Arab defeat began coming in. General public opinion was diverted from the Jews when [the Arabs] were drunk with success, but as the myth of an Arab victory began proving false [the government having claimed victory during the early days of the war], the authorities and the mob poured their rage out on the Jews. Dozens were arrested and jailed on ridiculous, trumped-up charges. . . .
>
> The charges ranged from collecting donations for Israel to engaging in activities in the service of imperialism. A medical student was arrested and accused of collecting 15,000 dinar for Israel. Presented as evidence were "tape-recordings," allegedly of her voice, from a Dictaphone machine. A representative of a German television equipment company was arrested on charges of using the Shield of David as a closing broadcast signal, generated by the equipment he sells. This accusation is patently false. Over time, some of those arrested were released; several Jews are still in jail, but the source was unable to name an exact number.
>
> After the wave of arrests abated, an official anti-Jewish incitement campaign was launched on radio and television, including religious preaching and interpretations from the Koran against Jews, claiming they have always been against Islam and Muslims. The Arabs have been called on to desist from cooperating or trading with Jews, to say nothing of maintaining social ties. This has its effect; even loyal friends of the source have resisted contact, partly out of fear, and partly having been influenced by propaganda.[13]

Today we know the situation was even worse. Max Sawdayee, born in 1932, lived in Iraq during the Six Day War and afterward, where he worked in advertising. His diary serves as an important testament and primary source in documenting the annals of the Jewish community at that time. He describes the fear that overtook the community immediately before and during the war, fear that kept them locked indoors, afraid to go to work, or send their children to school. The situation only became worse when the extent of the Arab defeat became known, and Jewish persecution quickly took on economic and social aspects. As Sawdayee wrote in his diary:

June 10, 1967: Today my Moslem partner tells me never to attend the business again. He's afraid lest both of us should get arrested. I've actually expected that, not without the heart-breaking sorrow and pain for a very successful and profitable work I've faithfully served and cherished, and in which so much time and effort have been invested.

June 25, 1967: Jewish pharmacies have been made to close for good. Many of their owners have been thrown into jail. More Jewish employees have been expelled from public and private offices. Most telephones in Jewish offices and homes have been cut off. It seems that in a matter of days the rest of our telephones will also follow suit. Jews suddenly discover that they cannot sell their property any longer. They have difficulties in drawing money from the banks too.

July 23, 1967: After paying my driver his salary and telling him that his job with me is over, I go to sell my new Chevrolet. I am afraid somebody may notice me. Besides, selling my car doesn't at all please me nor my wife, but we feel it's necessary for two important reasons: first, we can have some cash in hand; second, it isn't advisable to have such a big car at our door under the circumstances. For a Jew to sell his car isn't funny. Nor do I know whether it's possible in the abnormal conditions we're living in. Even if it is, it can be dangerous. Anyway, it's all right at the dealer's premises. It's rather interesting too, because there happen to be two army colonels with huge mustaches and plenty of medals and decorations, hotly engaged in a loud argument which borders on a quarrel, on the subject whether Moshe Dayan lost his left eye in a boxing ring or in a brawl over a girl in a Tel Aviv night club! The two are tumultuous, so much so that the occasion offers a rare piece of entertainment, a welcome relief indeed!

Back to my selling the car. It's more difficult at the traffic police headquarters, as it seems I'm the first or second Jew to sell his car after the Six Day War. They keep asking me bothersome questions, but happily they seem to ignore all new regulations connected with Jews. With over 2,000 dinars in my bag to finance our expenses for another seven or eight months, the risk is worth while.

August 19, 1967: A vast number of personalities in government and other circles wouldn't like to see Jews continue to work or do business anywhere in Iraq. Many hints are made to this effect. However, some Jews are still attending businesses or working in small or odd jobs. They must earn a living, anyway. They're taking all the risk of being noticed by official or interested agents who can do them a lot of harm.

August 23, 1967: The ways of making our livelihood are thinning out. Money becomes the most precious commodity. There's almost no means at our disposal to make money even to cover our current expenses. Stocks, shares and immovable property are all frozen so far as Jews are concerned, and banks do not make it easy for us either. The police, the State Security and army intelligence headquarters arrest or kidnap Jews at will. . . . Only in the past four days more than 15 persons have been arrested.

September 7, 1967: A vehement anti-Jewish campaign is taking place in this country. Television, the radio and the press find nothing more useful or interesting than to attack the Jews of Iraq, though indirectly, yet in the most dreadful manner ever done by these media.

October 30, 1967: The world awakes. A big campaign against the inhuman treatment of Iraqi Jews has taken fire during the last few days in several freedom-loving countries. The *New York Times, The Daily Telegraph, Le Monde* and other renowned newspapers have published detailed reports and articles about the detention of many Jews in Iraq, the sacking of employees, the closing of Jewish pharmacies and shops, the cutting-off of telephones from Jewish homes and businesses, the freezing of Jewish money and property, the rumors that we shall be consigned to concentration camps, and all other relevant subjects. Humanitarian Jewish and Christian institutions in America and Europe hold meetings and their leaders deliver moving speeches about the brutal treatment of Jews by the Iraqi government.

November 11, 1967: The wave of arrests and detention has slackened. Some forty Jews have even been released and sent home, exhausted and depressed. Various factors might have contributed to this turning of the tide in government policy. The recent campaign in the outside world must have undoubtedly done much, but the pressure from certain directions within the country must also not be underestimated.[14]

1968: ECONOMIC AND SOCIAL PERSECUTION ESCALATES

The new year brought no relief to the Jews. Quite the opposite: With every passing month their situation only got worse, mainly due to political developments in Iraq. In March 1968, the government issued several edicts that increased economic persecution. Jews were forbidden from selling real estate, mortgaging real estate as a guarantee on loans, leasing real estate, giving it as a gift, or renting it out for longer than one year without special permission from the Minister of the Interior.

Government ministries, government companies, and private businesses were forbidden to issue payments to Jews without special permission from the Ministry of the Interior. They were allowed to pay monthly salaries of up to 100 dinar—not enough to properly support the average family.

The regulations granted the Minister of the Interior total authority over money owed to Jews and income on sales or leasing of Jewish-owned property. As in 1951, Baghdad again refrained from officially confiscating property to avoid paying compensation, but the intention was clear. Jews were prevented from obtaining import licenses, all Jews were fired from government or public companies, in certain regions the government imposed a partial boycott of Jewish-owned shops. Needless to say, Jews were stripped of their civil and political rights, and they were forbidden from leaving the country.[15]

Additional first-hand accounts of Jewish persecution in the year following the Six Day War were provided by Israeli scholar Yitzhak Bezalel, quoting an Iraqi woman émigré to Israel who wished to remain anonymous:

> The most serious restrictions placed on Jews at that time were economic. The government measures made sure that, within a short amount of time, most Jews would be unemployed. Jews were fired from their positions in offices, companies, public and private enterprises like government ministries—which in any case, employed only a few Jews, and none in senior positions—insurance companies, banks, public enterprises and enterprises in key sectors. Jews were sent home from work without any official notice.
>
> In the same way, Jewish-owned pharmacies were closed, and some pharmacists jailed. Among those pharmacists arrested was my husband's brother. He was released a month later, and reopened his pharmacy, but that same day received notification from the Ministry of Health, revoking his license [to practice] and informing him that he must close the pharmacy within two weeks, and sell off his equipment and inventory. . . .
>
> In some cases, the authorities ordered the Jews to liquidate their privately-owned businesses. My husband's oldest brother was a partner in a company that imported batteries and drills from Japan. Suddenly he and his Jewish partner received a notice from the Government Registrar of Companies, telling them to close the business, which they did, of course. There were businesses that shut down because the owners were jailed, and once released, couldn't revive them. On the other hand, at this stage, Jewish businesses with Arab partners weren't touched—my husband's business, for example—but their numbers were very small.
>
> Doctors were among the few professions permitted to keep working. Maybe because even the government of Iraq couldn't stop Jews from getting sick, and they preferred that the Jewish sick get treatment from other Jews. . . .
>
> In total, these limitations forced a situation where most Jews had no work at all. Of course, most Iraq Jews had savings, assets or property in different forms—land, jewelry, expensive dishes and more—so when they were forbidden from working, they lived off these means, or the sale of property. But restrictions were placed on these as well. Jews couldn't sell their own real estate, and their securities were frozen. The banks made it difficult for Jews to draw money from their own accounts. The result was families left without anything, everything dwindled down until they reached their last crust of bread, after the savings were gone. The authorities' appropriation of Jewish assets was a success, because Jews at that time didn't dare oppose these decisions or try to get around them. They were afraid of being imprisoned.

As the days passed, and the economic edicts remained in place, the number of Jewish families in need increased. As the needy grew in number, there was not enough in the community chest to help them. And so, women who had never worked in their lives, were forced to support their families. These occupations were limited to sewing at home, teaching or giving private lessons, but demand was low.[16]

Why was Iraq persecuting its Jews, when it had not been beaten by Israel this time? Bezalel makes the convincing argument that internal politics were involved, citing traditional xenophobia of all minority groups, including Jews, in combination with a deteriorating A'ref regime: ongoing military conflict against the Kurds to the north; to the south, continued tension with the Muslim Shi'ite minority; and the failure of agrarian reform and nationalization to improve economic conditions for most Iraqis. The masses took to the streets in protest of the government, but also held, as a matter of course, anti-Jewish and anti-Zionist signs. "The Jews were a scapegoat for the Iraqi government to use to divert public opinion from the country's many real troubles, and to appease extreme and opposition elements," Bezalel says. Seen in this light, he adds, it is clear why Baghdad did nothing to hide its anti-Jewish actions—actions that clearly violated international civil rights principles—and instead made sure that everyone knew.[17] But even worse was in store, in the near future.

SHOW TRIALS, HANGINGS, AND CONFISCATION OF PROPERTY

In July 1968, the Ba'ath party came to power headed by General Ahmad Hassan al-Bakkar, as usual after a military coup. Behind the scenes, Saddam Hussein was beginning his ascent; in 1968 he had taken control of the Ba'ath Party militia and its secret service. From the early 1970s on, Saddam emerged slowly as Iraq's true leader.[18]

As early as the winter of 1968, half a year after the coup, Jews in Basra were imprisoned and tortured. On December 14, Iraq announced it had uncovered a major spy ring aiding Israel and the United States, whose members were Jews, former military officers, and former senior diplomats. One month later, a show trial commenced in Baghdad behind closed doors, where the twenty persons accused (some of whom were Jews) were charged on four counts: membership in a spy ring trained by Iran in terrorism, murder and destruction, including poisoning water reservoirs (an old anti-Semitic claim going back to the Middle Ages); blowing up a bridge in central Basra and planning additional acts of terror; receiving large sums of money from Israel via Iran and allocating funds to Kurdish rebels and other government opponents; broadcasting military information from Basra to Israel using a transmitter hidden in a Basra church. Bezalel notes: "This political profile, assembled to fit the spy ring, reflects to an amazing degree everything the Iraqi regime hated at that time: Israel, the United States, Iran, the Kurds, and Iraqi opposition elements both in and outside the country. Add some satanic elements like poisoning wells, and broadcasting from churches, and there you have it—the perfect monster."

In late January, nine Jews and five non-Jews were executed in Baghdad's main square. The Jewish victims were Naji Zilka, an upstanding merchant from Basra; David Dallal, a Basra high school student; David Ghali, also a Basra high school student, and the son of a well-to-do money changer; Yehezkel Sallah Yehezkel, a Basra high school student; Na'im Kaduri Hillali, the only son of a Basra cigarette dealer, one of the country's wealthiest and best-known Jews; Ya'akov Namurdi, a clerk from Basra; Sabbah Haim, a Basra spare parts dealer; Fuad Gabai, an agent with the Basra Customs Authority; and Charles Horesh, a well-to-do merchant from Baghdad. As execution by law also meant confiscation of property, it may be no coincidence that these false accusations were levied, for the most part, against wealthy Jews.

An Iraqi paper, which published a chillingly disparaging account mocking the Jewish victims' final moments, termed them "subhuman"—the same term ("untermensch") used by the Nazis against the Jews. Relatives of the condemned, who had not seen them since their arrests over a month earlier, were not allowed to see their loved ones one last time. Two hundred thousand Iraqis crowded into the main square, chanting hysterically and led by President Bakkar and Minister of Defense Hardan al-Takriti. The mob spit on the corpses, threw mud, jumped up to reach out and strike their lifeless, dangling legs. Dozens of blows rained on the mother of one of the victims as she clung to her son's body and kissed it, while the mob chanted: "Mother of a traitor! Mother of a spy! Whore!" They stopped only after the miserable woman lost consciousness and was dragged away by three military officers.

The Jews feared making the traditional visit to mourners and also feared making their feelings known. At the University of Baghdad, says a Jew who was a student there at the time, signs were posted that read: "We want more!" The same Arab students who studied together with Jewish students now laughed in their faces, saying: You're next in line. When the bodies of those executed were buried the next day, thousands of Muslims protesters gathered alongside the Jewish cemetery and threw rocks at the mourners.[19]

While the arrests and trial were conducted almost in secret, the government of Iraq did not try to hide the punishment: hanging and confiscation of property belonging to the accused. As Charles Horesh's widow, Simha Horesh, relates:

A few days after my husband was jailed, an official announcement appeared in the papers with a long list of names, including his, [stating that] their property was frozen by the authorities. After Charles was hanged, a sort of announcement or warning was issued, [stating that] anyone convicted of espionage would have their property confiscated. I was familiar with my husband's business, because I worked with him in his office for a long time. He had a range of businesses: insurance, export of wool, leather and other products. He started out as an employee and made his money all by himself. Maybe that's why the Arabs were jealous of him.

The day after his arrest, I went to his office and saw the safe was open and emptied of all money, papers and documents. The people who arrested him took everything. After that, I would go to the office almost every day, to continue managing the business. I wanted to maintain what we had, and I also put in new orders, in the hope that when my husband was released, he would be able to continue managing his affairs, but after his death I sold the business. We didn't have a lot of property to confiscate; the authorities tried twice to take the furniture and rugs from our house. The authorities were almost inhuman regarding their confiscation on property owned by the victims. It was said that the authorities seized the property belonging to one Jew from Basra, who had been condemned to death, and afterwards forced his family to buy back all the confiscated furniture, at full price.[20]

A mere seven months later, Jews were again executed in Baghdad. This time, they were Yitzhak Dallal and Yehezkel Ya'akov, hanged on August 25 without a trial. They died without a visit from a rabbi, but at least the authorities did not leave their bodies hanging on display. Nine Muslims and four Christians were hanged alongside them, also accused of espionage and sabotage. As in January, the executions were again accompanied by looting of property. Yitzhak Dallal's widow Odil Dallal relates:

After my husband's death, I was left without any source of income; 2,500 dinar was all I had. Of course, the financial difficulties started with my husband's arrest but while he was in jail, I didn't think about them, I hoped these troubles were temporary. While he was in jail I received a little cash from his partners, and people who owed him money. Now that was all gone. The government froze my husband's property and assets, under the law [pertaining to] those sentenced to death for espionage, and we became indigent overnight.

One week after the *shiva* [Jewish ritual seven day mourning period], I was summoned to appear before the government appointee charged with confiscating my husband's property. The property included two factories, one for sweets, another for cosmetics; import agencies for goods manufactured abroad, including a radio and electronics factory in Japan, and other imported goods; plus loans my husband made to various people.

One of Dallal's partners, Tahsin Hassan, cooperated with the authorities in confiscating the property, and was rewarded by being made part owner of the candy factory.

"The authorities began, in essence, to take hold of my husband's property while he was still in prison," Odil continues. "For example, all the money coming in from Japan, and other companies abroad with whom he had commercial dealings, were confiscated by the authorities. On the day my husband was hanged, and—I have reason to believe—some time before that, the authorities seized control of his factories, and took inventory of the merchandise and the account-books. In all, the government confiscated 70,000 dinar in property and cash that belonged to my husband."

The government appointee interrogated Odil Dallal, for an extended period of time, about the business of her husband, hanged less than two weeks earlier. He was particularly interested in Yitzhak Dallal's commercial ties outside of Iraq and emphasized that all assets deposited abroad in his name now belonged to the government. Odil answered that she was a housewife who had never been part of her husband's business dealings, adding that it was her legal right to take back, out of the property, the dowry she had brought with her into the marriage. The government appointee referred her to the Ministry of Finance where she was told she did have this privilege, even though her husband had been executed. The legal precedent was none other than the widow of Regent Abd al-Ila'a, who was slain in the 1958 revolution. The court had granted the widow priority before the government in collecting what was hers out of her husband's confiscated property. But another shock was in store for Odil:

> Encouraged, I went back to the government appointee and told him the Ministry of Finance's response. He looked embarrassed, scratched his head, and asked to see my marriage license. He stared at it for a long time, then said: "I'm sorry, but this document is not in order; this document was issued by a religious group. Iraqi law does not recognize this marriage, and the children born out of this marriage are illegitimate."
>
> I was stunned by what he said. His statement was, of course, outrageous and unfounded, as every Jew in Iraq was married by a rabbi—if what he said was true, then every Jewish marriage in Iraq was illegal. I hurried to the Chief Rabbi, Sasson Kaduri, [who had expressed his support of the government after the January hangings], and asked him to issue a document stating my marriage was legal. But Rabbi Kaduri refused, claiming this went against government policy, and he could do nothing on the matter.[21]

A few days after the executions of Dallal and Ya'akov, a foreign journalist arrived in Israel, after having spent a two and a half months in Baghdad. His account of the Jews' situation was reported anonymously in Israeli daily *Ma'ariv*:

> The overwhelming majority of Jewish wage-earners in Iraq haven't worked since the Six Day War. Heads of households had their sources of income taken from them, and their property confiscated. Before the war, Jews with bank accounts could withdraw up to 100 dinar per month. Today, bank accounts have been confiscated, and they can withdraw nothing. If the authorities hear that a Jew has found work, they arrest him and send him to jail. . . .

The 2,500 Jews still living in Baghdad have all become beggars, living in terrible conditions. They have only one another to turn to for help. Many are well-educated, they once had respectable positions, but under today's enforced unemployment they sit at home. A Jew seen walking streets of Baghdad wearing nice clothes can expect to be arrested, and held for a long time, perhaps accused of being a Zionist traitor spying for Israel or the US. Detectives and police make nighttime raids on Jewish houses, interrogate Jews on where they keep their meager resources. . . . Because the economic situation is so grim, the Jewish community leaders have turned to the International Red Cross, asking for care packages as they are dying of starvation.[22]

THREE MONTHS OF FALSE HOPE

Given these conditions, it is not surprising that there was a revival in illegal emigration from Iraq over the next few months. This followed a three-month period during which it seemed that Jews might be allowed to leave legally, but the illusion was quickly dispelled. Max Sawdayee diligently described those weeks in his diary. It all began on May 1, 1969, with a Radio Baghdad announcement:

"The Iraqi government finds that Jewish community members were persecuted and unjustly treated by the former hated regime. So it has decided to take the following measures in order to make amends for all the damages caused and wrongs done: (1) Restrictions to freeze shares and bonds pertaining to Jews will be lifted off as from the coming Saturday, and the Jew can sell, buy and dispose of his shares and bonds, as every Iraqi can; (2) Restrictions to freeze Jews' money in the banks will be lifted off as from the coming Saturday, and the Jew can withdraw or deposit money as much as he wishes, as every Iraqi can; and (3) Jews can sell their immovable property as from the coming Saturday, as every Iraqi can. Later the speaker also announced that "Jews wishing to leave the country must register within the next few days in a special department assigned for this purpose in the Passport and Identity Card official bureau."

Sawdayee, like all of Iraq's Jews, was surprised and pleased. He felt that the granting of exit permits—the most important of all the announcements made by the government—was due to the Jewish community's disassociation from Iraq. Perhaps, he thought, it was the result of a secret agreement between Israel and Baghdad. But another line in Sawdayee's diary may provide the real reason, certainly in light of what was to come in three months: "Now that there's hope for an exit out of the country for his family and himself, the Jew does not care much about his money, his share, his bonds, his property. He'll be happy to quit, leaving everything behind. And the sooner, the better."

Two days later, on the day the new rules and regulations were due to go into effect, dozens of Jews crowded around the special passport and identity card bureau. Sawdayee, sick with flu and a thirty-nine degree fever (Celsius), dragged himself there and was amazed at the polite service provided by officials, who even took an interest in his health. Just one week later, Jews thronged by the hundreds to register for exit permits. Everyone was there:

> Old men and women, some of them over ninety, who I'm sure haven't left their homes for many years even to stroll at the adjoining streets. They're tired and shaking, yet excited and happy. Their only wish is to arrive to Jerusalem alive.
> One also meets wealthy Jewish landowners or business men, whose property is still frozen as the government has not lifted off restrictions yet, all delighted to quit and leave everything behind. Also to be seen there are pharmacists, engineers, technicians, shopkeepers, former clerks, and other, all jobless since almost two years and would like to quit the soonest possible. One meets even physicians, who officially are still working, yet eager to leave and settle elsewhere.

Yesterday's problems of subsistence gave way to concerns for tomorrow: Where shall we go? Which country has the best economic opportunities? What's the best place to continue studying? How should family finances be managed until we leave? And even: Should we buy new clothes suited to Iraqi weather, or other? By June 23, more than 2,500 out of Iraq's 3,500 Jews had registered—all filled with hopes for the future.

> Men, women and children, roam our main Rashid Street, one of the most elegant streets in the capital, looking in shops for lovely suits and dresses, underwear, shoes, and other things necessary for the coming trip. But they need cash to buy everything they require for the big journey as well as their daily expenses. As they can't sell any shares, bonds or immovable property (despite the government's announcement to the contrary), they start to sell off whatever they can to obtain the maximum of cash possible. And that unleashes the funniest of sales! Women sell their jewels, gold and silver belongings. Men sell their home, carpets and furniture. Students sell their books. And so on! It isn't infrequent to meet university students on vacation, and other young men, selling kitchen copper utensils in the copper market, or cotton at 50 fils [one-half dinar] a kilo in the used clothes market or in the flea market!
> [My] brother, on vacation, can't bear hearing father forbidding the sale of anything from the house. But whenever father is out, brother helps mother look for something to sell. Copper utensils, cotton out of used pillows and mattresses, or anything else that comes to hand! Selling such things becomes an amusing obsession to the Jews. It kills time, provides some money and a sort of occupation.

Suddenly, on July 29, Sawdayee wrote in his diary: "The planned departure of Jews from Iraq is already forgotten. It is declared definitely dead. At the special department allocated to Jewish emigration in the Passport bureau, a small piece of paper hangs today, reading: 'This bureau is closed for the registration of Jews wishing to leave the country, until further notice.' The government, and surely every Jew in Iraq, knows precisely what that means. The hope for an exit out of the country was a momentary glow. It was just a flicker in the dark." The Jews were to remain imprisoned in a country where their destiny was certain to be humiliation, torture, and death.

What happened? Sawdayee theorized that the Iraqi government's see-sawing policy resulted from internal strife between the military and the Ba'ath party, between the military and the government, "or anything of such a nature and magnitude." As Iraqi government records are inaccessible, we can only guess at reasons, and Sawdayee's assumptions make sense. Along the same line of reasoning, two more theories arise: Either the exit permit farce was yet another cruel stage in the government's systematic persecution of the Jews, or it was intended to force them into selling off their property, yielding a fast profit to the State, and its non-Jewish citizens, and causing the Jewish community to collapse completely.[23]

THE CRISIS REACHES ITS PEAK

Some weeks later, Dallal and Ya'akov were hanged. Dozens of other Iraqis, the overwhelming majority non-Jewish, were tortured mercilessly, accused of various and strange crimes, then most of them were executed. In the street, arrests and torture became the topic of macabre jokes. In the open market, the grocer told Max Sawdayee's wife Sa'ida: "Don't be surprised if you don't see me here next time! Just listen to the radio, or call up the hangman at the central prison—then you'll know where I've gone!" In October, Sawdayee wrote of the deteriorating economic situation:

A new factor—logical, crucial, merciless and determinant—emerges out of a long period of idleness to dominate and to worsen our conditions. It is the shortage of money. The Jew, without any income since almost two years and a half, dispossessed, paralyzed by the government which compels him to sit idle and forbids him from disposing of his property, if any, could not but live on his cash reserve and consume it. He hasn't ignored the problem through-out, but expected, or at least hoped for, a change to come. There was also the dreamed-of possibility of leaving the country, sooner or later. But when all his hopes, dreams, and later on even the mirage of departure did not ma-terialize, the Jew finds himself on the brink of having no money left, deprived of all kinds of resources, and facing complete ruin. Starvation begins to stare him in the face. . . .

Everybody avoids working with him or employing him lest he himself should incur the displeasure of the government henchmen, with all the consequences that follow. Nor does anybody wish to lend him money and invite unexpected risks. At the same time the Jew takes into consideration the probability that he may be arrested any moment, or jailed, or murdered, and that his family must have some adequate cash reserve to carry on with. That badly needed reserve is exhausted or nearing exhaustion. Even if a few happen to save some money abroad, they dare not draw on it in the circumstances, when people are sent to the gallows for far minor reasons or for no reason, whatsoever.[24]

On December 7, Sawdayee returned to this subject. This time, his words remind one of descriptions of the European ghettoes during the Holocaust:

Winter breaks out. It catches us in a very critical circumstance. Amid other major problems, many in our community have run completely out of money. First cases of hunger begin to show up in the Jewish Frank Ini School. A number of Jewish personalities, especially those physicians still working, are donating sandwiches to be distributed among hungry children, some of them doing that daily. The best known neurologist in the country, a Jew, [apparently Dr. Jacques Abudi Sha'abi], is donating sacks of wheat and rice to be distributed among poor children or their families. The Jewish Community Center is also doing its best to send some foodstuffs to the school or to nearby families.

Electricity and gas bills become difficult for many families to pay, and rented houses find their tenants in a very destitute position. A number of them move to settle with brothers, sisters or parents, after obtaining special permission beforehand from the nearest police stations to this effect. For many persons pocket money isn't easy to find, and women face a real problem in meeting their daily expenses.

A lot of cunning is exercised to discover new ways and means of saving the maximum possible by reducing expenditure to the lowest minimum. We even joke sometimes on how to discover another astute method to save money from our daily spending! Except for fewer than a dozen physicians still officially permitted to work, no more than 20 Jews are working in the market, having business relations with decent Moslems and Christians. Some other four or five are having small jobs in private companies.[25]

Two weeks later, a short entry reads: "The Jew, sad, forlorn, broken-hearted, is therefore left to meet his desperate end, an end that we can truly call a slow death or extinction."[26]

The situation got worse from day to day. On May 5, 1970, Sawdayee wrote another diary entry reminiscent of the Holocaust, even the concentration camps: "The situation of the Jews in Iraq deteriorates still more. Jewish homes are closely watched, and the people inside are highly tense and deeply apprehensive. The shortage of money has reached an appalling ebb. Many families are at a severe loss to eke out a living. Our nerves are on the verge of total collapse. . . . It is not scarce to see Jews walking slowly in the streets, trudging with listless steps, or staring emptily, or moving with complete absent-mindedness. Their eyes are lifeless. Their faces are dead. Their gait is automatic. They are more like wax statues than human beings."[27]

HUNDREDS OF PENNILESS FAMILIES FLEE IRAQ

But Sawdayee and many other Jews decided during the coming months that they were not prepared to accept an end filled with suffering. The solution: Run away from Iraq. There is no accurate data regarding the number of escapes that took place in the late 1960s and early 1970s, but one gets the impression that hundreds of Jewish families left in this fashion. Some had been the victims of direct persecution, others were simply unwilling to wait until the moment they, too, would be victimized. In both cases, they left behind their remaining property: real estate, bank accounts and more, property that was confiscated several years earlier and never released.

Among the first to escape were relatives of Yitzhak Dallal, who was among those hanged in August 1969. Later on, Odil Dallal learned that, a day after her husband was executed, one of Iraq's richest Jewish families escaped over the border to Iran. Other wealthy Jewish families soon followed. With undisguised amazement, Odil emphasizes that these families left their vast property behind and took only a few suitcases.

The Dallal family left Iraq in the summer of 1970. Odil sold, or gave away, as much as she could so that there would be nothing left for poachers. Clothes were given to the needy, furniture sold to a used furniture dealer for 150 dinar (the furniture from the children's room alone, Odil says, was worth twice that). The gold jewelry she received from her late husband was given to a Christian friend who promised he would transfer them abroad, but they never arrived, and the man later claimed they were lost in transit. She gave her mother memorabilia and photos of Yitzhak, along with his clothes, as she could not bear selling them. Into a single suitcase, Odil crammed clothes, documents and a few more of her husband's effects. "I took my husband's robe, two shirts, and two ties, so I could give my children something of their father's when they were grown. I also took six rolls of film with pictures of Yitzhak at home, with the children, at ceremonies, and family events. Those pictures are the only momento I have from the past."

The last day in Baghdad arrived. The furniture dealer and his team emptied the apartment of its contents, each item abounding in loving memories. Odil did not even pay a final visit to husband's grave, fearing that a visit so soon after the one-year anniversary of his death would arouse suspicion. "Nothing was more important to me than getting out of Iraq. I was sure my husband approved of my decision."[28]

Max Sawdayee decided to escape in March 1970, but for months he failed to find a way to get out. He did not change his mind, even after an announcement, issued by the Minister of the Interior on March 4, canceled the restrictions placed on Jews by previous regimes. The Minister of the Interior decreed that Jewish pharmacists were allowed to apply for permits to open pharmacies; phone lines would be reconnected to Jewish homes and stores; Jews fired from civil service were invited to reapply for their jobs and would even receive compensation for their period of unemployment.

But, as always, the reality was far different. Most Jewish merchants were afraid to start over, especially if the change was only temporary. Those who did go back into business were unable to obtain import licenses. Government and other public offices continued their practice of not employing Jews; the private sector took the hint as well. Most Jews opted to not reconnect their phones, fearing they could later be accused of using the phone for espionage. The only real relief was in property ownership: Jews were allowed to sell property (including real estate) and withdraw over 100 dinar per month from bank accounts. However, anyone withdrawing particularly large sums could expect to be interrogated regarding the intended use of the money.

But the most important change was in granting Jews permission to leave their cities of residence. This was the opening through which they could escape Iraq.

The illegal emigration of that time was not an organized movement and, as far as is known today, no Israelis were involved. Jews escaped solo, crossing the border at various points, assisted by different smugglers. Some were lucky enough to be helped by smugglers who were decent people or by Kurdish rebels. Others fell prey to charlatans, paid money for nothing, and had to go back home. Still others were caught and thrown in jail. The wave of illegal emigration hit a high point in late August and early September 1970, when the average number of illegal emigrants reached fifty per day.[29]

Sawdayee, his wife, and their two daughters managed to escape in June 1970. On June 8, Sa'ida Sawdayee packed two small suitcases—all they took with them. As evening fell, Max went up to a hideaway on the roof, where he burned his documents and books. His heart ached for the burning books but there was no choice: Caution required that books not be distributed, certainly not sold. The next day, at 4:00 A.M., the family left their house and took a cab heading northward. With the help of some local Kurds, they made an arduous mountain trek—partly on foot, party by mule—reaching Iran on June 15.[30]

During that time, the daughter of one of Iraq's wealthiest and most respected Jewish families fled the country. The family fortune was founded by the grandfather, a tea merchant, trader and more, who also bought land in the right places. Some was agricultural land, that was later rezoned as residential, and on which Baghdad's most expensive neighborhood was built. A section of Saddam Hussein's presidential palace now stands on land once owned by this family.

The daughter arrived in North America, where she found work as a stewardess for a major airline. "For twenty years I had no direct contact with my parents," she says. "I didn't know if they had anything to eat. Occasionally, I'd receive a letter three weeks after it was sent, and ask myself whether they were still alive. Sometimes, we'd fly to Bombay over Iraq, and I thought about them all the time."

The family fortune was vast: a house in Baghdad worth 100 million dinar ($80,000); 8 million dinar ($7,000) in land in Baghdad; 50 to 60 million dinar ($40,000 to 48,000) in land in Basra; 2.9 billion dinar ($2.3 million) in land in Baghdad; additional lands in Baghdad worth 10 million dinar ($8,000); miscellaneous lands worth 100 million dinar ($80,000); other lands whose current value is unknown, plus bank deposits. The low dollar value for most of the properties is misleading; in Iraqi terms these figures represent a fortune. In addition, the current trading value of the Iraqi dinar—due to international sanctions against Iraq, limited oil export, and a difficult economic situation—is far lower than in previous years.

But her parents were left almost without any means of support. When the grandfather died in 1967, his will divided the property among his children. But the authorities refused to act accordingly and forced the family to divide their inheritance according to Muslim law: two parts for every son, one part for every daughter. The government then ruled that property belonging to those who had left Iraq must be handed over to it. The parents were therefore left with one-eighth of the property—the government owned the remaining seven-eighths—and were forced to pay rent for the privilege of living in the house that was once rightfully theirs.

As we have seen, for many years Jews were forbidden from selling property. Later on, they were required to deposit the profits on property sales in closed bank accounts, from which they could withdraw £300 per month to live on. In 1990, the parents left Iraq, legally and openly, to join their daughter in North America. They left their affairs in the hands of an Iraqi acquaintance who was given power of attorney but apparently took advantage of this position to sell off their property for no profit. The daughter sums up the fate of the family fortune in five words: "They came out with nothing."[31]

Chapter 5

"Mother Locked the Door and Left"

The State of Israel Is Established: The Jews of Egypt Pay the Price

On Friday, May 14, 1948, David Ben-Gurion declared the establishment of the State of Israel. The following morning, police officers knocked the doors down at the Viddal family residence in Cairo's Ha'lwan neighborhood, ransacked closets and drawers, and arrested Habib Viddal on suspicion of Zionist activity. The officers told Habib's brothers that the family owed millions of Egyptian pounds in income tax, and therefore, the family print shop was to be sold at public auction.

"I was only nine years old," relates Levana Zamir (nee Viddal), "but even then I understood we were left without income, and that my uncle had been put in jail. With a child's sensibility, I understood that our lives were about to change and that nothing was ever going to be the same." Confiscating a business on trumped-up charges of income tax evasion was not an uncommon subterfuge. "Everyone knew that when the government wanted to get Jewish property, it enlisted the income tax authority. At the public auction, the print shop was awarded to none other than Sa'id, who was the foreman when we owned the business."

A few months later, the army officers turned up again, announcing this time that the house was being confiscated.

Until that morning in May, we were a well-to-do Jewish family, part of the upper middle class. My father wasn't a millionaire, but was certainly very well respected, a pillar of the community. We had a two-story house, modern by the standards of the day. There was a giant living room that led to eleven rooms, and a large kitchen.

The house was surrounded by a large stone wall. Mother cultivated a lovely front garden, with a gazebo covered by fragrant jasmine. Inside the gazebo were benches. During World War II, soldiers from the Jewish Brigade stationed in Egypt would come to our house. They would sit in the gazebo and sing songs from the Land of Israel. We were enchanted both by them and their songs. We looked at them admiringly. For us, they were part of a wonderful, desirable world.

The Viddal family matriarch was a Zionist, who for many years had wanted to move to the Land of Israel and had encouraged her husband to buy land there. The wave of persecution in Egypt, in the wake of the State of Israel's establishment, turned the dream into reality. The family did not remain homeless, as the father managed to organize a few Muslim friends who bought his house and allowed the Viddals to continue living there. But it was clear that it was only a matter of time before more decrees were issued.

"In July 1950, my parents told us in confidence that we were going to Israel and asked us not to tell a soul. I told my girlfriends at the Christian school where I studied, that we were going to Alexandria for the summer vacation and that we'd be back at the end of summer," Zamir continues.

I remember my mother sitting up at night, sewing big pockets into our coat linings, in which she hid her jewelry. I divided up my books, and the dolls I loved so much, between my cousins—with great sorrow. And to this day, I get heart pangs when I think about them.

From Alexandria we boarded a boat for Marseilles. Although Father found work immediately, my mother insisted we continue on to Israel. She said she didn't want her children living in the Diaspora again. We reached Israel in the winter of 1951 and were sent straight to the immigrant camp in Tiberias. It was a hard winter, lots of snow, and all our suitcases and clothes got wet. Father got a job in roadwork, while Mother hid her tears from us. At night, by the light of a lantern, we saw Mother treat the blisters on Father's white hands, hands so unused to hard labor.[1]

THE EGYPTIAN JEWISH COMMUNITY FROM THE FIRST TEMPLE TO THE UN PARTITION PLAN

The history of the Jewish people in Egypt begins with the biblical Joseph, the Children of Israel's enslavement, Moses, and the Exodus. Centuries later, with the destruction of the First Temple at the hand of the Babylonians (586 BCE), many Jews fled to Egypt. After the Muslim conquest of Egypt (640 CE) only a handful of Jews remained, but over the years, the community grew and flourished. The great teacher and physician Rabbi Moses Maimonides lived and practiced in Cairo under Muslim rule. Jews escaping the Spanish Inquisition added to the community; they were joined by immigrants from North Africa. At the end of the nineteenth century, there were over 25,000 Jews in Egypt. In 1937, the community reached a peak of 63,500 people.[2]

Egypt gained independence from Great Britain in 1922. However, London continued to have a great influence, with a massive military presence in Egypt, primarily safeguarding the Suez Canal. According to a 1937 census, 60% of Jewish wage-earners dealt in trade, and of these, many were small businessmen.

Concurrently, many Jews had entered the fields of banking, finance, and industry; the latter sector alone employed 21% of Jewish wage-earners. The third important sector in Jewish economic life was civil service (10%). Jews played a significant role in developing the textile and sugar industries, railway tracks, and the establishment and management of some of the country's largest banks, such as the Anglo-Egyptian Bank, the Egyptian Mortgage Bank, and the Farmers Bank.

As our story continues, we will meet some of the most important Jewish entrepreneurs of the day, chiefly the Smouha family of Alexandria, along with the Katawi, Di-Menashe, Ades, Mosseri, Harari, Rolo, and Suares families, plus others. Underneath them, a middle class had developed of self-employed professionals: lawyers, doctors, teachers, engineers, and clerks. During the 1930s and 1940s, Egypt's Jewish community was the richest of all the Jewish communities in the Arab world, although sharp social differences did exist between millionaires, the middle class, poor workingmen, and the thousands of poor peddlers and craftsmen.[3]

The first blow against the community, due to increased tensions over Palestine, came on November 2 and 3, 1945, the twenty-eighth year anniversary of the Balfour Declaration. Nationalist elements called for a general strike on November 2, more in protest of the British, (who, as mentioned, continued to dominate Egypt to a large extent), than in solidarity with the Palestinians, or against the local Jewish community. The first hours of the strike passed quietly, but at 1:00 P.M., a riot broke out. Jewish businesses located on Imad al-Din street near the Muslim-run al-Azhar University in Cairo were attacked and looted. Two Cairo synagogues, the Amir Farouk Street synagogue and the Ashkenazi Congregation, were burned down, and twenty-seven Torah scrolls destroyed. The next day, Muslim youths stoned Jewish stores in Cairo, but were dispersed quickly by police. Two days later, it was known there were 400 people injured during the riots, many Jewish homes and stores were looted, and other institutions, such as the soup kitchen, the home for the elderly, the shelter for the poor, and the Jewish hospital were damaged or destroyed.[4] It was a ominous sign of things to come, as the struggle over Palestine escalated.

The first economic strike against Egypt's Jews came as early as July 29, 1947. An amendment to the Companies Law determined that 40% of managers and no less than 75% of employees at every company must be Egyptian citizens. This move, intended mainly against British nationals, dealt a harsh blow to the country's Jews, as only 15% of Jews held Egyptian citizenship.[5]

The situation became graver still after the UN Partition Plan was announced on November 29, 1947. Up to that point, the issue of a Jewish state in the Land of Israel was a secondary subject on the national agenda, used mainly as a political tool in the internal power struggles between the government and the opposition. But British historian P. J. Vatikiotis says that Egypt's extreme factions now quickly took advantage of the mass rallies organized against the Partition Plan to further their effort to undermine the government. According to Vatikiotis, the Muslim Brotherhood successfully transformed the Arab-Jewish struggle in the Land of Israel—especially given the West's support of the Partition Plan—into a cause worthy of an Arab-Islamic *jihad* (holy war) against the infidel.[6]

ECONOMIC PERSECUTION AND CONSPIRACY WITH THE STATE OF ISRAEL'S ESTABLISHMENT

In early May 1948, right before the British Mandate in Palestine was due to expire, King Faruq declared that most of Egypt's Jews were loyal to their homeland, and the government would take action against the Zionist movement only. Yet the situation that ensued in Egypt after the State of Israel was declared, and Egyptian army's central role in invading the new state, all served to expose the Jewish community to danger. On May 14, 1948, the Egyptian government headed by Mahmud Nuqrashi Pasha, declared a military alert and began a wide series of arrests. Within a few weeks, 1,300 people were arrested, 1,000 of which were Jews held on charges of having ties with the Zionist movement.

On May 30, the government decreed it would confiscate the property of all Egyptians—whether resident or expatriate—if their actions jeopardized national security, as well as the property of anyone under arrest on suspicion of treason. According to the decree, the State could appoint a manager in charge of confiscated property, who would be given owner's rights. Until the end of 1949, a period during which Israel and Egypt were almost constantly at war, Jewish property, both private and community-owned, was confiscated. Professor Michael Laskier has compiled a list naming no fewer than seventy Jewish businesses impounded by the government at that time and emphasizes that this accounts for only the most major companies.

Among those victimized by confiscation, according to Laskier, were Levi Perez, Maurice Cohen, the Chemla Department Store, A. Gattegno Enterprises, Aslan Baruch, Rahamim David, Hezechiel Ibrahim Matalon, Albert Guetta, Marco Mosseri, Wolf Horowitz, Beno Levi, Leon Rosenthal, Salomon Levy, "Cinema al-Hilal," Charles Rossano, Maurice Benin, Markos Israel, Zygmunt Neumann, Emile Nessim Ades, Abram Aaron Reisfeld, Roger Oppenheim, Raphael Dowek, and Haim Dora. These businesses spanned the sectors: cotton, shipping, banking, general trade, pharmacies, movie houses, the film industry, and agriculture. The Jewish community's economic foundations remained intact, Lasker adds, but both business owners and employees became disheartened.

Over the next few months, persecution focused on the economic front. In June 1948—either under direct orders or after being given to understand it was in their best interests—the Jews donated money to a fund benefiting Egyptian soldiers, then engaged in fighting against the Israel Defense Forces. The Cairo Jewish community donated $160,000, and the Jewish community of Alexandria, $80,000. On July 19, bombs went off near the Jewish-owned Cicurel Department Store; similar explosions occurred on August 1 near the Gattengno and Ben-Zion stores. Dozens were hurt, and there was heavy property damage. Yet no one was arrested; the police even hinted that Zionist agents might have had a hand in the blasts.[7]

On October 1948, the Middle East Division of Israel's Ministry of Foreign Affairs reported there were clear indications that the Egyptian supervisors in charge of confiscated Jewish property were firing Jewish workers employed by those businesses. At the same time, the authorities refused to issue citizenship papers to Egyptian-born Jews, and many were left without citizenship—a fact that would gain in significance several years later, after the Sinai Campaign, with the expulsion of foreign nationals and Egyptians without papers.[8]

THE JEWS LOSE THEIR PROPERTY AND REMAIN TRAPPED IN EGYPT

In early 1949, after the battles in Israel ended and a February cease-fire agreement between Egypt and Israel was signed, some of the restrictions on Egypt's Jews were lifted. The confiscation of property was terminated, and some property already confiscated was returned. A report released during those months by the Research Division at Israel's Ministry of Foreign Affairs stated: "The opinion shared by all is that there has been a vast improvement in the situation since the end of the war, especially since confiscation of several important Jewish companies was suspended. In effect, the authorities have retreated from their vicious attacks on foreigners, first and foremost being the Jews."

And yet, a nameless American Jew visiting Egypt in January 1949 submitted a conflicting report with the Jewish Agency. The man first noted that he had lived in Germany during the Nazi regime and had witnessed the Jewish persecution there firsthand. But, from what he had been told, the Egyptian Jews were far worse off in some respects—at least up until Prime Minister Nuqrashi's assassination in December 1948 by the Muslim Brotherhood. Persecution in Germany had been organized, he explained, while in Egypt gangs ran riot in the streets. Things improved slightly during the man's visit to Cairo: Nighttime raids on Jewish houses stopped, some Jewish prisoners (mainly those with foreign citizenship) were released and deported, and Jews whose only sin was being pro-Zionism were not arrested again.

Despite all this, the man reported, Egypt's Jews continued to live in a state of terror, primarily due to the military situation, which gave the authorities permission to censor and limit communications and confiscate property. In contrast to the Ministry of Foreign Affairs' report, this eyewitness said in no uncertain terms that the policy of confiscation continued, albeit at a relatively slower pace, of only ten during the few months that had elapsed since Nuqrashi's murder. Among these was Haim Dora's property, estimated at £5 million. The move made the Jewish community lose all faith in their economic future; Dora was an anti-Zionist, a fact that had no bearing when one of his workers brought false charges against him. The man further told the Jewish Agency that he had asked Egyptian Minister of Justice, Ahman Mursi Badder Bay, why Dora's property was confiscated. The answer was that Egypt feared that if Jewish capital were exported illegally out of the country, the economy would collapse; confiscation was the only sure way to prevent this from happening.

Jews are afraid of expressing their opinions, and refrained from filing even ordinary commercial lawsuits against non-Jews, the source continued. The limitations placed by the new Companies Law on businesses owned by foreign nationals, or noncitizens, were still in effect. Recently, many Jews had been fired for this reason, and the persistence of these limitations made it hard to find other work. Similarly, Egyptian citizenship was required in order to practice medicine or stock exchange trading. At the same time, there was an unspoken bias against Jews bidding on government contracts, or looking for civil service positions. Jews were also unable to obtain the permits necessary to sell real estate.

The most serious problem was the difficulty in leaving Egypt. Jews with foreign citizenship were able to get exit papers via their consulates, but only if they left Egypt for good. They were also required to leave their property behind and were permitted by the Customs Authority to take out only £20 in cash; even the rule allowing emigrants in general to take up to £4,000 in valuables did not apply to Jews.

According to the same report, the government of France granted a good amount of assistance to its Jewish citizens leaving Egypt. As a result, hundreds of French-Egyptian Jews arrived in Marseilles, and most continued on to Israel. By contrast, the British not only gave no help to Anglo-Egyptian Jews, but—convinced this would earn them points with the local regime—actively assisted Egypt in blocking their passage. For example, many Jews held British passports because their parents were from India. The British consulate in Cairo now maintained that since the Indian subcontinent had been divided, and Pakistan established, those passport-holders should apply to the

Pakistani consulate. Pakistan, a Muslim country hostile to Israel, refused to help the Jews who remained trapped in Egypt.

The man continued: Jews who were Egyptian citizens, or had no citizenship, could not leave the country. Over the previous months, hundreds of Jews had applied to leave, but only ten had been granted permission—those, incidentally, who had enough cash on hand to pay a respectable bribe. But willingness to bribe was not always enough. One wealthy Jewish banker, the source said, was prepared to pay a huge amount to be able to visit his sick son in Paris, but the request went unanswered. Most of Egypt's Jews were stuck in the land of their birth, living in constant fear of being arrested and their property confiscated.[9]

A rare Mossad le-Aliya Bet document, apparently from late 1949, outlines the manner in which, despite the difficulties, local Jews helped to get hundreds of their fellow Jews out of the country. One of the country's largest travel agencies, the Egyptian Travel Office, was owned by the Sitton brothers. The document outlines the company's smuggling activities as follows:

In 1948–1949, the travel agency worked to bring new immigrants to Israel, at the expense of private individuals, and that of the [Jewish] Agency. Some of those Jews who have escaped Egypt, with the company's assistance, are still in France as they are people of means. The company succeeded in smuggling Jews during the hardest of times, under Prime Ministers Nuqrashi Pasha and Ibrahim Abd al-Hadi, thanks to their excellent ties with officials at the Bureau of Emigration, the Ministry of the Interior, police officers from the Political Division, etc. On two occasions, each person was charged 1,000 Egyptian pounds for an exit visa. Ordinary visas used to cost 100–200 Egyptian pounds. That was in 1948. The dirty work, paying bribes in return for the permits, was done by a lawyer named Anbar Fahmi, a Coptic Christian who used to work for the travel agency.

All arrangements were made with the shipping companies, and low-ranking customs officials, who received a monthly salary [from the company] of ten Egyptian pounds. Their role was to turn a blind eye as the emigrants went through customs before boarding the ship. In cases where suitcases contained gold, jewelry, and silver—they would notify the officials ahead of time, and everything would be alright. In return, they received an extra payment from the company. The company bought Italian [and] French passports of dead people from the families [of the deceased], paid 50–60 Egyptian pounds, then changed the photos. They also arranged for false Italian passports.[10]

Over the next few months, the confiscation continued. In February, the military commander of Cairo, Fuad Sharin Pasha, issued an order evicting the residents of five Cairo apartments within forty-eight hours. The order immediately transferred possession of one apartment to an engineering corps officer; no details were given regarding the purpose of the other four apartments. The Middle East Division at Israel's Ministry of Foreign Affairs noted that Jews had lived in each of these apartments. One was registered to Emille Najar, Israel's representative in Paris; the others were inhabited by Yosef Weinstein, a lawyer; Ya'akov Weisman, who worked for the Shell oil company (and who had been arrested a short time earlier); Edgar and Eli Levy; and Marc and Chaim Najar. Two weeks later, the authorities confiscated radios and sewing machines belonging to Jews arrested some months before, and five major Jewish stores in Alexandria were also seized. A report from Cairo dated April 1949 stated that the Egyptian trustees continued to hold Jewish property and showed no signs of ever returning it to the owners.[11]

There exists a rare, firsthand account sent to Israel in April 1949, with the arrival in Marseilles of 80 new immigrants, on their way from Egypt to Israel—the first group of this kind since the 1948 war began. Mossad le-Aliya Bet emissaries interviewed thirty individuals, all holding foreign passports, and all from Cairo or Alexandria. These people—members of the middle class, clerks and small businessmen—said that in February, the Egyptians began granting exit permits to foreign nationals; within two months, 10,000 applications were filed. British citizens were allowed to take out 5,000 Egyptian pounds per person, while other nationals were allowed only 1,000 Egyptian pounds per person.

"We estimate that hundreds of Jews will leave Egypt after Passover," the emissaries reported.

> The Jews' situation in Egypt improved after the Rhodes cease fire agreement [in February 1949], and the Muslim Brotherhood arrests [in late 1948 and early 1949]. Open persecution in the street has stopped, and joint commerce [between Arabs and Jews] is starting. But the continued lay-offs of Jewish clerks [in accordance with the Egyptian law limiting foreign nationals in official positions to 25%] in Jewish and foreign-owned enterprises, and the constant fear of riots, intensify the desire of Egypt's Jews to leave.[12]

That same month, the official Egyptian government gazette published an order canceling the policy of Jewish property confiscation. The government returned property belonging to the brothers Cahanof of Cairo; to Eli Ades, also of Cairo; and gave the al-Hilal cinema back to its owners. But, judging from Israeli documents, this directive was the first and last of its kind. The property of dozens and maybe hundreds of wealthy Jews was never returned.[13]

DIRE STRAITS AND MIGRATION—1949 TO 1950

Between May 1949 and the summer of 1950, 20,000 Jews left Egypt. Some went to Israel, but many chose to live in Europe, due to Israel's poor economic situation. Many of the new immigrants to Israel were without means and might have preferred to settle in Europe but lacked the money to do so. Lasker presents two months as a representative example. In December 1950, 430 Jews left Egypt, of whom 68% were of employable age (15 to 69). However, 213 (half of the total number of emigrants and 72% of the employable) had no skills; in other words, they were unemployed or worked only occasionally. Very few had professions that placed them in the middle class or higher: four worked in textiles, five were clerks, one was in medicine, one in law, and two in education. In April 1951, there were 119 emigrants, of whom 56% were employable, but once again, half had no skills. Among those of employable age, 88% had no skills.[14]

Over the years to come, the situation remained the same as described by the Jewish Agency by July 1949: "According to Egyptian monetary law, one may officially take only 300 Egyptian pounds to France, or 150 Egyptian pounds to Italy. Some emigrants find some way of getting their property out. By contrast, the overwhelming majority are people for whom the pack on their back, and the little money recorded in their documents, is their entire fortune. We have not encountered many instances where Jews with property left it behind in Egypt, out of a desire to escape." A month later, Haim Zadikov, a former Jewish prisoner, released and deported to Italy, testified that he and other prisoners like him were allowed to leave Egypt only on condition that they relinquish all claims to their property. For this reason, 300 people who would not agree were still in jail.[15]

Very few could reach out and help the Jews of Egypt. Israel was preoccupied with a critical security situation, immigration from all corners of the globe, and financial problems that threatened its young economy with collapse. The Jewish Agency dealt mainly in life or death situations. The world was indifferent, aside from one country: France, which took an unusual step in October 1949 when it filed suit against the Egyptian government with the International Court of Justice in The Hague.

The word *Jew* is never mentioned in the lawsuit, as the French government was acting to protect all its citizens, regardless of religion, but almost all those involved were Jews. The suit stated that after May 15, 1948, Egypt arrested forty French citizens, four of whom were still under arrest in August 1949: Gastan Ben-Simon, Doria Nadia Hazan, Mohamed Ismat Badawi, and Jacques Cherbit. The others were released on the condition that they would leave Egypt. At the same time, Egypt confiscated property belonging to French citizens: the Messiqua family of Alexandria, Jacques Abu Chemla, Jacques Charbit, Marc Mosseri, Albert Guetta, and Alfred Cohen.

France stated clearly that Egypt's actions were connected to its war with Israel and claimed that as far as Cohen was concerned, there were no grounds for touching his property, even according to the standards set by the government of Egypt.

After 15 months of fruitless diplomatic negotiation, Paris turned to the Court, asking that it order Cairo to reverse its actions and compensate the victims. But the French lawsuit did not last very long. In February 1950, the government of France notified the International Court that, as the actions related to the suit had been canceled, it wished to withdraw the lawsuit.

The government of Egypt had no objection, and the lawsuit was withdrawn a month later.[16]

LEAVING EGYPT WITH NOTHING

In November 1949, the Jewish Agency decided to cut back on immigration from Egypt in order to increase quotas from other countries. Mossad le-Aliya Bet emissaries in Cairo tried explaining the impact of this action to their colleagues in Jerusalem. In doing so, they gave singular details on the new immigrants' finances.

> We are in enemy territory, all our activity is underground, and our employees are followed by the police. Our situation is that thousands of [potential] new immigrants have sold their houses, left their places of work, and await visas for passage either by ship or plane. A mob of them burst into our offices where we work, in the port city, broke the windows and wrecked the office. We were

Jewish refugees from Egypt arrive at the Greek port of
Piraeus, January 1957 (Central Zionist Archives)

barely to stop the police from coming, which could have had far more serious
results . . . in no way can we delay the emigration of people who already hold
visas. They have sold everything and are waiting, suitcases in hand.[17]

This statement is an apparent contradiction of the data showing the immigrants were impoverished. There are several possible explanations. First, the
emissaries might have exaggerated slightly in order to convince their superiors to increase quotas (an attempt that failed), and second, that even the
poorest of emigrants had sold off property—clothes, furniture and so on.
In the current situation—no work, no property, and only a little money, intended for a fresh start in the State of Israel—they had no source of income
and plenty of cause for despair.

It is clear that the property was sold at ridiculously low prices. In June
1950, the Aliya Department at the Jewish Agency requested information on
an Egyptian Jew named Yosef Perdo, apparently because it intended to en-
list his aid in matters of emigration to Israel. Members of his community now

Jewish refugees from Egypt arrive at the Greek port
of Piraeus, January 1957 (Central Zionist Archives)

in Israel told the Jewish Agency that Perdo was a wealthy Jew and the son-in-law of Itzhak Liskowitz, head of Cairo's Ashkenazi Jewish community. "Perdo worked for Jewish immigration from Egypt to Israel and helped in different ways," said one source. "One way was in transferring money. You have to assume he didn't lose anything on the transactions, because by changing money he made a profit, albeit indirectly." An ardent Zionist, Perdo was arrested by the authorities after the State of Israel was declared, and two months later, was released on bail (simply put: a bribe) posted by his father-in-law. Liskowitz sold his villa, worth 25,000 Egyptian pounds, for a mere 5,000 Egyptian pounds and received permission to transfer the money to Switzerland. Although the document does not say, it is very likely that the two then left Egypt.[18]

Others were not so lucky. Russian-born Y. Kogan, who had lived in Egypt for 40 years, managed to emigrate to the United States in the spring of 1950. In June, he wrote to Israel's Minister of Foreign Affairs, Moshe Sharett, a tale of woe of what happened to him at the Customs Authority at the Port of Alexandria:

> At 11:00 A.M. I arrived with my family, my three children, at the Customs House. The ship *Atlantic* was set to sail at 2:00 P.M. The customs official searched all eleven of our suitcases. When he finished, we were required to open them again for another official. Five officials, one after another, did the same thing, took out every item, ripped the stitches out of hat linings, shoes etc. But they achieved their primary goal: We were late for boarding. The officials kept saying there were lots of boats.
>
> We had in our possession three Credit Foncier Egyptien securities, each one worth £20. We asked the official if we could take them with us. He said, We'll see. Five hours later, after finding no gold or silver, they grabbed the bonds, and ordered us sent to jail. I pleaded, pointed out that we hadn't concealed the papers, had notified the official, and asked for permission to take them. But the official in question denied it. I added that these papers were worthless, and could not be sold outside Egypt, that I was permitted to take 100 Egyptian pounds with me, and so these securities were covered. But the clerk replied that I was not permitted to take securities with me, and sat down to compose a long police report, satisfaction written clearly all over his face. The fact that half my body was paralyzed due to a seizure had no effect on him. He kept saying, over and over: This Jew pretends to be travelling to the United States, but he is really going to Israel.
>
> I lived in Egypt but I had no idea that the penalty for taking silver or gold out of Egypt was five years in jail. We, and other Jews in Cairo, thought they simply confiscated the money you were trying to take out. It's very important that you tell all the Jews in Egypt, through the radio, that they could be imprisoned for every crime they commit. Many emigrants take pride in knowing all sorts of places to hide their money or gold. But if they knew that, if it's discovered not only will the money and gold be confiscated, but they will also be jailed for five years—meaning, certain death—maybe they would be

more careful. One is forbidden from taking salable items, one can take only used goods. There is a prohibition on taking out new clothes, china, machinery, etc., unless the emigrants have a permit stating exactly what items they are taking with them.[19]

Felix Mizrahi, today a violinist in his seventies, was among the poor leaving Egypt in the early 1950s. His father, Ibrahim, was a violinist and conductor of an orchestra that performed all over Egypt and Syria until his death in 1940. Felix was born in 1929 on Darb al-Kuttab Street in Cairo's Jewish quarter. The family lived for a number of years in Tunis and Alexandria, returning finally to their old house. "Playing music was the most important thing in our family. We all learned to play. We were considered lower middle class, and our financial situation was reasonable—no more than that." Felix came to Israel in 1950, and was joined two years later by his brother and mother Aziza. "Mother walked out of the house, locked the door and left. Out of everything we left behind in Egypt, the only thing I regret is my father's violin; I have no idea what became of it. Apparently, they wouldn't allow them to take even that out, but now it's too late to find out. I never asked my mother what she did with the house and the property. She never said, and I never pressed her for an answer. I suppose it was too painful to talk about."[20]

Chapter 6

"An Evil Duplication of Hitler's Aryanism"

The Sinai Campaign: Egypt's Jews Are Banished and Their Property Taken

On Friday, November 23, 1956, a few hours before the Jewish Sabbath was to begin, Shlomo Zalman Shragai was hurrying toward the Israeli embassy in Paris. The head of the Jewish Agency Aliya Department wished to transmit the following message to Jerusalem as quickly as possible: "Shragai has received reports from two different sources that the Egyptian authorities have told thousands of Jews without citizenship that they must leave the country within four days, if not—they will be sent to prison in the desert. They are 15,000 in number."[1] Thus began the most dramatic chapter in the modern history of the Jews of Egypt, a chapter in which they were required to leave the land of their birth with almost nothing.

THE OFFICERS REVOLUTION, THE SUEZ CANAL CRISIS, AND THE SINAI CAMPAIGN

The roots of this second Exodus from Egypt can be traced back to the revolution of July 23, 1952. Years of incompetent parliamentary rule, corrupt politics fueled by money and power, a weak economy, a backward industry, rapid population growth, an ever-widening gap between rich and poor, the 1948 military defeat to Israel, and internal strife between progressive elements and Muslim fundamentalists—all led to a total collapse of the royal sovereign government. A group of officers, led by General Muhamad Naguib and Colonel Ghamal Abd al-Nasser, toppled King Faruq, banished him from the country, and installed his infant son Prince Ahmad Fuad as figurehead. In January 1953, the junta disbanded all political parties and established a single party regime headed by Naguib and Nasser. Five months later, sovereign rule was abolished, and Egypt became a republic. Naguib was named president and prime minister, while Nasser became vice president. One year later, Nasser had become the true leader of Egypt, as Naguib vacated his position in favor of Nasser, who—until his death in 1970—was Egypt's undisputed ruler.

The Jews of Egypt were cautiously optimistic during the initial period of military rule, as the new regime demonstrated no inclination to take action against them. Their incomes improved, and the number of pupils in Jewish school increased. And yet, when interviewed in depth, members of the Jewish community admitted that they did not believe that the situation could last long and that many had begun preparing for emigration to Australia, France, Italy, and other countries in Western Europe.

During the new regime's first three years in power, international affairs were fairly restrained, as expressed by its policies on the two main international fronts. The border with Israel was quiet, and agreements were signed with Great Britain, granting independence to Sudan and ensuring the British Army would withdraw forces from its Suez Canal bases by July 1956. But in the mid-1950s, Egypt adopted a policy of nonalignment with either the Western or Eastern blocs, at a time when Western policy dictated that anyone who was not pro-West was, by default, pro-Communist.

Egypt's neutral stance infuriated the United States and its allies, chiefly Britain and France. In 1955, the United States and Great Britain initiated the Baghdad Pact (together with Iraq and Turkey), deemed the pivotal element in protecting the Middle East from the USSR. Egypt was invited to join the pact, but Nasser refused. In 1955, Egypt signed an arms deal with Czechoslovakia, which was backed by the USSR. The deal was viewed with a great deal of suspicion in the West, and in July 1956, the United States and Britain withdrew their willingness to provide funding for construction of the Aswan Dam, while at the same time, the USSR announced it would provide funding. Egypt reacted immediately by nationalizing the Suez Canal—which was, up to that point, under British-French ownership—and announcing that revenues on the canal would be used to fund the Aswan Dam.

At that same time, Egypt adopted a more extreme policy toward Israel, providing shelter and aid to infiltrators who terrorized, destroyed, and killed the inhabitants of Israeli border settlements. Israel took retaliatory measures, assuming that Nasser would then restrain the infiltrators. Among the Israeli leadership, calls were increasing for a preemptive strike against Egypt before it gathered strength—reinforced mainly with Soviet weapons—and launched an attack on Israel, as Nasser repeatedly declared he would. Additionally, Egypt blocked Israel's access to the sea from the south, preventing Israel from entering the Suez Canal and obstructing traffic entering and exiting of the Gulf of Eilat.

In the fall of 1956, the interests of Israel, Britain, and France converged. On October 29, Israel invaded Sinai, dropped paratroopers over the Mitla Pass, west of the Suez Canal. Twenty-four hours later, having coordinated beforehand, Britain and France demanded that Israel and Egypt each retreat to a distance of ten miles from the canal. Israel agreed and halted its troops at the agreed on distance, but Egypt—as the strategists expected—refused. On October 25, British and French warplanes began bombing Egyptian airfields. In response, Nasser ordered a full blockade of the Suez Canal by sinking ships along the waterway. On November 5, with the Israel Defense Forces (IDF) already in complete control of the Suez Canal, French and British paratroopers landed near Port Said, where the canal meets the Mediterranean Sea. The following day, they conquered the city.

The United States, however—incensed at not having been informed secretly of the campaign, which took place in the final days of its presidential election—pressured the three countries towards a cease-fire. The USSR was threatening to use nuclear weapons against Israel, while at the same time, there was increasing domestic opposition to the campaign both in England and France. London was forced to back down, and France could not continue alone. In December, British and French troops withdrew from Egypt, and Israel withdrew from Sinai in March 1957. UN observer forces entered the Sinai peninsula; until the eve of the Six Day War in 1967, they prevented further infiltrator attacks and ensured free passage to the Gulf of Eilat.[2]

CONFISCATION OF JEWISH-, BRITISH- AND FRENCH-OWNED PROPERTY

The Sinai Campaign was the turning point for the Egyptian Jewish community. The first indication that the regime was taking a considerably harsher attitude toward the community was the mass imprisonment of Jews. By December 7, at least 900 Jews were jailed, primarily on grounds of "anti-Egyptian activities." It was clear to all that the charges were false: Among those arrested were elderly people, and a nineteen-year-old girl, arrested previously on the same charges during Israel's War of Independence when she was twelve. It can be construed, therefore, that the arrests were made according to a prepared list and were not due to any actual crimes.

On November 1, 1956, at the height of the Sinai Campaign, Nasser decided that all British- and French-owned property in Egypt should be confiscated. The order, signed by Nasser personally, forbade Egyptian citizens from both direct and indirect trade with British and French nationals, or from fulfilling standing obligations. These foreign nationals were forbidden from filing suit against Egyptians or continuing lawsuits already in process, if the matters related to trade in any way. Nasser ordered his Minister of Trade to appoint two general trustees over confiscated property, who would determine what modifications were required regarding the property. The trustees would take inventory of the confiscated property, manage it, and replace the owners in all way, shape, and form.

The trustees' primary authority was their right to sell property and dismantle the companies they now managed, subject to approval by the Ministry of Finance. From those profits, the government of Egypt would then be licensed to take whatever sum it deemed necessary to compensate the victims of British and French air raids, as well as assist British and French citizens in leaving the country. Similarly, the trustees were permitted to take 10% off every financial asset and 10% off revenues from all other properties to cover their own expenses. British and French nationals were required to hand all their property over to the trustees, without exception. Employers were ordered to fire all British and French employees without severance pay and without advance notification.

On November 3, Nasser expanded the order, redefining it to include all Jews in Egypt who were neither British nor French citizens. Nasser ruled that the order would apply to citizens under arrest; anyone classified as "under supervision"; anyone who, while abroad, was involved in activities damaging national security; any company or corporation owned by a person falling under the aforementioned categories; and any agency or branch office of a foreign company managed by a person falling under the aforementioned categories. As seen in Chapter 5, similar classifications made in 1948 enabled Egypt to confiscate a large amount of Jewish property.

The trustees appointed were Hassan Mar'i and Ahmad Mansur, who moved quickly to bring in their own representatives to head the major British and French companies operating in Egypt. These included Credit Lyonnais, Credit d'Orient, Prudential Life Insurance, the Phoenix Insurance Company, the Marconi Company, Shell Oil, the Anglo-Egyptian Oil Company, and others. Research conducted at that time by U.S. experts showed that, according to official Egyptian records, out of 486 properties confiscated within the first few weeks of the new policy, at least 95% were Jewish-owned. It is estimated that between November 1956 and March 1957, 500 Jewish-owned companies were confiscated, and another 800 companies frozen. A few Jews managed to preserve some of their property by entering into 50% partnerships with non-Jewish Egyptians with influence.[3]

There was a partial respite in December 1956, when Egypt allowed the owners of confiscated property to sell off their furniture and personal belongings, excluding jewelry, precious stones, and cars. It was further determined that possession of furniture belonging to people already outside Egypt, or leaving in the near future with no time to sell, would be transferred to the Swiss Embassy, which now represented Britain and France in Egypt. The Embassy would be responsible for liquidating the furniture within two weeks, selling it, and transferring the proceeds to a trustee in charge of depositing them in owners' accounts.

One month later came the ruling that all banks and commercial enterprises must be "Egyptianized" within five years; in other words, control was to be transferred to Egyptian citizens. In practice, the authorities demanded that "Egyptianization" take place within one year, with extensions made available only in extraordinary cases. Within this framework, non-Egyptians were also forbidden from having management positions in these companies. In April 1957, the government allowed the sale of confiscated banks and insurance companies; at the same time, it set up a national holding company for State-owned shares in the confiscated companies.[4]

The measures were, first and foremost, damaging to British citizens. There were 13,200 British citizens living in Egypt during the Sinai Campaign, with an estimated £179.4 million in property (nominal value for all pound sterling amounts presented here), not including goodwill. About one-quarter of this property, £45.4 million, was irrevocably nationalized, and the remainder confiscated (ostensibly, this move was temporary, but in fact the property remained forever with the Egyptian government; Chapter 7 deals with the amount of compensation paid). British refugees exiting the country over the coming months left behind property valued at £80 million. The nominal value of property confiscated from French citizens was said to be 400 million Egyptian pounds, of which £300 million were shares in the Suez Canal Company.[5] The value of Jewish property will be discussed at length later, but it should be noted from the outset that no official figures exist. However, Egyptian Jews most certainly lost billions of dollars in property when they were banished from the land of their birth.

EGYPT'S MOTIVE: DESIRE TO RID THE NATION OF JEWS

As the Egyptian national archives are not open for research, it is impossible to know for certain what made Nasser decide to deport all of Egypt's Jews. Michael Laskier mentions a long-standing Egyptian policy to rid itself of Jews, implemented both through direct deportation orders (these instructed family patriarchs to leave the country within seventy-two hours and effectively deported the entire family), and through economic persecution and psychological warfare that caused Jews to leave the country on their own volition. On November 22, Nasser signed an order defining "Egyptians" as those persons living in Egyptian territory on a continual basis from January 1, 1900, and onward, and who did not hold foreign citizenship. This peculiar definition, coupled with the fact that only very few people had any records extending back that far, enabled the authorities to decide at will who was Egyptian and who was not; Jewish persecution was now legally sanctioned. The same law stated clearly that Egyptian identity cards would not be given to known Zionists, and that ID cards would be taken from so-called

Zionists—here too, the authorities could decide, as they saw fit, who fell under this category.

At the end of November, Israel's Minister of Foreign Affairs Golda Meir, appealed to the president of the United Nations General Assembly, asking that the UN intervene on behalf of Egypt's Jews. Meir reported that prior to the Sinai Campaign, there were 50,000 Jews in Egypt, of which 16,000 held foreign citizenship, 15,000 had no citizenship, and the remainder held Egyptian citizenship. Even theoretically, she emphasized, only a small portion of the community could continue living in Egypt once their property was repossessed, and they were ousted from their homes and workplaces.

"Bank accounts have been frozen, property sequestrated, industrial and commercial concerns taken over by the Government, and Jewish employees generally dismissed," said Meir in summing up Egypt's economic measures. The official Egyptian list of confiscated properties, as of November 8, numbered in the hundreds, and included some of the most well-known Jewish-owned business: department stores belonging to the Cicurel, Chemla, Hanau and Chalon families; banks owned by the Zilka and Mosseri families; and the Pinto cotton concern. Meir claimed that a modest estimate of this confiscated Jewish property put its value at $100 million.

Meir continued:

> Across Egypt, all hope of income has been taken from the Jews, not only by direct government measures but also through unofficial measures taken by the government. On Friday, November 23, preachers in mosques throughout Egypt read a long proclamation issued by Sheikh Hassan al-Bakuri, Egypt's Minister of Religion. This proclamation explained to the Egyptian public that all Jews are Zionists and enemies, who would all leave Egypt in the near future and that in the meantime, they, the Egyptians, were not to cooperate with any Jew. Similarly, the press—which is censored by the government—has shrilly attacked the Jews as traitors, and government radio, including the central propaganda station Voice of Arabia, broadcasts anti-Jewish discussions calling all Jews "Zionist agents."
>
> Immediately following Bakuri's proclamation, the Egyptian physicians' union issued an announcement calling on all Egyptian citizens to boycott Jewish doctors, while a number of shops hung up signs saying they refused to serve Jewish customers. After having taken away their businesses, homes, access to bank accounts and private property, a few thousands Jews are left with nothing, while at the same time, they are unable to leave Egypt because they are forbidden to travel.

Meir also claimed that the Egyptian government's actions were not a "reaction to events" (meaning the Sinai Campaign initiated by Israel), but were part of a plan that was put into effect at the appropriate moment. She said the Jewish Division at the Egyptian Ministry of the Interior had, for a long time, kept files on every Jew and every Jewish-owned business. All the information needed to initiate actions against Jews was collected in an orderly fashion, as evinced by the rapid implementation of mass imprisonment. Moreover, Meir noted, the Egyptian government had, at its immediate disposal, a workforce trained to manage the confiscated businesses—more proof that these measures were planned ahead of time. She concluded: "In this regard, it is significant that the Egyptian government has benefited for a number of years from the services of several hundred former Nazis whose importance, influence, training and methods have infiltrated the highest echelons of the army, government and propaganda machine." By late November, Prime Minister David Ben-Gurion had already told the Knesset that Egypt's actions were reminiscent of those of the Nazis.

The idea that Egypt was taking measures that had been planned well in advance was expressed as early as December 1956 by an anonymous source, a man active in an international organization operating in Egypt, who apparently filed a report with the heads of England's Jewish community. The source noted that, although there was no overt official policy intended to rid Egypt of Jews, there was no doubt that this was the goal, to be attained by stripping Jews of their property and conducting a battle of nerves against them.

The Joint Distribution Committee also claimed, in February 1957, that Egypt had learned from the Nazi's mistakes and were therefore not openly announced a plan to systematically destroy the Jewish community, but were in fact carrying one out without legislation, incitement via the media, or bombastic slogans. A year later, the World Jewish Congress maintained that Egypt's actions were deliberate and premeditated, similar to those of the Nazis.

"Egyptianization is an evil duplication of Hitler's Aryanism plan, which resulted in the total robbery, and eventual mass murder of six million European Jews," stated the WJC. In comparing Nasser to Hitler, the organization mirrored concepts expressed by British Prime Minister Anthony Eden, whose memories of Britain's policy of appeasement in the 1930s played an important role in his current policy toward Nasser.

For its part, the Egyptian government claimed emphatically that it had no anti-Jewish policies. In late November, the Egyptian Embassy in Washington issued a statement referring to the reports as "propaganda." Egypt declared that no Egyptian citizens had been deported or lost their jobs due to religious discrimination, claiming these false accusations were disseminated by those who hoped to conceal their own barbaric misdeeds against Egyptian citizens—in other words: Israel, Britain, and France. Egypt's Ministry of the Interior released a similar statement, adding that security measures had been enacted only against foreigners, a few of whom happened to be Jews. Egypt's Chief Rabbi, Haim Nahum Affendi, was forced to issue a statement in the same vein saying, among other things, that Egypt's government assisted the needy among those foreign nationals forced to leave the country.

Economic persecution played an important role in Egyptian policy. During the first month that property belonging to foreign citizens was confiscated, the government seized assets belonging to between 470 and 500 Jewish residents of Cairo, Alexandria, Port Said, and Ismailia. The Jewish employees of those Jewish-owned companies were fired immediately. Jewish traders discovered they could no longer work, as the government refused them the necessary permits. Professionals such as doctors, lawyers, and engineers were thrown out of their professional organizations and could no longer engage their professions. Jewish stores were seized by various and sundry officials, often without any sort of legal permit. Jewish clerks were laid off from their jobs, usually after the police paid a visit to their place of work, and made it clear to the bosses that the Jews must go. Other officers made their appearance in Jewish homes late at night, or early in the morning; some terrorized the family members, others administered beatings, very few were humane. But the message from all directions was clear: It would be best if the Jews give up their property and leave Egypt as soon as possible, sparing themselves any further violence or crueler measures from the authorities.

Between November 22, 1956, and June 30, 1957, more than 22,200 Jews left Egypt. The wave of emigration began with thousands of frightened Jews gathering at the Rabbinical Council offices in Cairo, which also housed the offices of Jewish community leadership. Others began pounding on the doors of foreign embassies, asking for aid in escaping Egypt—either technical (such as visas) or practical (cash). The Port of Alexandria and the Cairo Airport were flooded with refugees. Customs officials took advantage of the opportunity to confiscate most of the valuables; we will never know how much property found its way into their pockets and those of their superiors. Many Jews left with only the cotton robes on their backs.[6]

A BRUTAL EXPULSION AND ALL PROPERTY
LEFT BEHIND

The expulsion, a traumatic action in itself, was also carried out brutally. On November 27, a ship sailed into the harbor of Toulon carrying 174 deported Egyptian citizens, half of whom were Jewish. They related that on November 1, the Egyptian authorities had taken one member from every Jewish family in Port Said hostage (where there were 300 Jewish families) and transported them to an unknown destination. Despite the risk to their personal safety, some had stayed behind, hoping that the hostages might be released. London's *Daily Express* reported: "One young woman bewailed her lonely existence after her pharmacist husband was arrested, their son having died only a few months ago." A report from Rome said that the Egyptian Jews were ordered to vacate their homes within two hours, and fined six Egyptian pounds for every hour overdue.

These reports are apparently exaggerated. There is no evidence of hundreds of hostages taken from Port Said, and deportation orders gave between forty-eight hours and one week, and occasionally these were extended if the deportees could prove their intention to leave. But the reports provide clear evidence of the fear that gave rise to such harsh rumors. Other reports told of Jews who, on exiting Egypt, were required to sign declarations stating they would never return to Egypt, even as tourists, and that they had no claims on the property left behind. Sometimes, citizenship papers and deeds to property were torn up right before their eyes. They were forced to give details about foreign bank accounts, and customs officials searched their bags thoroughly, looking for jewelry. The first deportees were allowed to bring a single suitcase with them; others later on were allowed a bit more, but still movable goods only. Their real estate was left behind and confiscated.

The most reliable report was received in December by the Israel consulate in Berne, in a conversation with Swiss diplomat Max Hoenig, who was sent to Cairo at the height of the Sinai Campaign to handle British and French citizens. Hoenig told of seeing "many cases of Jews being brutally beaten, to force them to sign declarations regarding confiscation of their property, and their desire to leave the country. . . . Many of the deportees are visited by army officers who informed them that, by official decree, they and their families will be moving into the deportees' house. This announcement is generally accompanied by a paltry sum, set by the officer himself, 'compensating' the deportee. Upon receiving the sum, the deportee must sign a document declaring the house was 'sold' legally." Eliyahu Tavor of the Israel consulate in Berne noted that those methods were like those of the Nazis; Hoenig responded with silence. When Tavor asked what was the amount of Jewish property confiscated, Hoenig said he believed the economic foundations of the Jewish community were destroyed, and its future prospects were almost hopeless.[7]

An eye-witness account submitted in January 1957, by A. Sheftel of the Jewish Agency Aliya Department, tells of how the international Jewish organizations came to the deportees' rescue:

The exodus from Egypt began one night when the Egyptian authorities sent the secret police to Jewish homes. They knocked on doors after midnight, searched the houses, and ordered the residents to report to the Ministry of the Interior the following morning. The authorities knew where Jewish residences were located, according to a plan that had been prepared three or more years ago, which [the Egyptian government] had waited for the first opportunity to execute.

Among other questions, the Ministry of the Interior officials asked the Jews if they wished to leave the country or remain in Egypt. Those who requested to stay for a certain length of time were beaten and told that they must sign a statement that they wished to leave Egypt. These people told the other Jews what the authorities were doing; after that, Jews ordered to the Ministry of the Interior signed the document on their own volition, afraid they will be beaten like the ones before them.

These people received an order to leave the country within two days, a week or two weeks. As they hold no passports, lack the means and ability to leave Egypt, as many of the leaders of the Jewish community were in jail, or under house arrest, they have no choice but to appeal to the International Red Cross, whose offices are located in the center of town. The Red Cross initially came to their aid, but upon seeing the stream of people was increasing, it turned to the Rabbinate, asking for its help in organizing matters. Many officials at the Rabbinate volunteered for the task, and the Red Cross hung up a sign saying: "All Jews with citizenship, or without citizenship, or Egyptian deportees, or non-deportees wishing to leave Egypt, must go to the offices of the Rabbinate to arrange their affairs."

Then, the mass movement of Jews leaving Egypt began. Thousands submitted forms requesting passage. According to statistics, two weeks after the deportations began, 4,000 have requested passage, of which only 200 have been deported officially. This number includes only a few without citizenship and a small number of Egyptian citizens. (Egyptian citizens are afraid to submit a request of this type as they may be punished by the Egyptian authorities.)

However, after only a few days, a terrible tragedy occurred. It became clear that many families had both citizens and noncitizens. In one case, the mother is French and the father has no citizenship, or the reverse. The mother was to be deported to France, but the father could not accompany her because he had no visa. This tragedy was going on for ten days,

until the Red Cross intervened and convinced the Italian Consulate to grant both family members visas for nonresidents.

Sheftel continued: "The exit began about the first week in December 1956. Thousands set sail on foreign ships, or planes, but not Egyptian ones." Seventy-five percent of the requests to leave were from noncitizens, refused visas by all embassies and consulates. "For days and weeks, these Jews ran from consul to consul to no avail." After two weeks, Holland agreed to grant 200 visas to the elderly, women, and a few lone Jews. A week later, Italy agreed to grant visas to noncitizens, "and only then did the mass flight of noncitizens begin."

The problems did not end there. Only a third of the deportees could afford to fund their exit from Egypt; the others needed outside assistance. The Jewish community could not bear the expense; most of its assets were not salable (synagogues, schools, and the like), and its only significant liquid asset—shares yielding dividends—were needed for ongoing expenses. In any case, under the current conditions, the shares could not be sold for a reasonable price. Owners of confiscated property were sometimes allowed to use their property to finance their emigration, while foreign nationals could obtain assistance from their consulates. But most deportees were penniless noncitizens; in the end, funding came from international Jewish organizations, the Red Cross, and the local Jewish community itself. Sheftel notes with emotion that all Jews wanted to help their brothers in need—not just the rich, but the middle class as well. Officially, Jews were permitted to take 200 Egyptian pounds out of the country, but in fact they were allowed only £100, equal to 112.5 Egyptian pounds. Each child was allowed £50. A married woman was also allowed to take jewelry worth 50 Egyptian pounds; single women were allowed 20 Egyptian pounds in jewelry. This right was exercised only occasionally; in the end, much depended on the bribe given to the customs official at the port.[8]

THE DEPORTEES' SUFFERING IN EARLY 1957

The situation eased slightly in early 1957. The deportees were allowed to take a few more personal effects with them, and some confiscated property was returned to its owners. In April, the order allowing further property confiscation was canceled. A portion of property that had already been confiscated was again returned, but most Jews did not benefit. The reason: The Egyptian government demanded that the original owners sign a document releasing the authorities from all obligations to damage caused during the months of seizure. In many cases, but particularly in cases of businesses, the damage was so heavy that nothing could be done to revive the company after its return; getting back the business therefore had no real significance. In addition, the officials involved managed not to return all the property and even confiscated other Jewish properties, here and there, on various grounds.

The Jewish Agency attributed the change in attitude to international activity on the part of Israel and the Jewish organizations. M. Haskel, an emissary from the Jewish Agency Absorption Department visited the *Misr,* one of the first ships on which the deportees sailed, upon its arrival in Marseilles. In January 1957, he reported to Shragai: "It does not mean that the situation has improved, but the methods have changed; torture and beating, if not stopped entirely, has at least lessened. The Egyptians' current method of operation is primarily economic persecution; they systematically eliminate the Jews means of survival, and in this way, force them to leave the country."

According to the data that Haskel collected, 500 Jewish households had their property confiscated, management of their businesses transferred to Egyptians, and they were allowed to withdraw only 75 Egyptian pounds per month from their bank accounts. Upon leaving Egypt, most of them were required to sign a sworn statement waiving all rights to their property. There were also 800 families on a blacklist: Their properties were confiscated, they were forbidden from selling them, and could withdraw only 75 Egyptian pounds a month. Other Jews were allowed to withdraw 200 Egyptian pounds a month, but if they withdrew more, or sold property for a significant sum, they too were blacklisted.

Haskel added:

> The Jewish clerks and officials at large companies, banks and the like, were all
> fired. Some of the managers at the more important companies were not fired,
> but were sent on vacation for an undetermined length of time, without pay.
> There have been cases where people were called back to work, but this should
> in no way be seen as a change for the better; it is done out of necessity. [The
> owners] assign an Egyptian clerk to this person, who learns the job so that
> [the Jew] can be sent off again. Some clerks working at smaller companies do
> continue to work, but it is clear Egyptians will replace them, should they learn
> to handle the job. The situation of clerks working for small, privately-owned
> factories appears better, for the time being. Merchants and small businessmen,
> whose businesses have not yet been confiscated, continue trading for the mean-
> while but if they need an import permit, or any other type of permit, funding,
> etc., they cannot get it.

Haskel summed up, saying that almost all of Egypt's Jews had been sepa-
rated from their sources of income and would therefore be forced to leave
the country. He estimated that 70% to 80% of the Jews would leave Egypt,
of which 75% would come to Israel. Haskel made note of the warm attitude
the Egyptian Jews had toward Israel, but warned that Egyptian "horror stories" about Israel's economy had nonetheless filtered through. The Jews were
frightened "mainly of Israel's financial constraints," but also feared they
would not be allowed to leave Israel once they became new immigrants.[9]

That same month, however, the Red Cross in Cairo filed a report saying
the Jewish community's situation was getting much worse. The Egyptian
authorities had not kept their promise to bring laid-off clerks back to work.
To make matters even worse, the firings continued. Most of those Jews not
leaving Egypt, the report said, were forced to stay only because they lacked
the means to emigrate, as selling their belongings was not enough to finance
emigration. The Red Cross estimated that emigration costs per individual
were 17 Egyptian pounds, and that at least 6,000 to 7,000 Jews would need
assistance to emigrate. Concurrently, all community institutions were shut
down—either because the authorities had confiscated the properties, or simply taken them over—and could provide no assistance.[10]

HANDLING THE DEPORTEES AND SOURCES
OF FUNDING

The immediate problem posed by the deportation was how to handle these
Jews who, overnight, had become homeless, penniless expatriates. The problem was particularly serious due to a combination of factors: the surprising
immediacy of the expulsion, its size, and the lack of funding for emigration.
A breakdown of these problems into dollars and cents revealed dozens more
problems for the Jewish Agency, the Joint Distribution Committee, and the

other Jewish organizations dealing in migration. These included permits, visas, transportation, security, and funding—all of which required quick answers in a hostile environment in a state of war. Moreover, in October 1956, the Soviets invaded Hungary and vanquished the local liberation front; there too, thousands of Jews needed to be evacuated rapidly.

Initial assistance was provided by several countries, chiefly France, Italy, Greece, Holland, and Switzerland, all of whom permitted the emigrants to enter their borders. France, Israel's ally in the Sinai Campaign, provided the bulk of assistance, allocating a significant portion of its budget to assist the deportees. Most of the Jews continued on to Israel (13,500 by the end of 1957); other went to the United States, Canada, Australia, and South America (mainly Brazil). Some were allowed to stay in their host countries, primarily France. In Egypt itself, where the Jewish organizations were forbidden from operating, the assistance received from the Red Cross was of great importance. The Inter-Governmental Committee for European Immigration agreed to cover most of the cost associated with continuing the journey from Europe to Israel, or other destinations. At the same time, many deportees were assisted by the UN High Commissioner for Refugees. Other sources of funding included the Jewish organizations, chiefly the Joint Distribution Committee (also known as "the Joint") and the Hebrew Immigrant Aid Society (HIAS), whose budget came mostly from contributions to the United Jewish Appeal.

Michael Laskier's meticulous research reveals a number of factors regarding costs shouldered by the Jewish organizations: $151,563 was spent on organizing emigration to Latin America (Brazil, Venezuela, and Argentina); $601,943 on emigration to Israel. The Joint spent $551,000 on assisting Jewish immigrants from Egypt, and another $163,979 to help Jews remaining in Egypt. In all, direct aid (not including absorption) totaled almost $1.5 million, or $10 million in current values.

At the same time, the UN High Commissioner for Refugees, Auguste Lindt, tried to save the deportees' property. Backed by the Joint Distribution Committee, Lindt appealed in January 1958 to Egyptian Minister of Foreign Affairs, Mahmud Fawzi, asking that Egypt release the deportees' property. Lindt explained that the Commission was investing significant resources in resettling the Egyptian Jews and that transferring these assets to their new countries of residence would assist the UN greatly in fulfilling its task. However, Lindt and the Commission did not go out of their way to convince the Egyptians. In his letter, Lindt expressed only his hope that Cairo would respond to his request; the Commission was in no way empowered to actually force Egypt to do its bidding. And so, the request went unanswered, and the refugees received none of their property. This situation would change only slightly upon the signing of agreements between Egypt, France, and Great Britain, to be dealt with in the next chapter.

It should already be mentioned, however, that these agreements related only to citizens of Great Britain and France, while Jews who were either Egyptian citizens or noncitizens received nothing. Egypt naturally paid nothing, either to individuals or organizations, to compensate them for the enormous expense of resettling the deportees. In January 1957, the Red Cross estimated the cost of Jewish emigration at £23 per individual: £15 on travel costs from Egypt to Piraeus, £3 in border fees, £2 for a visa, £2 in travel costs from Cairo to Alexandria (most Egyptian Jews lived in Cairo), and £1 on miscellaneous expenses (transportation to the dock, and so on).[11]

Simple addition shows that by June 1957, the cost of moving 22,200 Jews out of Egypt reached at least £510,000, or £6.63 million in current terms. In any case, the Egyptian government should have borne the cost—whether it was covered by the deportees themselves, or by other sources—as it had forced the Jews to leave the country. It should also be noted that £23 per person refers to minimum costs and does not represent the cost to those who could afford a better class of transportation.

A breakdown of the refugee population by profession demonstrates why they could not be counted on to fund their own emigration. According to a report prepared by an Israel-based Association of Emigrants from Egypt, the poor comprised 10% of the entire Jewish community before 1956 and were supported by community funds and the wealthy. The middle class, meaning tradesmen, businessmen, and clerks, constituted 40%; craftsmen and professionals, such as doctors, pharmacists, engineers, architects, machinists, nurses, and social workers made up another 20%; the well-to-do, who owned large enterprises or were factory partners, also comprised 20%; and 10% were rich, (this group included 40 millionaires).[12]

RESTRICTIONS ON TAKING PROPERTY RESULT IN ITS LOSS

All the deportees, rich and poor, had one problem in common: the strict limitations on taking property out of Egypt. The result of these restrictions was that the overwhelming majority of Egyptian Jews lost their property overnight, and an ancient community was robbed of its wealth. All property left behind was appropriated by the Egyptian government, which divided it among its own or sold it for pennies and pocketed the profits.

A random sampling of documents preserved in the Central Zionist Archives in Jerusalem gives some idea of the problem. Hundreds of new immigrants sailed on the *Hermes* from Greece to Israel in the spring of 1957. The 126 families who arrived in March had 500 suitcases—an average of four suitcases per family. A few months later, 85 families arrived carrying 300 suitcases—an average of three and one-half suitcases per family.[13] Even assuming the figures refer to very large suitcases or trunks (the term used in the original documentation is "accompanied baggage," which gives no indication as to weight or size), there is no doubt the travelers came with only the basics: clothes, books, games, momentos, and the like. There were limits to the amount of financial assets one could take (as will be expanded on shortly), and furniture, naturally, could not fit into ordinary baggage.

Many of the emigrants took out travelers checks in an attempt to salvage something of their property. The 103 deportees on the ship *Misr*, which docked in Marseilles in January 1957, held a combined total of 100,000 Egyptian pounds in travelers checks. During the first few weeks, it was unclear how these were to be handled: British banks agreed to honor them, even outside England, but only on condition that they were held by British citizens. What would happen to the travelers checks owned by citizens of other countries, or Jews without citizenship, was unknown. The Jewish Agency announced that it was most likely that Thomas Cooke travelers checks would be honored in Israel. The Joint, for its part, learned that Thomas Cooke and Barclays Bank agreed to honor up to £100 in travelers checks per person, even if the bearers were not British citizens, as opposed to the £20 American Express had agreed to pay non-British citizens.[14] The documentation does not deal any further with this matter, and what happened in the end is unknown.

Another way of taking property out of Egypt was via a letter of credit, especially from the Britain's Midland Bank, or Societe Generale of France. In January 1957, Yehuda Dominitz of the Jewish Agency Aliya Department said he believed "chances were well-founded" that the new immigrants would be able to cash in their letters of credit "for a minimal sum," if they were issued by French or Italian banks. By contrast, things were very confusing and unclear regarding letters of credit and travelers checks issued in pounds sterling. That same month, Jerome Jacobson of the Joint announced that British citizens would be able to cash in these documents at up to £100 per person, and other citizens, up to £20. Later that year, the British banks decided they would only honor letters of credit presented in England, and refused to honor them abroad. Up until June 1957, French banks cashed all travelers checks and letters of credit on presentation in France, but later discontinued the policy, leaving the Jewish refugees stranded with a total of 3.63 million francs in credit. Only after Great Britain and Egypt reached an agreement in early 1959 (to be discussed in Chapter 7) were most of the letters of credit honored. Even then, they were not cashed in at full value, but according to a relative value, determined by the agreement.[15]

There were suggestions, here and there, about how things might be facilitated to enable the deportees to bring at least a little of their property to Israel. In January 1957, Dr. M. Bitan was sent by the Jewish Agency to examine the situation of a group of Jewish deportees from Egypt who had reached Italy. In his report, Bitan emphasized the need to offer these future new immigrants to Israel some economic and financial solutions:

We must make contact with the Egyptian Jewish émigrés who have lived for a prolonged period of time in France and Italy, most of whom, if not all, are business persons, and give them information about investment opportunities and business in Israel. They will spread this information among newer émigrés with capital who generally come to consult with them. This information campaign will be conducted through lectures, discussions, short condensed bulletins, but mainly via a special emissary who will impart, in person, information on these possibilities, give advice, and guide those interested. This way, we can break the ice, draw capital and people to Israel. . . .

We must arrive at some sort of an arrangement with the Ministry of Finance regarding investment, and transfer of capital belonging to the new immigrants from Egypt. We must take into consideration the fact that most if not all have left most of their property there, and understandably, it will be hard for them to cope with the little they managed to smuggle out. The State of Israel, more than any other country, must take the plight of these refugees into account, come to their aid, and encourage them from an economic standpoint. A special exchange rate should be set, for transfer of their capital, and breaks given to those who wish to set up factories, businesses and the like. At the same time, I must once again emphasize the urgent need for a person to act as a special emissary of our department [apparently the Jewish Agency Economic Department] to Italy, who will visit all camps where refugees from the Land of Goshen [Egypt] can be found, give them information and news on what is happening in Israel's economic field, and explain and provide guidance on investment opportunities and business in Israel. This person will also help the refugees regarding capital transfers in the form of cash or securities.[16]

A similar opinion was expressed in March 1957 by Judge Emanuel Yadid-Ha'levi, chairman of the Israel's Association of Emigrants from Egypt, after having spent many weeks with his countrymen in Europe. "We met with some of them [wealthy Egyptian Jews] and explained the economic situation in Israel and opportunities for investment, both in existing enterprises and by establishing new ones." Some planned on, and are still planning, to visit Israel as tourists, and make contact with financial institutions, and the Ministry of Trade and Industry in Israel, in order to discuss the possibilities for investment in Israel.

Our organization has brought the matter to the attention of the Ministries of Trade and Industry, Foreign Affairs and the Economic Department at the Jewish Agency, that they must find the most suitable way, using appropriate promotional methods, presented by Israeli persons of note—especially immigrants from Egypt with contacts among the wealthy deportees—to motivate them, from a business point of view, to come to Israel, found their enterprises and industries, and provide them with attractive conditions. This action will also provide a significant solution to the problem of employing the new immigrants from Egypt, as each Egyptian investor will absorb a number of new immigrants of his acquaintance in his factory. This will assist the Jewish Agency and the Labor Exchanges, who are facing difficulties in finding sources of income for the aforementioned new immigrants.[17]

DIFFICULTIES IN ABSORPTION FOR THE NEW
IMMIGRANTS FROM EGYPT

In the end, very little—if anything—was done to encourage investment in Israel on the part of Egyptian deportees. The result was that the deportees of 1956 encountered problems of subsistence similar to those experienced by their countrymen a few years earlier. Israel's economic situation in the latter part of the 1950s was better than the former, but new immigrants still faced the difficult challenges of finding housing and income—not to mention the sudden necessity of adapting to an alien society in an unknown land. The result was letters of complaint sent by the new immigrants to various Israeli government ministries and the Jewish Agency, although it should be noted that the amount is low, certainly relative to the number of immigrants. One possible explanation is that the new immigrants were absorbed finally into Israeli society, or at least understood that the alternatives were far worse. However, one gets the feeling that most new immigrants were too preoccupied to bother to complain officially or they were unused to this option, having lived all their lives under undemocratic Egyptian rule.

In 1960, Yosef Gohar, father of eight, from the Jesse Cohen neighborhood in Holon near Tel Aviv, wrote a letter of appeal to Prime Minister Ben-Gurion. He told of what happened in Egypt during the Sinai Campaign:

> When rumors of an Israeli Army victory reached [the Egyptians], they got heated up and looked for some way to let their feelings go, breaking down the doors to our apartments in the middle of the night, entering our bedrooms with guns drawn. . . . The men were taken to prison with treatment [an apparent reference to torture]. There was no limit to the lawlessness of their house searches. Children were taken from their beds, women in their cotton nightdresses, forbidden from getting dressed on the grounds that they [might conceal] arms or espionage equipment, and whatever they wanted, they took from our homes. Then from jail—straight to the ship. Shops were broken into by corrupt government officials who did whatever they saw fit. . . . My financial situation is very difficult now, and because of these troubles, I have a heart condition, diabetes and rheumatism. [Israeli public housing company] Amidar is threatening to evict us from our apartment due to irregular mortgage payment, and seven banks do not stop sending me warning notices.

Gohar asked the Prime Minister to compensate him out of Palestinian assets held by Israel.

Upon receiving no reply, Gohar turned to Minister of Finance, Levi Eshkol, in January 1961. In an unusual move for that time, this letter put forth a claim of ethnic discrimination against new immigrants from Arab countries, as compared with European immigrants. Gohar noted that as an Italian citizen, he had the right to migrate to that country, but because he believed in Israel he preferred to come there. Now, however, he was in danger once again of being thrown out of his house—this time by Jews. Added Gohar:

> As I had once worked with a doctor in an Egyptian hospital who was well-known to the Ministry of Defense and the Egyptian government, there was not enough evidence to hang me. They settled for stealing my property and deporting me, together with my family. In fact, this was worse than death, as it is written "They that be slain with the sword are better than they that be slain with hunger." It is upon the government of Israel to renew me and my family, if it has a bit of goodwill. I do not want payment for my services rendered to the government of Israel, as it is every Jew's responsibility, but I do not wish to be discriminated against. Our Ashkenazi [meaning, of European extraction] brothers receive better absorption conditions than we do, even though Israel is only a way-station for them, en route to America or Germany, while I have put my entire faith and future in Israel.

Gohar said he hoped his debts could be frozen until he received his property from Egypt or until he migrated to Italy. There is no reply to be found in the files.

In December 1960, Shmuel Attia, also of Holon, sent a letter of supplication to Ben-Gurion, several government ministers, and the Jewish Agency. Three of Attia's sons had come to Israel before the Sinai Campaign, leaving him in Alexandria where he dealt in textiles and was "the chairman of the needleworkers' union." Attia said he was the second Jew in Egypt to be arrested when the war broke out, as he was considered "an overt Zionist," his sons most likely in the Israeli Army ranks fighting against the Egyptian Army ("To my delight, they did," said Attia.) As his wife and the rest of their family had already been deported to Israel in 1951, the authorities found proof "that I sent thousands of young people to Israel." Attia was arrested, his "apartment locked with a padlock, with fine furniture inside. My property was confiscated, my stores and workshops. Stripped bare of everything, I was put on a ship after a month and a half in jail." Once in Israel, Attia received loans from the Jewish Agency and the Israel-based Association of Immigrants from Egypt. He tried to reopen his tailoring enterprise but failed, sold the sewing machines, along with jewelry and rugs his wife had brought with her in 1953. In his letter, Attia added details about his personal distress and asked the recipients to freeze his debts or assist him in immigrating to France.[18] No replies to the request have been recorded.

Not that it would have comforted the deportees, but Egypt too was suffering as a result of the Jews' expulsion. The stock market was damaged within the first few days of the Sinai Campaign, as 98% of the market players were foreigners or Jews (who alone represented 60% of all traders). The arrests and deportations were so damaging that Nasser was forced to release a portion of the jailed Jews so that they could go back to work. Later on, the stock markets in Cairo and Alexandria were nationalized, and all their employees were required to hold Egyptian citizenship—a restriction that, of course, immediately brought about renewed layoffs of Jews.

Two reports on the hard times in Egypt were sent, in January 1957, by Jewish Agency representatives in Paris to the Aliya Department in Israel. D. Asa'el wrote: "As the Jews occupied key positions in Egypt's economy (stock market, cotton, management of major trade companies, technicians), and the negative effects of measures taken were felt, the trend now is towards lifting restrictions. Several major businesses which were under [government] supervision, [have been] confiscated, and an Egyptian trustee nominated, have now had these restrictions lifted. A large Cairo factory for cement pipes [had been] managed by a Jewish engineering team; they have now been called back to work."

A. Sheftel reported: "After all the recent upheavals, the economic situation in Egypt has revived significantly. Egypt's economy had been concentrated in Jewish hands, with a high percentage of Jews among the French and British [players]. Therefore, [with the arrests and deportations] all of Egypt's financial institutions stopped working. Because this situation might have been irreparable had it continued longer, the government was forced to single out the Jews, and promised them improved conditions, to attract them and give them a feeling of security."[19]

But these reports were both exaggerated and fleeting. Jews did hold important positions in Egypt's economy but were not as indispensable as Asa'el and Sheftel thought. More importantly, the effect of their exodus on Egypt's economy was apparently short-lived, as the authorities took no real initiative in stopping the remaining Jews from emigrating or bringing back some of those who had already left (as Iraq had done a few years before). In the longer term, Egypt no doubt profited a great deal from confiscating Jewish property: Millions were stolen in broad daylight and made their way to the local government coffers.

Chapter 7

"We Had No Home"

The Egyptian Deportees Register Claims with Partial Restitution for Some

One day in the early 1920s, a steam locomotive crossed the plains of Alexandria. In one of the cars sat Joseph Smouha, a wealthy Egyptian Jew with British citizenship, together with a local friend. The latter turned suddenly to Smouha, pointed to the stretches of mud flats passing by the window, and said "Mr. Smouha, do you see those swamps? You could drain them and make something out of them." "Why?" Smouha asked. His companion replied that when Napoleon's fleet had retreated from the British in the battle over Abu Kir, 120 years earlier, the French flooded the region to stop the British advance, and originally this was excellent land. "Why tell me this?" asked Smouha. "Because you've helped me in the past, and now I'm returning the favor," was the reply. Smouha continued to press: "Why don't you do it yourself?" "Because you're a British citizen with connections who can bring in engineers, and I'm an Egyptian who can't," was the answer.

And so, Smouha City was born—an exclusive neighborhood in the center of Alexandria, owned privately by this Jewish family whose roots were in Baghdad. In the late nineteenth century, Joseph Smouha moved to Manchester, England, where he dealt in textile and prospered. He also formed his first contacts with Egyptians, who raised the finest long-fibered cotton in the world. In 1917, at the height of World War I, at the request of the British government, Smouha went to Egypt. He had close ties to His Majesty's government and its representatives in the Middle East. He was also one of those backing Lawrence of Arabia's efforts to spark the fires of nationalism among the local residents of the Arabian peninsula.

After the war ended, Smouha left the cotton business, settled in Alexandria, and began dealing in enterprise. The fact that he quickly became one of the richest people in Egypt did not change Joseph Smouha. He remained an unassuming man, who never gave interviews to the press, did not request a favored seat along the eastern wall of the synagogue, and had no official role in Jewish community leadership. Smouha unfailingly contributed to charity (mainly hospitals, welfare, and religious institutions) and donated very large amounts—hundreds of thousands of pounds sterling were mentioned in a rare news article about him—all in complete anonymity. Even after the area was developed, the family lived on Alexandria's seashore in a house that was pleasant, but not grandiose, with a staff of workers and servants. Their lifestyle was not ostentatious: There were neither yachts nor big parties.

When Smouha decided to develop the swamp region, he first brought in British engineers who concluded the idea was a viable one. Smouha then turned to the Egyptian government and entered into the strangest of negotiations, unlike any other. Smouha wanted to buy the land. The official answer was, Take it. Smouha said, Wait a minute, you don't understand, I'm going to do something very nice with this property. The officials responded with, Good idea; you can have the land for free. Smouha insisted, No, I must pay for it, because this is going to be a very exclusive neighborhood. Alright, the officials replied, Pay us a symbolic fee. Don't talk nonsense, Smouha said, I'll pay much more than that. An extraordinary argument then ensued with Smouha trying to raise the price, and the officials trying to keep it low. They finally reached an agreement, which forty years later served the Smouha family well. Egypt confiscated Smouha City after the Sinai Campaign and refused to compensate the family, first on the grounds that the land had been given free of charge and later claiming it had not been paid a fair fee. But the family had proof to the contrary, which in the end enabled them to receive at least partial compensation.

Beginning in 1924, the Smouha family operated as a sort of privately owned regional development authority, first draining the swamplands, then paving two-lane roads. An industrial zone sprang up near the Ford assembly plant already standing in the area. For the residents' convenience, a golf course was built, along with tennis courts and a race track. Tracts of land were sold to private investors who wanted to build their homes in the area, which rapidly turned into the most exclusive neighborhood in Alexandria. Among the residents were members of European royalty. Egypt's King Fuad, a friend of Smouha's, told him the area should be called "Smouha City," and the nickname stuck.

During World War II, Smouha's three sons served in the Royal Air Force. One son, Edward, was promoted to Wing Commander and was acting commander for British air freight in the Middle East. Joseph Smouha contributed heavily toward the purchase of Spitfire planes, the aircraft used in the first line of attack to protect Britain's skies. When German troops advanced across the Western Sahara towards Egypt, posters appeared in Cairo listing the names of the first ten people who would be hanged on Field Marshall Erwin Rommel's entry into Cairo; Joseph Smouha was number one on the list. The British Embassy in Cairo, which effectively ruled the country, summoned Smouha and ordered him to leave Egypt. The family moved to the Palestine and lived for six months in Ramallah, north of Jerusalem. They then returned to Egypt, even before the German threat had abated. Edward and his brother Ellis, who had passed their bar exams before the war, worked in the family business, then returned to their law practices after the war. Today, Edward's son Brian is a senior partner at major international accountancy firm, Deloitte-Touche, in Washington, D.C., and serves as auditor for the World Bank.[1]

THE WEALTHY FAMILIES WHO WERE HARMED: SMOUHA, ADES, AND CICUREL

In 1956, when Egypt confiscated properties belonging to British and French citizens, and very soon after that, those of the Egyptian Jews, Smouha City headed the list. But the Smouha family was certainly not the only one to leave their riches—in some cases, vast riches—behind.

In early 1957, only 50,000 Jews remained in Egypt, mainly those who wished to preserve their property. The government was allowing some owners of confiscated businesses to continue running them, even canceling some of the property seizures, but collectively, the Jews had lost their faith in the future. The feeling among the Jewish organizations was that, in the end, almost all would leave Egypt. Official persecution had ceased, reported emissary Eran Laor in April to the Jewish Agency in Geneva, replaced instead by informal harassment with the same intent: To force the Jews to leave. "By law, all deportation orders have been canceled, people sitting in prison released, and a large portion of business confiscation, canceled," wrote Laor, "but in practice, people cannot continue running their affairs." Bank accounts remained frozen, and Jews were still allowed to withdraw money only in the amount required to cover day-to-day subsistence.[2]

In late 1958, the British Foreign Office drew up a detailed list of British property that had been nationalized or confiscated, with a total value exceeding 178 million Egyptian pounds. The value of property belonging to Joseph Smouha and his family was assessed at 14.3 million Egyptian pounds—the largest private claimant by far. In effect, there were only two private claimants (individuals, not companies) on the list of those claiming over one million Egyptian pounds. The second, also Jewish, was the Ades family (to be discussed later on). The vast size of the Smouha family fortune is even more outstanding in light of the fact that the value of those British oil companies in Egypt, according to that same document, was 55.6 million Egyptian pounds; British banks in Egypt had assets valued at 4.6 million Egyptian

The entrance to the Rambam Synagogue in Cairo, March 2000 (Author's Collection)

The interior of the Rambam Synagogue in Cairo, March 2000 (Author's Collection)

pounds; Prudential Life Insurance had a 1.9 million Egyptian pound claim; while telecommunications company Cable and Wireless claim totaled 1.6 million Egyptian pounds.[3]

The Smouha family's main problem was that almost all their assets were in Egypt. Over the years, Joseph Smouha had forbidden his sons from transferring funds abroad, telling his son Edward, "If we were to take out a worthwhile amount, we would cause Egypt harm. Egypt is the source of the money, and we have an obligation to keep it here." Many years before, King Fuad said that Joseph Smouha was the only foreign national he knew who invested his money in Egypt and never took even one cent out of the country. But when the confiscation policy was enacted, no one remembered Smouha's acts of charity, honest business practices, or patriotism toward his country of residence.

The Suez crisis came when the family was in Europe; the Smouhas lived in Egypt between October and May and summered in cooler Europe. But in 1956, the family did not return from Europe, as the international crisis over the Suez Canal was already heating up. The Egyptian government re-zoned Smouha City as agricultural land, claiming its value was only £1 million. In the end, the family received only £3.1 million, in accordance with a Anglo-Egyptian agreement, dealt with later in this chapter. To this day, the Smouha family has suits, both pending and suspended, against the Egyptian government. Occasionally they win, sometimes receiving a paltry sum in compensation money, but in all, the family lost more than £10 million in 1960s terms, or over £100 million in current values.[4]

As previously mentioned, another wealthy Jewish family severely damaged by the Suez crisis was the Ades family. These were distant relatives of Shafiq Ades, the merchant hanged in Baghdad in September 1948 after a show trial. The assets confiscated from the Egyptian branch of the Ades family were valued at more than 1.4 million Egyptian pounds. Most assets were held by David Ades & Son, a company that operated in Cairo and Alexandria. Additionally, there was the family's private property. British paperwork documents only the personal compensation paid to four family members, who received a sum total of 1.2 million Egyptian pounds, with no mention of compensation for the loss of the business.[5] To this day, the Ades store in central Cairo continues to sell children's clothes under the original name; it is now government-owned.

The Cicurel family was one of the best known and wealthiest of Cairo's Jewish community. Their claim to fame was primarily a chain of department stores, bearing the family name. "Cicurel and Oroco" began in 1910 as a small shop near the Opera Square, adjacent to the city's best hotels. Later on, the chain's flagship store was established, not too far away, on the street now called "July 26th"—honoring the date in 1952 when the ousted King Faruq left Egypt. The family fortune enabled them, in 1920, to participate

The Jewish school in Cairo, which currently houses a government-run school, March 2000 (Author's Collection)

Abandoned building, formerly Cairo's Ben Ezra Jewish orphanage, March 2000 (Author's Collection)

in the founding of Bank Misr, from which emerged an industrial group by the same name. Selector Cicurel, who had transferred a large amount of capital out of Egypt before the Suez crisis, managed to sell the department store chain to an Egyptian family named Jabari for 600,000 Egyptian pounds, or $150,000, before leaving Egypt in March 1957. The chain's true value was in the millions of pounds, meaning Cicurel took an almost complete loss on value of the property. But he was one of the lucky few who managed to transfer a significant amount of money out of Egypt. A good number of store managers also left Egypt, and only two family members were left to continue managing whatever businesses were still owned. In 1961, the authorities nationalized the department store chain, taking it from Jabari. The store on July 26th Street is still called Cicurel, and as these words are being written (in March 2000), the government of Egypt is planning its privatization.[6]

JEWS FILE FOR COMPENSATION ON LOSS OF PROPERTY AND WAGES

Many more details about other Jews who lost their property to Egypt can be found in the British Foreign Office files dealing with implementation of the compensation agreement between Great Britain and Egypt. Under the terms of this agreement, the British Foreign Ministry established a framework for examining claims filed by British citizens whose property was confiscated. As Egypt paid a bulk sum, which covered only a relatively small percentage of the total claims, as we will see, a thorough investigation claims was necessary to determine who met the criteria stipulated by the agreement.

In his damage claim, Albert Joseph said that he lost his job, a respected position (not specified precisely) at the British Consulate in Ismailia, where he was employed between July 1955 and August 1956. At that point, he said, he was forced to leave Egypt due to the nationalization of the Suez Canal; the document does not make clear the connection between the two events. Secondly, Joseph lost his one-quarter share in a family clothing store, whose annual sales were 4,000 Egyptian pounds and annual profits were 1,000 Egyptian pounds. Thirdly, Joseph said, his father's house was destroyed in a "military action," and as a result, he had lost 250 Egyptian pounds that were in the house at the time. His father, he explained, dealt in foreign exchange and tended to keep large amounts of cash around the house.

A committee comprised of Clifford Middleton and Sir George Lowe handled Joseph's claim in November 1962, and ruled that, as he had left Egypt before the Sinai Campaign, Joseph was not entitled to compensation under the Anglo-Egyptian agreement. They could not accept his demand that he be paid a salary for the four additional months he was to have worked at the consulate. Joseph said the position was held for him over that period of time, during which he was allowed—according to the terms of his passport—

to return to Egypt. The committee's decision is clearly logical; Joseph apparently tried his luck, but failed.

On the other hand, the committee accepted Joseph's two other claims. They accepted the figures submitted regarding the family store's profits; and with the addition of the accepted interest rates, they ordered that Joseph be paid £560. The claim regarding the cash in his father's house was accepted mainly in light of the fact that Joseph was able to present a letter from the British Admiralty, according to which his father had received on retiring from this office, £320 for his services. The connection between the father's pension and the son's foreign currency stash is unclear. The impression is that the committee tried to accommodate Joseph as much as possible and was apparently satisfied that the Admiralty's letter provided sufficient proof that his father did keep cash on hand for the purposes of exchange. Joseph received an additional £256 for this claim.[7]

Another claim on lost wages was filed by Joseph Levi-Castro, age 67 when C. Montgomery-White and William Temple dealt with his case in December 1962. Levi-Castro worked for the Egyptian Salt and Soda Company since 1915. He started out as assistant to the chief accountant; eventually he himself became chief accountant. In March 1955, he signed a 22-month contract as an advisor to the company on accounting matters. The contract was to have expired at the end of 1956, but in November of that year, the company notified him that his work was to be terminated immediately. He continued to receive a salary until the contract expired.

On the face of it, the arrangement was fair: Levi-Castro was fired but received what was due to him, therefore he had no claim. But Levi-Castro maintained before the committee, that he was about to have signed another 22-month contract with Egyptian Salt and Soda, as the allotted time period was not long enough for training his replacement. What was the damage? Levi-Castro earned 125 Egyptian pounds a month, and in his last year of work was awarded a bonus of 110 Egyptian pounds, in all, 1,610 Egyptian pounds. He managed to find work in England but on retiring in February 1959, he had earned only £1,240 over a two-year period, amounting to under 700 Egyptian pounds per year. The committee ruled that there was sufficient evidence that Levi-Castro's contract was to have been renewed and assumed he would have earned wages similar to the previous year. From this amount the committee subtracted (justifiably) his income in England and set the final amount of compensation at £2,059.[8]

The logical approach used by Montgomery-White and Temple also applied in the case of Victor Levis-Romano, an upstanding Jew who managed a large animal feed manufacturing and export plant. The company, A.S. Sarpakis Factories, was established in Cairo in 1948 by Sarpakis, Hefni Mahmud, and Fuad Serag al-Din. The latter two were influential Egyptians, each of whom invested 20,000 Egyptian pounds in the plant. Levis-Romano himself invested 8,000 Egyptian pounds.

Levis-Romano had a high salary: 100 Egyptian pounds a month, enough petty cash for anything he desired (500 Egyptian pounds a year at first, and 1,000 Egyptian pounds later on), plus a bonus of two Egyptian pounds on every ton of animal feed exported by the company. According to agreements presented to the committee by Levis-Romano, there were 3,000 tons in exports for 1952–1956, for which he received a 6,000 Egyptian pound bonus. Levis-Romano's representative, Ian Percival, argued before the committee that his client's average annual income was 4,000 between and 5,000 Egyptian pounds.

Levis-Romano's claim was divided into four items: loss of his investment in the company, loss of income, loss of his position, and payments levied by the Egyptian government out of the confiscated property; this last item was already settled prior to the committee hearing in March 1963. Regarding the loss of property, it transpired that in December 1956—a few days before being forced to leave Egypt against his will—Levis-Romano signed an agreement with the company management, selling his share in the company for which he would receive 12,400 Egyptian pounds: 400 Egyptian pounds in cash and the remainder in payments of 100 Egyptian pounds each. But, argued Percival, the contract was signed under the pressure of deportation, when Levis-Romano needed to ensure he had some form of income, especially for the care of his handicapped son. Percival allowed that his client won a case in the Egyptian courts, and his 8,000 pound investment was returned, but claimed that the real value of the investment at the time of the deportation was far higher.

Montgomery-White and Temple ruled unequivocally that the agreement of December 1956 was signed under duress and with no alternative and could not be taken into account in calculating damages to Levis-Romano. They ordered he be paid £9,734, both for the loss of the bonus promised him on animal feed exports and for loss of income. Compensation was calculated according to a two-and-a-half year period (and not five, as Percival had requested), at a salary of 2,200 Egyptian pounds per year with full bonuses on exports.[9]

CLAIMS OF HARDSHIP PRESENTED TO
THE BRITISH COMPENSATION COMMITTEE

The hardship experienced by the Egyptian deportees is almost never mentioned in the summary reports of the compensation committee, but it is reasonable to assume that such claims were raised—if only out of emotion—in the hearings themselves when claimants appeared in person before the committee. Occasional hints of what the deportees went through may be found in a lengthy decision written by Middleton, Temple and Lowe, in February 1963, on the matter of the Lagnado family who ran tour boats along the Nile. The dry language used in the claims filed by the family nevertheless hints at what was happening in Egypt in late 1956, particularly at the ports where masses of stunned deportees had congregated, trying to take out at least a few of their possessions before encountering the local customs authority. The Lagnado family story makes it plain that the customs officials blocked the deportees and took all their valuables, especially jewelry. Whether these items ever reached the government coffers in Cairo or remained in the officials' pockets will never be known.

The committee's summary report opens with the matter of the family tour boats, which sailed twice a day on Sundays in the summer season and every other night in winter. The family proved its average profit on every trip was 73.25 Egyptian pounds, but the committee noted that trips were canceled when the Nile overflowed its banks, and this must be taken into account. It was also determined that the family had not invested in advertising, and therefore the reputation of the business could not be assessed. In all, the four family members (David Isaac Lagnado, Victor Isaac Lagnado, Fortunee Lagnado and Gaston Isaac Lagnado) received a total compensation of £6,753, to be divided among them according to their relative share in the business.

The family members also filed separate claims for compensation of personal property lost during their expulsion, either stolen from their apartments, confiscated by the customs authority or taken by the banks. At this point, the protocol of the hearing allows us a glimpse, slight though it may be, into the events of those days. Victor Lagnado said that when he was banished, all his furniture was left in the apartment. At customs, his camera, stamp collection, gold ring, and gold chain were taken away; things of great sentimental value, in addition to being the sort of portable valuables that many deportees tried to take with them. The committee ordered he be paid £500 in compensation for these items. Victor also received £933 for the loss of income from his work as a private French teacher, calculated for a two-and-a-half year period, the meticulous committee having determined that 5 Egyptian pounds should be subtracted on monthly expenses for the lessons. On the other hand, the committee rejected Victor's claims for compensation on expenses connected with emigration and legal fees, as the agreement between Britain and Egypt did not provide funds for this sort of compensation.

Some Lagnado family members lived together in an apartment, and according to their accounts, the furniture belonged to Fortunee Lagnado. The committee assessed the value of the stolen furniture at 500 Egyptian pounds, and the value of Fortunee's wardrobe—her clothes were also taken—at 150 Egyptian pounds. Fortunee also lost her jewelry to the customs officials, but these were not itemized and the committee awarded her 150 Egyptian pounds. The committee further ruled that Fortunee was entitled to compensation of £1,579 for bonds also confiscated by the customs authority, and £799 in compensation for having lost her job at the Ottoman Bank. The committee rejected Fortunee's claim for severance pay and a pension from the Ottoman Bank, having clarified that Fortunee, or a representative in Egypt, had already received a check covering this claim. It is unclear whether Fortunee had submitted a parallel claim regarding this item or whether the arrangement in Egypt was reached after the claim in Britain was already filed.

The committee next dealt with the matter of Gaston Lagnado. The committee ordered the British government to pay £330 for Gaston's furniture and personal effects, £779 for bonds left behind in the apartment during the expulsion, £138 for cash stolen by the customs officials, and £232 for lost of income as an salesman. On the other hand, the committee rejected Gaston's request for compensation on emigration expenses and legal fees (as mentioned previously, the Anglo-Egyptian agreement did not cover these). In all, the Lagnado family received a respectable £11,564 in compensation payment.[10]

Another look into the dark days of expulsion is afforded us by a failed claim submitted by Jacques Dwek, who said that after receiving a deportation notice in December 1956, he rushed to the bank and withdrew all his money in cash. He then made his way to the Swiss embassy, which represented the interests of Britain in Egypt at the time of the Suez conflict. In general, the embassy agreed to accept 300 Egyptian pounds from each deportee, but Dwek said that in his case the embassy had agreed to safeguard 2,000 Egyptian pounds and had even issued an official receipt. In addition, Dwek said he deposited currency and jewels worth 6,850 Egyptian pounds with a Swiss clerk named Rieter, a temporary employee at the embassy, who promised these would be transferred to Switzerland.

Dwek told the committee in detail how he had traveled to Switzerland in early 1957, a short time after arriving in England, in an attempt to receive his property. After a good deal of difficulty, Dwek located Rieter who told him the money had been deposited with "some organization," and that the moment he, Rieter, received the money from that organization, he would return it to Dwek. From the outset, Dwek had been naive in entrusting his money with Rieter; now he realized his mistake. He reported the incident to the British Consulate in Geneva, who turned to the local authorities. Rieter was arrested and admitted he received the cash and jewelry. But the Swiss authorities decided there was insufficient evidence to bring Rieter to trial on charges of theft, and he was released. In the end, Dwek managed to get £2,638 from Rieter, but failed in his attempts at getting the remainder through the Swiss courts. Dwek was therefore requesting that the British government compensate him, under the agreement with Egypt. The committee, however, determined that the agreement did not apply in this case.[11]

SEVERAL WEALTHY JEWISH COMMUNITY
MEMBERS FILE CLAIMS

The British compensation committee occasionally dealt with major claims filed by wealthy deportees, including some of Egypt's richest Jews. One of these was Moussa Shaoul, who died before the committee hearing regarding his claim, and was represented instead by his brother Zaki and nephew Charles. Charles said his uncle had been a healthy man, who rose every morning at 6:00 A.M. to work as a horse trainer. But deportation had broken his heart, and England's cold, rainy weather also contributed to his early demise.

The claim itself was over Shaoul's horse training enterprise. Sir Miles Lampson (Lord Killearn), the powerful British Ambassador to Egypt in 1936–1947, was one witness. He said Shoul had "a reputation of the highest degree" in his profession, with a thriving business. Lord Killearn himself had eight or nine horses in Shaoul's care, and testified that he would not be surprised if Moussa Shaoul's annual income came to 6,000 Egyptian pounds.

The family was represented by Ian Percival (who also represented Levis-Romano), who described Shaoul's professional accomplishments in detail: he owned two stables, one in Heliopolis near Cairo, the other in Alexandria (on fields rented from the Smouha family for 350 Egyptian pounds per year). His income came from several sources: regular payments for his services as a trainer, a 20% fee on prizes won by horses he trained, and illegal payments (as Percival himself put it) from other trainers hoping to someday inherit Shaoul's business. In fact, according to Percival, Shaoul was engaged in deceit as, early in the 1950s, he designated his nephew Charles as his heir.

In any case, the business flourished. The heirs assessed its annual revenues, just prior to confiscation, at 7,500 Egyptian pounds. They estimated a loss of 17,364 Egyptian pounds in revenues for the period between late 1956 and the passage of the Anglo-Egyptian agreement in early 1959. Shaoul's success was also expressed in his standard of living: he owned two cars, a new Ford worth between 400 and 500 Egyptian pounds, and a 1932 Rolls Royce worth 1,000 Egyptian pounds. He owned expensive rugs and furniture that decorated two rooms in his brother's apartment where he lived.

In his testimony, Shaoul's brother Zaki related that, immediately after the enactment of property confiscation, his apartment with all its contents was sealed for six months. Eighteen months later, the furniture was moved to a warehouse so disorganized that it was impossible to distinguish between the two brother's belongings. In the end, the furniture was sold at public auction, and Zaki paid Moussa 200 Egyptian pounds for the lost property. At the same time, it transpired that two expensive carpets from the family home, one worth 4,000 Egyptian pounds, the other 4,500 Egyptian pounds, were severely damaged after being held by the Egyptian authorities. Repairs cost

500 Egyptian pounds, and the rugs' collective value fell to just 1,000 Egyptian pounds.

The family members assessed the value of Moussa Shaoul's personal property at 2,900 Egyptian pounds and the value of equipment at the two stables at 1,367 Egyptian pounds. The latter figure was derived from an estimate prepared for the compensations claim and was approved by Shaoul himself before his death. He also approved the estimates of annual turnover and profits for 1953–1956, as prepared by his nephew Charles and his accountant, Jacques Attal, also for the compensations claim. Percival summed up: "This was a growing enterprise that was eradicated."

The committee, which included Middleton and D. Eifion-Evans, decided the Shaoul family was entitled to £32,198 in compensation. Among the items were 900 Egyptian pounds for the two automobiles, 2,500 Egyptian pounds for the loss of the horses, 150 Egyptian pounds for trophies and momentos left behind in Egypt, and 1,500 Egyptian pounds for the ruined carpets. The main element for compensation was the estimated loss of three years income, at 28,742 Egyptian pounds. Moussa Shaoul, however, died of a broken heart, and never had the satisfaction of receiving even a single penny.[12]

Five members of another well-to-do family, the Shamas, filed claims under the Anglo-Egyptian compensations agreement. They were Dina Shama, Raymond Shama, Giselle Shama, Marie Shama, and Gustave Shama. The family business was centered around the Raymond Shama Company, which dealt in lumber importation and marketing of various wood products. The business was confiscated in October 1956 and released in February 1960, but poor management on the part of the government-appointed trustee meant, effectively, that the business and all its assets were lost. The family filed for compensation on loss of property, loss of income, and loss of goodwill as was the accepted practice.

The company financial reports presented to the committee showed a business with an annual turnover of 143,000 Egyptian pounds in 1956. But for the last two months of that year, the business was under the management of Egyptian authorities who "successfully" managed to knock turnover down from a peak 216,000 Egyptian pounds in 1955. Profits also declined from 10,255 Egyptian pounds in 1955 to 8,055 Egyptian pounds the following year. In his summation, claimant representative Gabriel Cohen said: "From the days of sequestration onwards, no profits were made but losses were incurred and on desequestration, very little of the business remained."

Raymond Shama went into the lumber business at age 18, when he became a salesman for a company in the field. In 1943, he was drafted into the British Army. After his service, he was put in charge of lumber at the Egyptian Commercial Import and Export Company. After seven years there, Shama took out a loan and set up his own company, based in Alexandria, and allocated shares to all members of his family. In his testimony, Shama noted that, were it not for the Suez conflict, the company would have received a contract worth 50,000 Egyptian pounds for exports to Sweden, plus a local contract worth 14,000 Egyptian pounds. He estimated company goodwill at 50,000 Egyptian pounds, but the government trustee had sold the company for 10,300 Egyptian pounds—enough to cover bank debts, worker compensation, and tax payments. Shama himself received only 250 Egyptian pounds.

After some complicated calculations regarding company revenues, profits, and unrecovered debts, Middleton and Temple concluded that the Shama family members were deserving of £65,215 in compensation for the loss of their business and its revenues. Over half the sum was paid out to Raymond, according to his share, and the remainder went to Dina, Giselle, and Gustave, who were partners in the business. The family also received a return of 1,144 Egyptian pounds, a charge levied by the Egyptian government for management—very poor management, as mentioned—by its appointee. Marie Shama requested a return on a 1,450 Egyptian pound loan made to the company, but the committee ruled there was no proof this sum was stolen when the government authorities confiscated the business.[13]

Other claims are documented in letters sent by the deportees to the British Foreign Office in the years following the Sinai Campaign. These included some very large claims, such as that of Gustave Joseph Goar, who claimed a total property value of £323,000, due mainly to lands and a warehouse worth £250,000. In addition, property was confiscated belonging to his parents—Edwin Nissim Joseph and Matilda Goar—valued at £348,000, including agricultural land, a residence and the surrounding property, furniture, objets d'art, and more.

Another major claim was filed by members of the Dwek family, owners of a Cairo factory. Moise Dwek itemized his confiscated property (buildings, shares, bonds, rights on property rental, bank accounts, cars, and more) valued at 234,661 Egyptian pounds. In 1964, the family managed to obtain the annual report of the now-nationalized company, which put the value of assets at 123,000 Egyptian pounds, and net profit at 103,000 Egyptian pounds. The Egyptian accountant had even listed the shareholders—eleven Dwek family members—headed by Moise Dwek. Another family member, Mourad Dwek, filed a claim for over £25,000: one half for his wife's jewelry; £4,700 on the value of his home furnishings; £2,000 for his life insurance policy; a car worth £1,000; a parcel of land worth £2,000; shares worth £1,000 and office furniture worth £5,000.

The smaller claims were often accompanied by a greater display of need, for the simple reason that these were filed by people with no money or connections outside Egypt, people whose entire economic foundation had crumbled because of their religion and nationality. Members of the Douek family filed a claim for £8,115, mainly for the value of their furniture and apartments in Alexandria and Cairo (£5,500), and the remainder for the loss of severance pay, savings and other wages.

The Cohen family of Cairo reported confiscated property worth £15,639. Each item was recorded in detail, including £8,280 on commercial inventory; £2,000 on store furnishing; £1,800 in savings at the Ottoman Bank; £400 in jewelry and watches left in a Banc Credit Lyonnaise safe deposit box (the key was deposited with the Swiss embassy), £1,500 on the contents of their home, and even three shares in the Panama Canal worth £6. For months, Joseph Isaac Cohen asked the British Foreign Office repeatedly for assistance, out of consideration that he must earn a living and could not stay with his children forever. The reply was always: We must await a settlement between England and Egypt.[14]

FILING THE CLAIMS MADE BY THE EGYPTIAN DEPORTEES

Within a few months after the deportation from Egypt, various Jewish organizations began recording claims made by Jews. These records are, in essence, the only reliable source for estimating the overall value of the confiscated property. In September 1957, the World Jewish Congress claimed the value was $200 million, but the estimate was unsubstantiated, and with hindsight, appears to be more promotional than factual.

The first organization to deal with recording claims was the Joint Distribution Committee, which in 1957, together with the Jewish Agency, World Jewish Congress, and the American Jewish Committee, established the Paris-based Central Registry for Jewish Losses in Egypt, headed by Jerome Jacobson. By June, the center, which was headquartered in Paris, had sent out 9,550 claims forms to the Egyptian deportees that were known to it, living mainly in Israel, France, England, and Italy. The center promised applicants that all information would remain confidential and would be used to centralize claims and enable the Jewish organizations to achieve a suitable compensation arrangement. It emphasized however that there was no guarantee the effort would succeed. The questionnaire was very specific and asked for details on family members who had left Egypt and how, who covered expenses, their destinations, property taken with them and property left behind, what assets were confiscated or nationalized, their occupations in Egypt, and more. Former prisoners were asked to give details about their sentences: dates, charges, locations, and conditions.[15]

The confidentiality clause is still in effect. The guidelines of the Joint Distribution Committee archive in Jerusalem forbid viewing of files containing personal information. This goes against the practices of most other archives in the western world, but as a private organization, the Joint is allowed to set its own terms, as it sees fit. For this reason, documents directly related to the claims were not viewed for this writing, only summary reports.[16]

At the end of its claims registration, in June 1959, the Joint collected 1,035 forms, which Jacobson estimated represented 5,175 deportees—about one-quarter of all Jews who left Egypt after the Suez conflict. Most claims came from France, Brazil, Israel, and England. It was also apparent that a few Egyptian Jews had reached Rhodesia, Mexico, Kenya, Iran, Austria, Argentina, Colombia, Holland, Belgium, and Uruguay. Of all those filing claims, 45% had no citizenship, 11% held Italian citizenship, a similar percentage were French, and 9% were British. The total value of assets claims was 11,279,270 Egyptian pounds, making the average claim 10,898 Egyptian pounds. Almost half the purloined property was commercial—companies, agricultural lands, office furniture, equipment and more. Real estate accounted for 17% of claims; apartment values, 8%; bank accounts, 7%; the remainder comprised jewelry, objets d'art, collections, libraries, automobiles, insurance policies, and more.[17]

At the same time, the Association of Immigrants from Egypt in Israel was working on similar lists, mainly in Israel and, to a limited extent, abroad. The motivating force behind this effort was the organization's vice president, Advocate Shlomo Cohen-Sidon (the association's chairman, Emanuel Yedid-Halevi, was a judge and could therefore not be involved in this activity). By late 1956, Cohen-Sidon had already appealed to Minister of Finance Levi Eshkol, saying it was necessary to document the vast amounts of property left behind by the Egyptian immigrants, along with the property they were forced to sell under duress, both before and after the Sinai Campaign. Eshkol agreed and in March 1957, established a committee for claims registration, headed by Cohen-Sidon. The committee put ads in the Israeli press, calling for all Egyptian immigrants to come forth and report their stolen property.

"Outside Israel, the news spread by word of mouth," says Cohen-Sidon. The committee worked for a year and a half, and registered over 3,500 claims. There is no backlog of claims files at the Jewish Agency or Israel's Ministry of Foreign Affairs, and only an interim report from November 1957 remains. According to this report, 640 claims were registered between July and September, totaling 5,531,755,370 Egyptian pounds, mainly on lands, securities, bank accounts and insurance policies. There were also claims for compensation on 8,735 days in prison. Most of these claimants naturally lived in Israel but hundreds of claims were also reported from residents of the United States, Canada, France, Brazil, and other countries. There were claims amounting to a few hundred dollars, alongside claims in the hundred thousand dollar range. Today, those involved in the registration project assess the nominal value of the claims at between $300 and 500 million, or between $1.5 and 2.5 billion in current values.

The claims are still not available to the general public, but several years ago, Israeli journalist Inbar Lagstein was permitted to view a few of the claims. One filed by Esther Cohen read: "I lived in Egypt, in the city of

Cairo, in the Harrat al-Ayhud neighborhood. My family had a three room apartment, furnished, with a bedroom. In 1948, they put dynamite in our building and blew it up. I was severely wounded in my left leg and head, and to this day my leg still pains me. . . . When I returned from the hospital we had no home, and today, a mosque now stands where our house once stood. So it was worth a lot of money."

Ze'ev Wexler related: "My father, of blessed memory, had property on Tursini Skanini Street in Cairo. This was a four-story building, eight apartment units, each one with four rooms, separate entrance, kitchen and bath. After my father died, my mother stayed in Egypt, and announced she was safeguarding the property. The Red Cross notified us of her death."

Albert B. concentrated mainly on his family's business: "My father had a garment piecework and tailoring workshop in Cairo, on al-Bosta Street number 7A. Left behind in the workshop were 12 sewing machines, four cutting tables, curtains, display and sale furnishings, various wool and cotton fabrics made in England, Germany and Egypt. There were finished suits and outerwear for men and boys. Securities and unfilled orders from merchants whose property was confiscated after the Sinai Campaign in the Suez strip [sic]. Also left behind in Egypt was our personal furniture, and my sister's furniture, worth 3,500 Egyptian pounds, which we were forced to sell for the ridiculous sum of 500 Egyptian pounds."

In addition to personal property, over the next few years, the committee also collected information on community property. A very conservative estimate, Cohen-Sidon wrote in September 1963 to Shmuel Ya'ari, deputy manager of the International Institutions Department at the Israeli Ministry of Foreign Affairs, set the value of communal property at between $92,924,900 and $72.53 million in Alexandria, $13.39 million in Cairo, and the remainder in Tanta, Mansoura, Damanhur, and Port Said. The most valuable piece of community property was the Jewish hospital in Alexandria, valued at $20 million.

The Jewish hospital in Cairo, valued at $7.5 million, was sold to the government for only $1.5 million. The value of the synagogues, which represented the bulk of community property, was far lower—a few tens of thousands of dollars each—as in any case, Jewish law forbids their sale, except under unusual circumstances and for clearly defined purposes. Alexandria's Elijah the Prophet synagogue was one exception; according to Cohen-Sidon's letter its value was assessed at $5 million.[18]

The Association of Immigrants from Egypt in Israel was not content merely to write things down, but also tried to obtain real compensation for its members. The organization claimed that Egyptian immigrants suffered from economic hardship in Israel, so much so that "we are prohibited from going to the movies, enjoying a good meal, or dressing [properly], and in general, from enjoying elementary things a person needs, we work solely to repay the interest on loans." It was only fair, said Cohen-Sidon, that the deportees benefit from the sale of Egyptian property in Israel, namely the railway station at Lod, which for some reason was registered under the Egypt government's name.

When nothing came of his appeals to the Israeli government, Cohen-Sidon filed suit against the State of Israel in early 1960, for a declarative ruling stating the Egyptian immigrants were deserving of a portion of Egyptian property. Representing the State was Hannah Even'or (later on, president of the Tel Aviv District Court), who declared to the court: "There is no doubt that it is the wish of the State of Israel, and the government of Israel acting in its interests, to arrive at an international arrangement that would provide suitable compensation to the plaintiffs." Cohen-Sidon—who, a few years later, would serve as a member of the 6th Knesset—said with a smile that he was reminded of a passing conversation with then Prime Minister Eshkol: "Eshkol thought that registering claims was the end of the story, and the suit certainly came as a surprise to him. He told me I was a wily fox—I started out with something small, and this is what happened." But Cohen-Sidon withdrew the suit after the State announced that, when the time was right, it would make sure that the rights of Egyptian deportees were not violated. As the next chapter will show, this promise was never fulfilled.[19]

PARTIAL COMPENSATION UNDER AGREEMENTS WITH BRITAIN AND FRANCE

During those years, Egyptian Jewish deportees with French and British citizenship received partial compensation, in accordance with agreements between Egypt and the two European countries. The agreement with France, signed in August 1958, stated that properties in Egypt confiscated from French citizens would be returned; if return was impossible then the owners would be compensated. French citizens were permitted to come back to Egypt with no damage to their economic rights, despite the long stay outside Egypt. The hitch was in the secondary clauses, which determined, among other things, that confiscated property would be returned only on proof of ownership; during the time between the claim and settlement, the property would continue being managed by the Egyptians; if it transpired that the property had disappeared, the Egyptians would make an effort to locate it—with no promise of compensation should they fail. The agreement stated further that if the confiscated property had been sold, payment would be transferred to the original owners. Although the agreement stated, in principle, that the transferred sum would cover the full value of the property at the time of confiscation, no arrangement for compensation was made in cases where full value was not a factor. In many cases, as we have seen, the Egyptians sold property at well below its actual worth. Small wonder, in light of these facts, that in June 1959, one year after the agreement was signed, the

Joint Distribution Committee reported that, up to that point, no claims had been settled regarding the release of confiscated Jewish properties.[20]

The agreement between Great Britain and Egypt, signed in February 1959, was different. This agreement also related to the return of confiscated property, but determined that Egypt was exempted from returning property already sold. Instead it was agreed that Egypt would pay Great Britain £27.5 million in compensation for physical and property damage caused to British citizens in Egypt. The list of property already sold, and therefore would not be returned, which appeared as an appendix to the agreement, ran over four pages and effectively included all major British assets in Egypt. There are mentions of lands owned by the Ades family, the Sasson family, Adolf Yacoub, Mary Josep Emanuel, Solomon Suares (a member of one of Cairo's most important Jewish families), Emil Ades, Jack Chalom, and Leon Levi, an estate owned by Nessim Ades, lands owned by Rene Levi, Edwin Nessim Gohar, and of course, the lands belonging to the Ades and Smouha families of Alexandria.[21]

The sum paid to Great Britain by Egypt was not enough to cover the 4,442 British property claims, which amounted to £72,376,404. For this reason, rules were needed for allocating partial compensation. The operating principle was similar to tax reckoning: X percent of one part of the claim, Y percent on the next part, and so on. Rankings were modified several times during the agreement's implementation, in accordance with the claims filed, and in the end were as follows: Claims of up to £10,000 were paid in full; between £10,000 to £40,000, 75% compensation; £50,000 to £500,000, 40%; £500,000 to £1 million, £265,000 plus 30% on the sum exceeding £500,000; £1 million to £2 million, £415,000 plus 25% on the sum exceeding £1 million; £2 million and up, £665,000 plus 20% on the sum exceeding £2 million. In this way, more than £35 million in compensation was paid out; it is not clear how the difference was covered, whether by Britain or from interest on the Egyptian payment.[22] This calculation makes it easy to see how the Smouha family received £3 million.

Yet, even with the signing of the agreements, Jews were still discriminated against. Although the British and French citizens had been granted the right to return to Egypt and control their property, Cairo forbade the Jews among them from doing so. The situation of Jews with Egyptian citizenship, or without citizenship, was even worse. No government ever negotiated on their behalf, and they never received any form of compensation.[23]

Chapter 8

"Our House Had Become a Ruin"

Community Property Lost, Private Property Stolen

Ghamel Abd-al Nasser decided to mark July 23, 1961, the ninth anniversary of the coup d'etat that brought him to power, with a dramatic announcement to his people: From midnight that night, most private property would be nationalized. In practice, the State laid claim to all import trade, most export trade, local insurance companies, and major commercial enterprises. Over the coming months, property belonging to Egypt's 600 wealthiest families was seized, this time not only Jews but Muslims and Coptic Christians as well. In March 1964, the last of the privately owned enterprises—the contractors—were also nationalized. The regime completed its transition to a centralized economy, styled after the most rigidly planned Communist system, and obliterated the power held by the rich and landed.[1]

THE FATE OF PROPERTY BELONGING TO WEALTHY JEWS

As stated previously, these measures were not directed solely against Jews. According to official data from Egypt, 820 companies were nationalized, although outside observers place the number far higher still. The official lists published by the Egyptians contained Greek, Armenian, Lebanese, and Syrian names as well as Jewish ones. Professor Michael Laskier says that nationalization severely damaged Jews outstanding in the fields targeted by the Nasser regime: banking, insurance, and export. The measures eradicated what little economic base was left to those Jews who remained in Egypt after the Sinai

Campaign. But what happened to the personal property of these wealthy members of the Jewish community? The answer is unclear.

In 1995, Israeli journalist Ronen Bergman published a long list of nationalized Jewish property in Egypt that had gone uncompensated. According to Bergman, the mansions belonging to the Cicurel, Mosseri, Castro, Mizrahi, and other families had been turned into embassies, residences for foreign dignitaries, and public institutions—all without the owners receiving a single penny. Bergman's list contained a number of interesting items: the Imbashi family house, which belonged to the parents of Suzy Eban, Abba Eban's wife; the house of Dr. Wolf Jacob Margolis, grandfather of Israeli government minister Matan Vilnai; and the Rolo family house, which was destroyed and the United States embassy built in its place.

Bergman devoted a good part of his article to describing the Suares family mansion, the owners of a large private bank who had laid the railway tracks between Cairo and Hilwan. According to Bergman, the mansion—whose current value is $3 million—had been acquired somehow by a lawyer named Muhammad Mahmud Halil Bay. After his death it was confiscated and used as the official residence of then-President Anwar Sadat. Today, it is an art museum. In his article, Bergman claimed that the Egyptian government was now prepared to pay compensation of only $2,500.

Bergman's article aroused a great deal of interest, but the accuracy of his reporting is in doubt. Egyptian journalist Samir Raafat, a leading expert in the history of Cairo, its historic figures and sites, states unilaterally: "Bergman made mistakes almost at every turn. The overwhelming majority of properties were nationalized, but were not confiscated from Jewish owners; they were taken from those individuals who bought them from the original Jewish owners." Raafat says this holds true in the cases of houses belonging to the aforementioned Cicurel, Mosseri, Katawi, Suares, Rolo, Imbashi, and Margolis, as well as houses belonging to Albert Carmona, Henri Prasker, Emil Jacob, and others.

According to Raafat, the mansion belonging to Advocate Emanuel Mizrahi—one of King Faruq's advisors—is owned today by his daughter Lydia (who lives in Paris) and is leased to the Mexican government as its ambassadorial residence. The story of the Suares mansion is well known: It was sold legally by Raphael Suares's heirs—he died childless—and was confiscated from Mahmud Halil Bay's heirs. The only important building that might have been confiscated directly from its Jewish owners (Raafat does not state this as a fact, but says it may be the case) is the Victor Castro mansion, where Anwar Sadat once lived and where his widow, Jihan, still lives.

But Israeli Middle East expert Dr. Yoram Meital calls attention to an important fact: When was the Jewish property sold, and at what price? "The sale of a large percentage of private Jewish property—mainly immovable assets, like the department stores—began before the Sinai Campaign. As early as 1953–1954, the owners sensed something in the air, began transferring capital abroad, and initiated contact with whoever might be interested in buying their property. In the end, they sold for a price well beneath real value. In a formal sense, Raafat is correct. There were agreements, these were legitimate sales, and during the nationalization of 1961 the property truly was taken from second and third owners. But I say these transactions must be viewed in their contemporary contexts. The Jews felt, and justifiably so as it turned out in retrospect, that if they didn't sell for the offered price—which wasn't much—they might not be able to sell at all. If a country creates an atmosphere where business-owners have no confidence their business will continue to exist, and they sell off their business at a low price because of this atmosphere—this is a problem."[2]

There is no doubt that the remnants of the Jewish community were subject to severe economic restrictions. Already in 1952, a law was passed requiring Egyptian companies to ensure that a majority of Egyptians held management positions. Over the coming years, quotas were increased, and other laws made eminently clear they were intended for "real" Egyptians, in other words: Muslims. (This also discriminated against the Coptic Christian minority that has inhabited Egypt for longer than the Muslim majority.) In 1959, Egyptian employees were made to carry a so-called worker ID card, which—on the second line after "name"—listed their religion. The authorities made it clear, unofficially, that companies would be wise to not employ Jews. When positions were available, companies were supposed to turn to the government employment service for suitable candidates, yet this service never recommended a Jew for any position. Another law, passed in 1959, obligated all those engaged in foreign trade—importers, exporters, and agents of foreign-owned concerns—to register at a special office set up for this purpose. This office did not reject requests filed by Jews, but for the most part, simply did not answer the requests.[3]

JEWISH EMIGRATION FROM EGYPT IN THE 1960s

Jewish emigration from Egypt continued during the first half of the 1960s, although naturally, at a far lower rate than immediately after the Sinai Campaign. According to Rabbi Aharon Angel, the chief rabbi of Alexandria until 1956, the only Jews remaining in Egypt by 1958 were the elderly and those who did not wish to give up their assets. And, at this point, there were not a lot of assets. Although confiscated bank accounts had been released, income for most Jews was constantly decreasing as elderly Jews retired from jobs and younger ones were passed over in favor of Muslims. Those who wished to emigrate discovered, after the wave of nationalization in 1961–1962, that it was a difficult task simply because most Jews were left with nothing to fund the move. But all in all, Jewish life went on peacefully, and the community even had a few well-to-do merchants.[4]

In 1962, the Harari family—one of Alexandria's wealthiest—left Egypt. The parents and eleven children lived in a spacious house in the city's nicest neighborhood. They owned a textile factory and fourteen buildings, each one of which had eighty rental units. Zaki Harari relates that when he married in 1955, he purchased a six-unit apartment building on Abu Kir Street near the Hippodrome in central Alexandria; the apartments were rented out and the ground floor unit leased to an Ottoman Bank branch. Harari himself owned and lived in a large villa, where he had two drivers at his disposal, gardeners, and a staff of servants.

> It was a 500 square meter house, with seven rooms, each one at least 30 square meters.
> In 1957, when all the Jews left Egypt, we decided to stay because of the property, but at the same time we decided to dilute it, and sold off parts at any opportunity. I sold my villa at 10% of its value, with all its contents. The buyers, who knew exactly why we were selling, took advantage of the opportunity to buy the house at a bargain. My new Opel car, that I paid £600 for, I gave to my driver as a gift. But instead of being grateful, he complained that he deserved more.
> When we left in 1962, I sold some of my buildings for £1,000 each, when today every apartment in that building is worth at least £1,000. When we left, my father still owned three buildings, each one with 80 apartment units. Before we could leave, we were made to sign documents saying we were leaving Egypt of our own free will and that we waived our claim on everything. We left Egypt with one suitcase and $100. At the port, they stripped us to make sure we weren't taking out anything more. Fortunately, we managed to get out some more money over the years, which helped us manage.[5]

The Six Day War and the Egyptian defeat only made matters worse. By the end of May 1967, during the tense period leading up to the war, Jews working in civil service and other official capacities were relieved of their duties, sent on vacation for an undetermined length of time, and later fired. During the first days of the war, 425 Jews were imprisoned without trial. Most were released gradually over the next six months, although there were some who remained in jail—without trial—until September 1970. A week after the wave of arrests, seventy-five of the prisoners with foreign citizenship were put on trucks, transported from Cairo to Alexandria, loaded on ships and deported from Egypt with nothing, naturally. Up until September 1968, Jews could leave Egypt on condition that they give up their citizenship, promise never to return to the country, and leave behind all their possessions aside from personal effects. Over the eighteen-month period between the Six Day War and the end of 1968, 1,500 out of the 2,500 Jews left. During the following two years, only freed prisoners and their families were allowed to leave, but they were denied permission to sell their property.

As a result, the number of Jews in Egypt fell to only 600 by the summer of 1970. The community pension funds were frozen, aside from being able to withdraw small monthly sums, and the community was unable to support its ever-growing elderly population. In 1970, the government of Israel claimed that Egypt's Jews were "close to starvation, after being robbed of their resources, including employment and property."[6]

EGYPTIAN JEWISH PROPERTY IN THE PEACE NEGOTIATIONS

During the Israeli-Egyptian peace negotiations that followed President Anwar Sadat's visit to Israel in November 1977, the issue of Egyptian Jewish property was not raised—until the last minute. Only at the Camp David summit in 1978 did the matter suddenly come up. It was September 7, during a meeting between Sadat, U.S. President Jimmy Carter, and Israeli Prime Minister Menachem Begin. Sadat took out an eleven-page document and read the Egyptian draft proposal for a framework agreement with Israel. The participants in the talks were stunned as they heard the most extreme document ever submitted by Egypt during the ten months of negotiation, calling for Israeli withdrawal from all occupied territories including Jerusalem, the evacuation of Jewish settlements in the West Bank, a prohibition on nuclear weapon manufacture, and the establishment of a Palestinian state. Toward the end of his ninety-minute speech, Sadat added an item that infuriated Begin: "Israel undertakes to pay full and prompt compensations for the damage which resulted from the operations of its armed forces against the civilian population and installations, as well as the exploitation of natural resources in the occupied territories."

When Begin, Sadat, and Carter met the following day, Begin rejected each of Egypt's demands, one by one, and said: "You demand that we pay compensations on damage to Egypt. We wish to remind you, Mr. President, that we are a nation who vanquished aggressiveness and defended its life. If you demand compensation, I want you to know that we too, have a demand for compensation from you. I will bring you a long list of damages that you caused us."

It is unclear whether Begin was referring obliquely to the fate of Jewish property in Egypt, which was most certainly not the main topic of discussion in those historic talks. But, indirect though it was, Carter and his aides did make note of this point. On September 10, the U.S. delegation composed a first draft of the agreement between Israel and Egypt stating, among other things: "Egypt and Israel agree to work with each other and with other interested parties to achieve a just and permanent solution of the problems of Palestinian and Jewish refugees." The last four words were emphasized by Carter's advisors in the document handed to him; in the margins they wrote: "Israel would like the reference to Jewish refugees and Egypt would not." The idea was, of course, to ease Israel into accepting the need for a solution to the Palestinian refugee problem, a sensitive issue unlike any other in Israel's foreign policy. A similar version was inserted in the Camp David agreement presented on September 17: "Egypt and Israel will work with each other and with other interested parties to establish agreed procedures for a prompt, just and permanent implementation of the resolution of the refugee problem"—without identifying nationality.

The arduous negotiation over the formulation of the peace agreement between Israel and Egypt was carried out over the next six months. The two sides argued over every word, including the article regarding compensation that was so peripheral, relative to the agreement's central principles. In the end, the peace treaty was finalized, including Article VIII: "The Parties agree to establish a claims commission for the mutual settlement of all financial claims." On March 26, 1979, the agreement was signed on the White House lawn.[7]

The Israeli immigrants from Egypt waited patiently for almost a year, hoping that the joint claims commission would be established, and they might finally be awarded some compensation. But in February 1980, when nothing had happened despite signs that relations between the two countries were normalizing, Shlomo Cohen-Sidon wrote to Begin: "Now, after the government has achieved a peace treaty at Camp David—an agreement approved by the Knesset—it is clear that in fact the government will fulfill its obligation to this item (the claims filed by Egyptian immigrants) both by balancing accounts, and by other means (mutual waivers on claims). Given these circumstances, the State is now responsible for paying compensations to those Israeli citizens who recorded claims at the time, through the committee nominated by the government for this purpose." Cohen-Sidon asked Begin to select someone to be in charge of handling compensations payments.

But Israel's Ministry of Foreign Affairs felt otherwise. Elyakim Rubenstein, then deputy general director of the ministry and currently Israel's attorney-general, responded to Cohen-Sidon: "As you know, in keeping with Article VIII in the peace agreement with Egypt, the two sides agreed to establish a claims commission for the mutual return of financial claims. When this committee is established, it will most certainly be possible for the government of Israel to include the issue you raise as a topic for commission's discussion." Rubenstein rejected Cohen-Sidon's interpretation that Jerusalem was now responsible for compensating Egyptian immigrants.

"When this committee is established," promised Rubenstein. Twenty years have passed and the committee has never been established. Egypt has never pressed for it, and for Israel it is certainly not a priority. Initially, the Egyptians realized that Israeli claims could leave Egypt "stripped bare" as one Israeli informed source says. Israel, for its part, feared that Egypt might file a massive claim for oil pumped from the Abu Roddes fields in western Sinai between 1967 and 1975. Israel's government, which for decades promised to handle the matter of properties taken from the Egyptian deportees—

a promise made in court that superseded the claims made by individual immigrants—did nothing.[8]

As a youth, Maurice Zacks was a member of an Israeli spy ring operating in Cairo during the 1950s, and decades later served as chairman of the association of immigrants from Egypt at the time the peace treaty was signed. Today Zacks says:

> The [Israeli] Ministries of Justice and Foreign Affairs had different excuses for not handling our affairs. Before the peace agreement was signed they said there was nothing to talk about. Afterwards, they said we had to wait until the joint commission for mutual claims was established. In the end, they claimed that at the time our property was taken from us, we were not Israeli citizens, and therefore, the state could not represent us. If memory serves, the European Jews who received reparations as part of the agreement with Germany were not Israeli citizens during the Holocaust. Why them and not us?[9]

THE FATE OF COMMUNAL PROPERTY AND JEWISH RITUAL ITEMS

Meanwhile, the Jewish community in Egypt steadily dwindled down to a pitiful few. At the time of this writing, the maximum estimated number of Jews in Egypt is 100—half in Cairo, half in Alexandria. The average age is 75;[10] therefore the issue of what will happen to Jewish community property is critical, chiefly the matter of the synagogues.

First, the matter is complicated from a standpoint of Jewish law, which forbids the destruction or sale of a synagogue, except in very limited and clearly defined cases. Egypt's Jewish community was and is aware of the problem, and tried to obtain permission to sell from important rabbis in Israel. Ronen Bergman, the first Israeli journalist to publish reports concerning Egyptian Jewish community, quoted the former head of the Jewish community, Emil Roso, who claimed that he held a permit issued by Israeli Chief Rabbi, Eliahu Bakshi-Doron, enabling synagogues to be torn down and the properties sold to developers. But Roso refused to show Bergman the permit, calling it a "community secret." Moreover, Rabbi Bakshi-Doron wrote to Roso that he was forbidden from selling synagogues except under unusual circumstances, and then only if the proceeds went toward constructing a new synagogue.

Roso was not the first to request a Jewish legal permit. His predecessor, Yosef Dana, discussed the matter with then-Israeli ambassador to Egypt Moshe Sasson, who suggested he turn to the Israel's chief rabbinate. But Dana preferred appealing to the French rabbinate and claimed that he too had received permission. Once again, the supposed permit-grantor denies having issued one. Rabbi Rene Sirat, who was Chief Rabbi of France during Dana's tenure in Cairo, told Bergman: "I don't remember any Dana.

I don't remember granting any permission to sell synagogues just like that, it's forbidden by Jewish law. You're allowed to sell only if a new site is created in its place. In any case, I didn't have the authority to issue that sort of permit. I would have turned it over to the [French] rabbinical court, which in my opinion, would not have wanted to interfere in the matters of another Jewish community; in any case, because it is forbidden by Jewish law, they would not have issued a permit like that."

Bergman's excellent investigative report described in detail the goings-on around the synagogue and the Judaica owned by the Egyptian Jewish community. In the summer of 1995, he reported, the synagogue at Port Sa'id was destroyed after Roso sold it for 450,000 Egyptian pounds—$150,000—to a local contractor who was going to erect a shopping center on the site. Jewish legal matters aside, a question of responsibility still arises: How did the head of Cairo's Jewish community sell the synagogue in Port Sa'id? Roso claimed that, in the absence of a Jewish community in Port Sa'id, the matter was under his supervision.

In the 1980s, an attempt was made to sell a lot adjacent to the Me'ir Einayim synagogue in Cairo's Ma'adi neighborhood, and perhaps the synagogue itself, but the attempt was blocked by Carmen Weinstein (today the acting chairman of the community's affairs), with the behind-the-scenes assistance of the Israeli embassy. But why sell synagogues at all? Roso claimed that the money went to community needs, mainly care for the elderly and medical expenses. But when Bergman asked to see the community's financial records, he was denied access on the grounds of "community secrets." It is important to note that the Joint Distribution Committee provides the Egyptian Jewish community with $50,000 to $100,000 a year in aid, a fact that once again raises the question of why the properties need to be sold at all.

And what of the sacred relics from synagogues that were sold or abandoned? Egypt's government forbids their removal from the country, arguing that these historic items belong to the Egyptian people. The last time Torah scrolls were openly taken from Egypt was in 1977, when Sadat allowed the transfer of eleven precious scrolls to England. In early 2000, Egypt's Minister of Culture Faruq Abd al-Aziz Husseini—"Not a champion of normalized relations with Israel, to put it mildly," says one informed Israeli source—rejected a proposal to establish a Jewish museum to house the Torah scrolls and other sacred relics. This means, says the Israeli source, that "the Torah scrolls will continue to deteriorate."

There was significant progress in 1989, when 25,000 books were collected from the synagogues and Jewish community offices and deposited with the library of the Historical Society of Jews from Egypt, next to Cairo's Sha'ar Hashamaim synagogue ("the Gate of Heaven"). There is also a Karaite library next to the abandoned Karaite synagogue named for Moshe Deri, which houses 4,000 books and Karaite manuscripts. In early 2000, the

Ben Ezra Synagogue, where the Cairo *genizah* was discovered, after its renovation in the 1990s (Author's Collection)

Sha'ar Hashamaim Synagogue, the only synagogue currently active in downtown Cairo (Author's Collection)

Karaite community requested assistance from the Egyptian government to renovate their house of worship. Today, the facade is in reasonable shape, but the vast inner chamber show decades of neglect. As of this book's publication, the Egyptian government has still not answered the request.[11]

Only a few items of Judaica reached Israel from Egypt, some of which are found at the Israel Museum in Jerusalem. This collection, the Yedid Bequest, was contributed to the museum in 1991 by Yitzhak Yedid, member of a family of synagogue superintendents at Cairo's Hanan synagogue, also known as the Etz Haim ("Tree of Life") synagogue. The collection includes Torah scrolls, the covering to the ark of the Torah, Torah scroll ornaments, and sacred books from the nineteenth and twentieth centuries, some of which came from Hanan (which closed in 1967) and others from a private synagogue the family held in its home. The Israel Museum says it does not know how the items reached Israel long before 1991, at a time when Israel and Egypt were still in a state of war.[12]

One exceptional Torah scroll was held openly until July 2000 by the government of Egypt, which had adamantly refused its return to Israel. The scroll was captured from the Bar-Lev Line, along the banks of the Suez Canal, during the 1973 Yom Kippur War, and was immortalized in a photograph showing Israeli soldiers carrying it on their way to captivity. For years it was on display at Egypt's Military Museum, which depicts a Yom Kippur War that ended after three days with a glorious Egyptian victory. The events of the days that followed, during which the Egyptian army was beaten, the Third Army routed, and the IDF stopped 101 kilometers away from Cairo, are not on display. The government of Israel has made several official requests that the Torah scroll be returned, but Egypt has refused each time, claiming that it was one of the spoils of war. The only so-called concession Egypt was willing to make was to change the description accompanying the display. Originally it read that each and every morning, the IDF soldiers stood in two rows and passed the Torah scroll down the line while shouting anti-Arab slogans. Later, the description read simply that it was the Torah scroll from the Bar-Lev Line. Only in July 2000, as a gesture by president Husni Mubaraq to Isreal's outgoing president Ezer Weizman, was the Torah scroll returned to Israel.[13]

Only a few Jewish sites operate in Egypt today. The most famous is the Ben Ezra synagogue in Cairo, where the famous Cairo *genizah* (storehouse of sacred texts) was discovered in the nineteenth century—120,000 manuscripts in Hebrew and Arabic, on subjects both sacred and profane. The synagogue was renovated extensively in the early 1990s, funded by Phyllis Lambert, sister of Edgar and Charles Bronfman (the former is president of the World Jewish Congress, the latter is a controlling shareholder in Israel's Koor Corporation). The renovation was done by agreement with the Egyptian government, which announced its intention to turn the entire area into a interfaith and intercultural center. Two important churches stand near the synagogue, and a short distance away stands Cairo's oldest mosque, attributed to Omar Ibn al-As, which has also undergone extensive renovation in recent years. There are no prayer services conducted at Ben Ezra, which today serves solely as a tourist attraction.

Only operating synagogues remain in Cairo: Sha'ar Hashamaim in the center of town, which was renovated by Swiss-Jewish millionaire Nissim Gaon, and the Me'ir Einayim synagogue in Cairo's Ma'adi neighborhood (the same neighborhood where the Israeli ambassador lives), whose renovation was funded by the Solzberg and Zupan families. Services at both synagogues generally take place only on holidays. On the Sabbath, and certainly on weekdays, it is almost impossible to assemble a quorum.

The headquarters of the Jewish Community Council of Cairo, headed by Carmen Weinstein, are located in the Abbasia neighborhood. Most of the office's spacious rooms are vacant and neglected. The Jewish school stands next door; it is currently rented out to the Egyptian authorities and serves as a public school. The same is true for the Jewish school in Alexandria; the combined rent income on both properties is 180 Egyptian pounds per month. The Maimonides synagogue in Harat al-Yahud (where the great twelfth century scholar Rabbi Moses Ben Maimon, also known as Maimonides or Rambam, worshipped), is closed, and on the verge of collapse due to waterlogged foundations. Cairo's Rabbinical Jewish and Karaite cemeteries, located in the Bassatine neighborhood, were left whole and untouched, but the marble on most of the headstones has come off. Some of the marble was stolen and "go know if it doesn't end up as someone's kitchen counter," says an informed source. Moreover, the "City of the Dead" phenomenon is alive and well here; hundreds of Cairo's homeless have made this their place of residence. By contrast, the Jewish cemetery of Alexandria is in good shape and remains off-limits to the homeless.[14]

At first, one might think of proposing that Cairo adopt the model used in Prague, where one synagogue (the famous Altneushul) is still used for daily prayer, and the city's other synagogues turned into magnificent museums documenting the Jewish community's illustrious history. But one visit to Cairo proves how difficult this would be, and not only for financial reasons. The only two synagogues that could be considered as museums, in terms of size and location (with easy access to public transportation) are the two active synagogues, Sha'ar Hashamaim and Me'ir Einayim. The other surviving synagogues are in bad shape and tucked away in remote alleys; it is unlikely that someone would be willing to buy them for the purpose of establishing a museum. There is also the Karaite synagogue, but it is uncertain that this offshoot of Judaism would be willing to give up this structure or that a joint museum could be established between the Karaite and Rabbinical Jewish communities. The only viable solution is to transfer the responsibility of synagogue upkeep to the Egyptian government, as was done with a large majority of mosques, but this too is difficult. First, giving up the synagogues would be hard from an emotional and symbolic point of view. Second, the Egyptian government may not be particularly interested in taking care of the synagogues, both out of budgetary considerations and matters of principle.

Meital openly supports this proposal: "The Egyptian Supreme Council of Antiquities is not prepared to oversee the Jewish historic sites without receiving ownership. In my opinion, if that is the price, transfer the sites to them. After all, in a few years, there will be only a small number of Jews in Egypt, with a large amount of cultural treasures in hand—Judaica, community archives and more. An arrangement must be reached with the Supreme Council of Antiquities to transfer these properties in an orderly fashion, for example, for the purpose of establishing a museum."[15]

NO SOLUTION TO THE PRIVATE PROPERTY PROBLEM

The problem of private property seems insoluble, although Egypt is the only Arab country that has a law for the handling of nationalized assets. The law was initiated by Sadat in the early 1980s and applies not only to Jewish assets, but to all properties nationalized over the years out of ideological or political considerations. However, the law does not obligate the government to return the property to its owners; it may pay a limited amount of compensation: up to 30,000 Egyptian pounds ($7,000) per person, and up to 100,000 Egyptian pounds ($25,000) per family. Compensation is calculated according to the property's value at the time of nationalization, not taking inflation into consideration. It is also hard to find lawyers willing to represent Jews in this type of action. The Egyptian Bar Association heads the list of local bodies opposing normalized relations with Israel, and its members tend not to distinguish between Israelis and Jews; they are unwilling to have a relationship with either.

Here and there in central Cairo one can still see remnants of Egyptian Jewish wealth. There is the aforementioned Cicurel department store on July 26th street, which continues to operate under the original owner's name. Farther down the same street is a building, topped by a rusty sign also bearing the Cicurel family name; today, it houses a hotel and some offices. Between the two Cicurel buildings stands Chemla, another well-known Jewish department store, which was sold to Kut al-Kulub al-Damradshia, and then nationalized; it continues to operate under the original name. Two Ben Zion department stores, located in the Ma'adi neighborhood and Mustafa Kemal square, as well as the Ades children's clothing store on Qasr al-Nile street, are also government owned yet continue being called by their original names. The Ades family name crowns an eight-story building (tall by Cairo standards) in the center of town; today it is a residential and office building. Near the Sha'ar Hashamaim synagogue one can find the Rivoli and Gattengno stores, also owned by Jews and subsequently nationalized.

The former Cicurel department store on 26 of July
Street, Cairo, March 2000 (Author's Collection)

The heirs are often blocked by various legal restrictions. In central Port
Sa'id stands a magnificent building owned by a Jew who left for Palestine
in 1937. The owner never gave up his title to the building, and the building was not confiscated after the Suez crisis, as the owners had in any case
not been in Egypt for a long time. The family's interests were represented
by a local lawyer, and later on, a younger female lawyer. The lawyers acted
on instructions given from Israel to Egypt via a family friend living in England. In the 1980s, the young lawyer told the family that the building was
in very bad condition and in need of repair, with only one potential buyer
who was willing to pay 60,000 Egyptian pounds. The heirs agreed to sell
and only later discovered they had been swindled by the lawyer; the building's
true value was 16 million Egyptian pounds, or $4 million. There were cer-
tainly grounds to sue the lawyer and request the court cancel the sale, but
under Egyptian law such claims are invalid, due to a one-year statute of
limitations.[16]

Building on 26 of July Street, Cairo, formerly owned by
Cicurel family, March 2000 (Author's Collection)

Professor Ya'akov Meron, former advisor on Arabic law to Israel's Ministry
of Justice and a leading Israeli expert on Jewish assets in Arab countries,
points to an additional problem: laws protecting tenants. "Egypt did not
invent the concept [that says] from the moment a person lives in a house,
after a certain period, they become a protected tenant and cannot be evicted.
But in Egypt, the concept is even worse, as rentals are unlinked to the con-
sumer price index, and remains at the nominal value it was when the Jews
were still here. Even if the authorities would agree to return the houses to
the Jews, the rents are worth nothing." Another problem: the statute of limitations. "This artificial pitfall known as the statute of limitations is used intentionally against Jews in order to block their claims. After all, it is clear
that during the many years of hostilities between the two countries Jews
could not claim their property."[17]
Even those who manage to win their cases discover that realizing their
victory is a very difficult task. This was the case with Odette Metzger,

The former Ades children clothing store in downtown Cairo, March 2000 (Author's Collection)

daughter of Albert Metzger, owner of Alexandria's luxurious Hotel Cecil. The building was nationalized after the Sinai Campaign, when the family members left for Israel and later for South Africa. Its current value is estimated at 150 million Egyptian pounds, or $35 million. After a legal battle that spanned eight years and three continents, the Alexandria court of appeals ruled in March 1999 that the building be returned to the Metzger family. But in 1988, the present owner, the Holding Company for Hotels and Tourism, signed a twenty-three-year management contract with French hotel chain Accor-Sofitel, which complicated matters. As of October 1999 it seemed the hotel would not be returned to the family, despite the courts definitive ruling.[18]

An unusual claim was filed in the New York courts by Raphael Bigio in 1988. The defendant was the Coca-Cola Corporation but the suit encompassed a vast amount of Jewish property in Egypt, confiscated in 1961 and nationalized in 1964. Bigio remembers the day the property was seized, when

Building in downtown Cairo, once owned by Ades
family, March 2000 (Author's Collection)

a phalanx of policemen surrounded the family factory in Cairo, managed by
Bigio's father, Josias. "A senior police officer waited at the gate. 'Mr. Bigio,'
he announced, 'the key, please. This place is confiscated under my orders.'"
The whole group entered the factory. "'Where do you sit, generally?' the
police officer asked my father. Father pointed to his armchair and the police officer sat down on it. He declared the chair was his from now own, and
he would manage things. My father was an introvert, quiet, peace-loving.
In his eyes, I saw the fear gripping him. I also saw the humiliation, the help-
lessness." The officer laid his gun down on the table, and asked for the keys
to the safe. "Father gave them to him immediately, as well as the combination numbers. Each movement was accompanied with great pain. The following day, he had a heart attack." While the father and son continued managing the factory on behalf of the government, they were required to pay
rent—even on their house, which was also confiscated. In 1965, realizing
there was nothing more for them in the land of their birth, the Bigio family
emigrated to Canada.

One of the stores once owned by Ben-Zion family, Mustafa Kemal Square, Cairo, March 2000 (Author's Collection)

The former Chemla department store on 26 of July Street, Cairo, March 2000 (Author's Collection)

The Bigio family had come to Egypt in 1901 from Aleppo. Raphael Nissim Bigio, grandfather of the plaintiff, set up a number of factories in Heliopolis. In the 1930s, the Egyptian branch of Coca-Cola rented one of the factories and set up the company's first production line in Egypt. The factory continued operating in the same location even after insurance company Al-Misr took it into receivership and leased it to the Al-Nasr beverage company, which continued to work with Coca-Cola.

Bigio claimed that confiscation of the family property was canceled in 1980 and that the Egyptian Ministry of Finance had admitted there were no grounds for nationalization from the outset. However, as Al-Misr refused to fulfill the order, the Bigio family filed suit in Egypt, although their lawyer warned that the case could take fifteen years. In 1993, the Egyptian government decided to privatize the Al-Nasr company, which held the Bigio factory along with twelve other beverage plants. Coca-Cola, together with additional partners, acquired control of Al-Nasr and in doing so, Bigio claimed, illegally gained control of his family's property. Therefore, Coca-Cola had participated in the campaign of persecution against Egypt's Jews, had benefited illegally, and therefore owed him compensation. Bigio demanded $100 million in compensation for damages and emotional distress.

New York district court Judge John Martin rejected the claim outright in 1999, after determining that the U.S. courts had no authority to rule on the matter. Bigio appealed, and his lawyer presented a long series of legal claims that stated, in principle, that the New York court did have the authority, and in any case, there were many material questions of consequence that could only discussed within the framework of litigation.

For its part, Coca-Cola vehemently opposed the suit, not only because the U.S. court had no authority on the matter, but because it claimed to hold only a minority share in the Al-Nasr company and was therefore the wrong target for Bigio's suit. Bigio presented a legal opinion prepared for him at Yale University by the International Association of Jewish Lawyers and Jurists, which in principle reinforced the claim that Egypt's actions violated international law, which would require a U.S. court hearing on the matter and all its ramifications.[19] The case continues as these lines are being written.

Very few can allow themselves the luxury of an expensive, drawn-out legal process. The majority of Egyptian émigrés are like Zaki Harari and Levana Zamir. Harari has never been back to the land of his birth. "To this day, I don't feel comfortable going there, and I'm afraid the emotional excitement would be too much. One of my uncles, who lives in the United States offered to sue the Egyptian government [in my name] for the property, to try to get back at least the money we left in the bank. I told him it wasn't worth the time, the effort, or the nerves. In any case, Egypt will pull out the piece of paper proving we gave up everything. If someone would promise an arrangement for all the Jews, that would be another story. But to go it alone— that's not for me. It's a waste of the lawyer's stationary."[20]

Zamir relates: "After the peace agreement with Egypt was signed, my mother and father refused to go and visit their old house. They claimed the trip involved a lot of excitement and pain. They knew everything had been confiscated, and it was useless to cry over a way of life that had disappeared. They told me they hadn't even taken their documents with them, because they never believed they would ever return."

Zamir herself, who chairs the Israel-Egypt Friendship Association, did visit the family's old house in Cairo's Hilwan neighborhood. "I knocked on the door and asked to come in, just to peek inside and remember. The lady of the house invited me in for coffee, and only afterwards, when her son came home, did I figure out that this lovely lady, Samiha, was the daughter of our gatekeeper, who moved in after we left. There were puddles all around the garden and jasmine arbor, apparently sewage that no one was taking care of. The fence was wrecked, and the beautiful balconies were almost completely destroyed. Our beautiful house had become a ruin."[21]

Chapter 9

"Poison, Hatred, and Destruction"

Persecution of the Jews of Syria upon the Establishment of the State of Israel

Two carpets. That's all the Chammah family managed to take from their home in Aleppo in northern Syria. "We owned three or four houses in the Jamilieh neighborhood, the most elegant Jewish area in Aleppo," says Ezra Chammah, today a New York businessman who is also author Elie Wiesel's translator into Italian. "There was a cafe, and over ten apartments. My grandmother lived in one of the buildings, the one that housed the cafe."

The Chammah family resided in Aleppo for 900 years, since the days of Rabbi Moses Maimonides, the Rambam. Ezra is particularly proud of his great great grandfather, Rabbi Eliyahu Chammah, head of the Aleppo Jewish rabbinical court, who wrote two books printed in Livorno 250 years ago. Ezra's grandfather, Eliezer Chammah, was a banker, and Ezra's father dealt in banking and textiles. Yet in 1940, the family was forced to flee to Beirut, where Ezra was born two years later; his father was a Gaulist and avowed opponent of the pro-Nazi Vichy government that ruled Syria under the French mandate following Germany's conquest of France.

Ezra's grandmother and the uncle who cared for her remained behind in Aleppo. His Aunt Sarah also stayed. While there, she photographed the Great Synagogue that housed the fabled Aleppo Codex (Keter)—one of the most important manuscripts on the bible—before the building was destroyed in the riots of December 1947. When Israel's War of Independence broke out in May 1948, the Syrian regime decreed that all the country's Jews were now State enemies. "They had to get a permit to leave their towns, of course they were not issued passports, and if someone did get a passport it was valid for one month only. Whoever didn't come back to Syria—his property was impounded and confiscated," Ezra Chammah says.

As part of the persecution process, the Syrian government nominated trustees over Jewish property; the situation remains the same today. The remaining Chammah family members were permitted to stay in the buildings they owned, but henceforth, the government allowed itself a portion of the rent collected from the other tenants and the cafe owner. In 1959, Chammah's grandmother died, and a year later, so did her caretaker son. The Syrian government never for one moment considered returning the property to the rightful heirs. Instead, the government trustee commandeered the buildings, and all movable goods were sold at public auction. A family friend managed to purchase two carpets for $1,000; they can now be found in Ezra's New York home. The rest was all lost. "We were forbidden from taking the books out of Syria; the library disappeared. There was no sense in buying the furniture, because the conditions of the auction required buyers to transport goods to their destination, which was impossible. The rugs were all we managed to save."[1]

CHANGES IN THE SIZE AND STATUS OF THE SYRIAN JEWISH COMMUNITY

The Chammah family was not the only Jewish family that had lived in Syria for centuries. Jewish had lived in this land continuously since the destruction of the First Temple in 586 B.C., and had increased significantly in number after the expulsion of the Jews from Spain in 1492. Throughout the generations, the main Jewish communities were to be found in Damascus and Aleppo, cities that were also major economic and administrative centers.[2] In 1943, Syria conduced a population census, and counted 11,000 Jewish in Damascus, 17,000 in Aleppo, and between 1,500 and 2000 in Kamishli, a city on the Syrian-Turkish border.[3]

When discussing the economic situation of Syria's Jews, writes historian Haim Cohen, a distinction should be made between the Damascus and Aleppo communities. The opening of the Suez Canal in 1869 caused a decline in Aleppo's stature as a major crossroads in international trade that affected its Jews directly. Many emigrated to Egypt and the United States. The majority of those remaining were poor, and by 1942, 40% to 65% required support from the Jewish community.

Cohen adds:

Most of the Jews in sixteenth century Damascus were tradesmen: shoemakers, silver and goldsmiths, and straw mat makers. There were also a great many peddlers, the sort forced to wander from village to neighboring village in search of income. But there were also those who became fabulously wealthy by trading with the Palestine, Egypt and Venice. In the nineteenth century as well, there were wealthy Jews to be found in Damascus. . . .

When Damascus lost its economic standing, Jews began migrating to Egypt. But because many of the city's Jews were tradesmen and workers, the effects of Syria's economic decline weren't immediately noticed, as in the case of Aleppo, which suffered an economic crisis due to a diversion of international trade via the Suez Canal. On the eve of World War I, the Jews of Damascus continued dealing in their traditional occupations: silver and gold smithing, weaving, dyeing, woodworking; few dealt in international trade, and their effect on Damascus's economy was limited.

The Jews of Damascus suffered a serious economic upheaval after the political events of 1925 [the Druse revolt], which created unemployment and mass migration among the Jews; many of those remaining required community support which was supplied mainly by the Syrian-Jewish community in New York. A short time after these events it was discovered that, out of 6,635 Jews in Damascus, 2,275 were wage earners, meaning one breadwinner for every three persons. Among these wage earners, 32% were tradesmen (mainly brass and copper-workers, the rest were weavers, tailors, shoemakers and laborers), 17% were clerks, 4% housewives, 14% peddlers, 9% traders and smiths, 1% were rabbis and the remaining 23% worked in various professions, most likely providing services. Over the years, economic conditions worsened for Jews of Damascus due to a fall in demand for hand crafted goods, and those remaining in the city after 1940 were mainly poor.[4]

ECONOMIC CONDITIONS FOR THE JEWS OF DAMASCUS ON THE EVE OF ISRAEL'S WAR OF INDEPENDENCE

In the mid-1940s, only 5% of Damascus's Jews were considered wealthy, 15% were middle class and the remainder was petit bourgeois and the needy. However, Jews with initiative could go far. One such man was Moshe Doar, who wrote in his memoirs: "In 1911, when I was a boy of 15, I left the Alliance school and began exchanging all sorts of coins and bank notes, gold pounds and more. I stood in the Hamidiya open market, next to my Uncle Raphael's store, and managed a business, like many other people. Meanwhile, as I was standing in the market that specialized in jewelry, where they bought coins for the purpose of extracting the pure silver, I met an older man, a Christian from Ramallah, north of Jerusalem who bought the coins for a good price.

> I asked whether he was willing to buy a large quantity, and when he answered yes, and also gave me his address, I collected almost every single coin of that type from the shops of Damascus, at all sorts of prices. I traveled to Beirut, to Hims, Hamah, and Aleppo, and collected as many coins as possible, sold them at a profit until I had a handsome sum of money. I made my first visit to the Palestine in connection with the sale of these *wazirs* [ancient coins]. In Ramalah, people hung those coins from chains which they would wear on their heads, which is why they were willing to pay more than twice the regular price.[5]

A street in the abandoned Jewish neighborhood in Damascus, 1994 (photograph by ABPix)

Other Jews had more conventional sources of income. Yosef Sakal related: "Before they began bringing imported brass- and copperware into the Jewish quarter, we made our living from engraving. We made gifts: vases, trays and all sorts of presents for export. Most were bought by Europeans, and the English would market these products in Egypt. Before the [First World] War, we opened a copper and brassware branch, which played a significant part in the economy of Damascus' Jewish community.

> There were also butchers, bakers and barbers who lived in—and made their living from—the Jewish community. There were also a few peddlers. A few Arab peddlers wandered the area with their wares: vegetables and the like, which they brought to our neighborhood. The Jewish peddlers would visit the Arab villages to sell their wares, then return home; they would leave on Sunday and come back on Thursday, bringing chickens and eggs, and everything the farmers gave them in exchange for products. And that's how the neighborhood made its living.[6]

The Jewish community of Kamishli, like the town itself, was new. Kamishli was established by the French forces to guard the Jezira region from Bedouin gangs and attack by the surrounding Kurds. After 1928, when it was decided that Jezira marked the borderline between Syria and Turkey, many Jews fled to Kamishli from the neighboring city of Nezivin, about 2 kilometers to the west in Turkish territory, mainly to avoid being drafted by the Turkish army. Most of the city's Jews dealt in trade: textiles, shoes, wool and dairy products. A few were farmers or craftsmen. Only a few families were wealthy, and most of Kamishli's Jews were lower middle class. In 1931, 200 Jewish families in Kamishli dealt in trade, and fifty families worked in agriculture. In 1943, as previously noted, the city had between 1,500 and 2,000 Jews.[7]

EMIGRATION TO PALESTINE IN THE 1930s AND EARLY 1940s

Worsening economic conditions increased Jewish migration from Syria in the nineteenth and twentieth centuries. Immediately after the Balfour Declaration in November 1917, Zionist sentiments were awakened to some degree within the Damascus Jewish community, and several of the city's wealthiest Jewish families—Mugrabi, Lalo, Romano, Turkiya, Akiva, Mizrahi and Doar—went to live in the Land of Israel. But these were exceptions; Palestine was not the main destination for immigrants in the 1930s, although the worldwide economic depression had increased migration overall. In 1934, Eliyahu Cohen wrote from Damascus to the secretariat of the Kibbutz Artzi Federation saying: "The situation is indescribable. Horrible unemployment. Families of six and more, wandering the street with nothing. Mass migration. The streets of the Jewish neighborhood . . . are emptying out. Not one bus leaves Damascus without Jewish passengers."[8]

There was an increased trend toward migrating to Palestine, where there was economic prosperity in the 1930s, mainly due to increased immigration of Jews of means from Poland and Germany. However, most of the Syrian Jews who came to Palestine were lower middle class, as reported by Eliyahu Epstein (Eilat) to Moshe Shertok (Sharett), head of the Jewish Agency's political department, in late 1934:

The economic deterioration of the Jewish communities of Beirut, Damascus and Aleppo continues. The economic situation in Syria . . . has provided the impetus for a large number of Jewish within the community to move to Palestine via any channel and means. From the very old to the very young, they say the words 'Tel Aviv' as a sort of heaven on earth they would all like to gain. It should be noted that practical approaches to the question of emigrating to the Land of Israel were raised by Syria's Jews only after they were left completely without income, and had lost all hope regarding Syria's future. Most emigrants to Land of Israel are real 'proletariats' . . . among the few wealthy Syrian Jews with occupations, almost none are emigrants to Land of Israel.[9]

Between 1932 and 1936, 2,868 Syrian Jews came to Palestine, while over the next five years, only 854 came—due mainly to the outbreak of the Arab

Revolt (1936–1939), which reduced the economic attraction of Palestine significantly.[10]

The Markus family reached Palestine from Aleppo with the outbreak of the Arab Revolt. The family patriarch, Avraham Markus, traded in textiles and had dealings all over the Far East, from where he imported silk, cotton, and bed linen sold to local Syrian and Lebanese dealers. The family was well-to-do and lived with its servants in a large house in the wealthy Jamilieh neighborhood, as did many other Jewish families.

But something happened in the 1930s. "My brothers went to the Land of Israel as part of the illegal immigration," relates daughter Frida Yadid. "My mother could not stand the separation from her children and decided to go to the Land of Israel. Taking me, my sister and another little brother, we set out on our way. My father stayed at home to sell the remaining property. I didn't take anything with me, not a doll, teddy bear, not my doll carriage, nothing. When we arrived in the Land of Israel, we went to my brother's house in Jaffa. I remember it was a Friday, and on Sunday the riots had already broken out. We ran away from the house, and when we returned, we discovered that our meager possessions, including the few clothes we'd brought with us from Aleppo, were all completely burnt."

Two years later, in 1948, Avraham Markus arrived in the Israel with nothing. "He told us how he got up in the morning, made a cup of coffee, drank it, took a small suitcase with a few clothes, and closed the door behind him. When the Arab neighbors saw him leaving, they entered the apartment and just took everything. My father had a few good properties, and my uncle also left all his property. They just got up, left, and didn't look back. Sometimes my parents reminisce about how good it was in Aleppo, but no more than that. I don't even have photos from my childhood. It was all left there."[11]

The situation changed in 1942, and 5,000 Syrian and Lebanese Jews came to Palestine over a six-year period. The primary motivation for the change was Great Britain's return conquest of the region in June 1941. For the Jews of Syria, this transformed Palestine from enemy territory into Allied territory. Palestine's economic situation had improved, the Arab Revolt was quelled, and British military activity in the Middle East had brought economic prosperity to the Jewish population.

But the gates to Palestine were bolted shut, under restrictions laid out by the White Paper of 1939. The situation on Europe clearly obliged the world Jewish establishment to turn its attention and energies toward saving European Jewry, and naturally, the quota for British immigration certificates to Palestine was filled entirely by members of communities otherwise destined for slaughter. The Jews of Syria, therefore, had no other choice but to cross the overland border illegally.[12]

There is no information today, among the available documents and testimonies, regarding the properties of those illegal immigrants. However, it may be assumed that most of it was lost, given the circumstances under which the owners came to Palestine. As stated earlier, their entry was illegal and preparations demanded absolute secrecy, as British troops were stationed in Syria, which was controlled by British ally France until the end of World War II. The possibility of bringing property into Palestine was extremely limited: furniture, rugs, and books could not be smuggled at night over the winding roads in the mountains of the upper Galilee, given the presence of British army patrols. The only option was to sell the property before setting out, which was difficult to do clandestinely.

Jews could sell their property before going to Palestine and claim they were migrating to another place; they would then have to hope no one would ask to see proof of their planned destination. These sales were also transacted under time pressure, especially in cases of illegal immigration that could not be planed months in advance; it was therefore not easy to receive the proper, maximum return on sales. It should also be borne in mind that most of the illegal immigrants were poor, and did not lose a great deal of property in coming to the Land of Israel—although the value of what property they had is nonetheless important. Given these considerations, it is clearly impossible to properly evaluate the value of property lost by the Jews of Syria during those years.

THE OUTBREAK OF PERSECUTION AND THE 1947 ALEPPO POGROM

Conditions for the Syrian Jews worsened drastically as the State of Israel neared its establishment. They could feel the violence bubbling under the surface immediately after the UN general assembly voted to partition Palestine on November 29, 1947. In December, a pogrom erupted in Aleppo. Yitzhak Pardes, a child at that time, recalls:

At that moment, I was on the balcony. I looked out and saw my uncle, his wife and their ten children walking our way, barefoot, wearing nightclothes—all of them—and crying. I said to my late mother, "Look, Auntie is coming with the children. What happened?" Then my uncle knocked on the door and said, "For God's sake, let us in." "What happened?" I said. [My uncle answered] "Can't you see?"

I looked and saw columns of flame that reached the sky. At 10:30 at night, I decided to go down and see what was happening. Then my mother shouted, "Tell me son, where are you going? They might be killing people down there!" I couldn't hold back. I went down. The synagogue where I used to pray was 500 to 600 meters from the house. I walked 300 meters and saw a man, an Arab, who said to me, "Yitzhak, where are you going? The synagogue; they've burned it all, and they're burning houses now; all the Jewish places are going up in flames. Go home!"[13]

Among Aleppo's wealthy at that time was A'ish Sabbah who, according to daughters Rachel Shushan-Sabbah and Aliza Totah-Sabbah, was "the most famous tailor in Syria and Lebanon. Among his many customers numbered military officers, Syrian and Lebanese government officials, for whom he would create the most elegant suits, of fabric he imported directly from London." Sabbah's elder son, Yosef, was an outstanding athlete who participated in one of the Maccabiah games and later immigrated to Palestine. His sisters recall the letters where he would beg them all to join him, as well as their father's reaction: "He said: 'The boy's gone crazy, what is he looking for in the Land of Israel.' He wasn't prepared to hear a word on the subject." A month after Yosef's latest letter, the Aleppo pogrom began.

"It was on Friday, December 2, 1947," Aliza recalls.

> The Muslims went to the mosque, and the Sheikh told them the Jews had taken their country, and they must take revenge. That same day, the Muslims burned thirty-one synagogues and Jewish schools. We lived opposite the Silvera synagogue in Jamilieh. We stood at the windows and watched the Torah scrolls flying through the air, going up in flames, all night long.
>
> In the center of town was a synagogue that was 3,500 years old, where for centuries great rabbis were buried. Tradition had it that the footprints of Eliezer, slave of Abraham the Patriarch, were there. That synagogue burned for three days and nights; we could hear shouts and cries throughout, although there was no one inside. To this day, I break out in a cold sweat when I think of it.
>
> Father and mother decided we should leave the house for period of time, because of the riots. My father had a lot of Muslim and Christian friends and one of them, Qarim Gabriel, hosted us for eight days until things calmed down. When my father went out of the house to see what happened to his property, he discovered the shop was burnt, along with the material, and the suits, each of which was worth 600 pounds.
>
> Father, who was very frightened by what had happened, decided we should go to Beirut, to my brother Yosef, who had started working there as a tailor. My father, my married sister and I stayed behind in Aleppo to collect debts. Father had a hard time leaving his possessions, which included not only the shop, but two lots—one 1,200 square meter lot in Fa'yid, and another twenty dunam [five acre] lot in Sabbil. More than anything, he had a hard time accepting the new reality foisted on him, and the knowledge that his entire world had disappeared. Father died of a heart attack in 1951, when he was fifty-four. From someone who was so important that all of Syria and Lebanon's wealthy came to his door, he became a broken, beaten man. It was hard for him to cope with the destruction of his business, his world, and so he died.

Aliza later moved to Beirut as well and from there traveled a number of times to Aleppo in order to try and collect debts and salvage something of the family assets. "According to my father, different people owed us 100,000 Syrian pounds, and another 10,000 in gold coins. I hired a local lawyer but managed to collect only a small portion of the money. People took advantage of the situation to refuse payment, or just ignored the debt."

In 1952, Aliza came to Aleppo and met an elegantly dressed man in her aunt's shop. "He said, 'Why don't you come back to Syria? We're your brothers.' I answered that my father died out of worry for his property, and my brothers did not wish to return and be drafted into the Syrian army. He introduced himself as Ahman al-Rifa'i, a government minister. I shook his hand, and he promised to help in handling the debtors who did not want to pay. In the end, he didn't pay back his debt, either."

Aliza finally gave up. Some of the Fa'yid lot was confiscated, and a street paved over it, while two large buildings were built on the larger Sabbil property; the Sabbah family, of course, did not receive a penny in compensation. After the Six Day War, when one of the sisters left Syria with a false passport, she and her family arrived in Israel with nothing; "They hardly had any clothes with them." Thus, the family's assets were reduced to nothing.[14]

A dry, factual report on the Aleppo riots was submitted by H. A. Shadforth, British Consul to Aleppo, to the British Embassy in Damascus. "Separate groups of rioters operating in the business and Jewish quarters attacked Jewish institutions, shops, and houses. The rougher element of the town low quarters, which were now more numerous than the students, did not need encouragement to enter synagogues, shops and houses and soon several fires were burning in the Jewish quarters of Jamilieh and Bassita and still Police and Gendarmerie were taking no preventative measures. In fact, some policemen are reported to have taken part in the wrecking of several Jewish shops. Ibrahim Bey Kessab, director of the Police and O/C Gendarmerie, Aleppo, was present when the A.B.C. Stores [neither owned nor patronized by Jews] were attacked and all goods therein set on fire; he made no attempt to order his men to stop the rioters. . . . Disorders went on throughout the day and part of the evening and it was only at about 8 P.M. on 1 December that the Mohafez [the district governor] sent troops to the town to restore order and give protection to Jewish property. From then on, [army] troops with the cooperation of the Gendarmerie were able to prevent further disorders."

In his report, Shadforth went into detail regarding the severe damage caused by the riots. Among others, the J. Benattar store was attacked; it belonged to a Jew with British citizenship. Twenty other shops and houses in the Bassita neighborhood were also damaged, two cars belonging to Jews were destroyed, and four synagogues were attacked. During the riots, the nineth century Aleppo Codex disappeared. It is one of the most unique and important documents of its kind, and only decades later were large portions of it recovered. Many of its pages are now housed in the Israel Museum in Jerusalem; many more pages were apparently destroyed in the riots.[15] Shadforth also noted his satisfaction that no Jewish or Communist lives were lost.[16]

Ya'akov David Hazan was the treasurer of the Jewish Community in Aleppo at the time of the riots. In 1961, Hazan was interviewed by Alexander Dotan of the Israeli consulate in Sao Paolo, Brazil, where he then lived. Dotan reported back to Yitzhak Ben-Zvi, then president of Israel, who was trying to uncover the whereabouts of the Aleppo Codex:

> The demonstrations, fires and acts of destruction in the synagogues lasted only one day. In the witness' opinion, Jews suffered no bodily harm, and their private property was unharmed [an erroneous opinion, as evinced by the British consul's report], but synagogues were burnt, destroyed, plundered or robbed of all their contents. The witness believes the demonstrators intended to express "outrage" by destroying synagogues, but not kill or steal private property. The witness has no doubt the demonstrations were organized by the Syrian authorities themselves. The authorities also made sure the demonstrators did not deviate from the framework "permitted" them. After the riots achieved their goal, military or police reinforcements were brought in to the city streets, to restore order as quickly as possible.

After three tense days, during which commerce in Aleppo shut down completely, stores reopened and Hazan accompanied the governor on a tour of the city's synagogues. The witness found all the city's synagogues ruined or burnt, arks of the Torah and sacred relics broken or burnt, Torah scrolls ripped up or burnt. The Great Synagogue in the old part of the city, where the Codex was kept, was completely destroyed, and in the courtyard was a large heap of steaming ashes, the remains of dozens of Torah scrolls burnt at the stake. The witness is convinced that the number of Torah scrolls kept in the synagogue's many 'temples' [referring to the arks] was close to 200.[17]

THE ROOTS AND ESCALATION OF SYRIAN ANIMOSITY TOWARD THE JEWS

Anyone who thinks that the UN Partition Plan was the reason Syrian Jewry suffered has the wrong idea. The following selections are from reports sent in June 1947 (when the UN began debating the Palestine issue), by a Mossad le-Aliya Bet emissary stationed in Syria, Akiva Feinstein, to his superior, Yeruham Cohen, in Tel Aviv:

> As you know, the prevailing spirit among the Syrian nation is an overt Nazi spirit,[18] although they were ashamed to reveal their true nature after being granted independence. But now, two years after independence, with the matter of the Land of Israel now transferred to the United Nations Organization, and not handled as they had hoped, they are now beginning to openly persecute the Jewish minority with all their might. . . . These are the conditions for Jews since the day the [French] foreign military withdrew from Syria:

All [Jewish] clerks working in the French bureaucracy were fired and not reinstated in the new system, as all are suspected of aiding foreigners. [Jewish] trade centered mainly around manufacturing stores [the reference is perhaps to tailor shops], and souvenirs that profited from a never-ending stream of foreign civilian and military clientele. But ever since the day this type of customer left the country, several of the shops have been forced to close, and the rest are struggling to survive, unsuccessfully. Business today is dead, local customers do not need luxury items, and discredit the stores owned by people of other faiths.

Peddling has a central position in local commerce. But once, peddlers were protected by the government authorities. Today, they [the Jewish peddlers] do not dare leave their villages and towns, and the government, for its part, is interested in reducing and forcing Jews out of this profession. The same is true of all other professions where one might earn a living wage in Syria, and so the Jew has no choice but to die slowly, as there are no sources of income, and leaving the country, not necessarily to the Land of Israel, is also forbidden.[19]

The situation had gotten steadily worse as a decision on Palestine approached. December 1947 was the turning point, for that was the moment that persecution was officially and openly sanctioned, beginning with a wave of lay-offs for Jews in civil service that ended on Israel's declaration of independence five months later. Needless to say, Jews were no longer accepted into civil service. On December 22, the government announced that Jews were forbidden from selling their possessions—real estate and movable goods alike. The meaning was clear: whoever tried to leave Syria would lose all their property.[20]

But even those willing to give up their property found themselves trapped inside the country's borders. In January 1948, the Minister of the Interior announced that all Jews applying for passage to Lebanon must receive a special permit. This might have been connected to a report submitted by the British Embassy in Damascus to the Foreign Office a month earlier, mentioning that several wealthy members of the Aleppo Jewish community had escaped to Beirut, out from under the Syrian authorities' very noses. But the Syrians had an excuse: "The Police inspector general claims that the new regulation was to the Jews' benefit, as they may prove their sincerity," in the words of the British Embassy report.[21] This short message did not explain the Inspector General's intent, but apparently the logic of his claim was as follows: If Jews set out for Lebanon after requesting and receiving permission, it was reasonable to assume that they were not running away; therefore the very act of requesting permission proved their intentions were pure, and they were loyal citizens.

In other cases, the Syrians engaged in overt anti-Semitism. In January 1948, the British Ambassador to Damascus reported to Prime Minister Clement Atlee that several Syrian newspapers claimed the country's current cholera epidemic broke out because Jews poisoned the water sources—a modern-day take on the medieval European Christian libel that accused Jews of poisoning wells and causing the Black Plague. Moreover, Syria's press also claimed that Jewish merchants were not contributing their share to funding the war against pre-state Israel, and some papers demanded Jews be forbidden entirely from receiving exit visas.[22]

ECONOMIC PERSECUTION AFTER THE STATE OF ISRAEL'S ESTABLISHMENT

If these were the conditions for Syria's Jews before the State of Israel was established, one can easily imagine how much worse they were after the War of Independence, with Syrian forces taking part in the battle. Shoshana Perez-Hilleli, born in Damascus and daughter of a Jew employed by the government storehouses, recalls:

> We were lower middle-class, but nonetheless lived in a large, beautiful house with at least twenty rooms. Instead of closets, there were niches that in winter were covered with blue velvet curtains, like the Torah ark coverings at the synagogue. In summer, we would change the velvet for gold fabric. The floor was Italian marble, and in the garden we had a pool and a fountain. My sisters were considered the most beautiful and elegant in the Jewish quarter of Damascus. My elder sister was a nurse in a hospital, and we were considered a very worthy family.

In 1942, Leah and Rivka Perez immigrated to Palestine, and one year later, came to visit their family, telling them excitedly how wonderful the Land of Israel was. The parents, who because of the World War feared for their daughters' safety, allowed Shoshana and her sister Olga to move to Palestine. With a smile, Shoshana recalls a piece of practical advice her mother gave her before setting out: "If a boy wants to touch you, let him go only as far as the elastic on your panties."

During the 1948 War of Independence, Shoshana says,

> My parents arrived in Israel, exhausted and drained after riding on donkeys. They told us the Arabs had burst into the synagogue, despoiled it, leaving them with no choice but to leave everything and come to Israel with nothing. We received [from the Israeli government] a room near the Hadar open market in [the northern port city of] Haifa, where we all lived, my parent, my sisters and me. Instead of a closet, we had an orange crate. Father worked as a porter in the Haifa port and later as a metalworker. Sometimes my parents would recall the house they left behind in Damascus and the good life we once lived. Mother liked to tell us about how our family was considered to have the most elegant, educated daughters in all Damascus. I tell my grandchildren it's too bad I can't show them the beautiful gold curtains and the large lanterns we had in our house. Since then, I have never seen such beautiful lanterns.[23]

In April 1949, Israel's Ministry of Foreign Affairs summarized the situation of Syria's Jewish community since the establishment of the State of Israel: "The Jews of Syria, who numbered 30,000 a few years ago, now numbers no more than 5,000, almost all living in dire poverty. Already in 1947, [members of] Damascus's small Jewish community began immigrating illegally to Beirut, and it is doubtful whether Damascus' Jewish quarter now numbers more than a few hundred. After the riots of December 1947, a similar illegal immigration began among the Jews of Aleppo, a much larger community than Damascus with relatively better economic conditions. Reports are that 3,000 Jews remain in Aleppo, as compared with the 25,000 that were before.

> Illegal immigration increased mainly upon Syria's entry into the war with Israel on May 15, 1948. It has come to light that Jews with means left Syria, some for Lebanon, others to farther-flung countries—mainly Italy. Rahmo Nehmad, head of the Aleppo Jewish community and member of the Syrian parliament for many years, is now in Italy with his family, along with many others. The Jews remaining in Syria represent the poorest class of Syrian Jewry, those without traveling expense money. According to Syrian statistics, 70 to 80 percent of Jews exiting Syria did so by illegal means, including forging passports, etc. . . .
>
> Clearly circumscribed anti-Jewish sentiment exists in Syria today. Because of censorship, not everything that happens to the Jews of Syria is reflected in the press. But from time to time, reports appear of attacks on Jews, skirmishes and outright theft, even though all these are not reported seriously. Early on during the war, 260 Jews were arrested in Damascus but were released over time. In Damascus, the Jews are essentially closed up in the ghetto that is the Jewish quarter, surrounded by police guards, which are also there to protect the Jews from attack by the mob. There is a Jewish prison camp in Dumair, east of Damascus, where a number of Jews accused of "Zionism" are held. Noteworthy among the methods of repression and dispossession used against Jews: A) In a process ongoing from December 1947 to September 1948, all remaining Jewish employees of government offices were fired. B) Any and all Jews are forbidden to enter Syria's borders. C) All property belonging to the Baghdad-Damascus Travel Agency owned by Iraqi Jew Haim Netan'el has been confiscated; Jewish employees of the company were arrested and accused of 'collaboration with the enemy' [meaning Israel]. D) Damascus' Alliance school was confiscated and is being used to house Arab refugees from Palestine. E) On December 22 [1948], the government of Syria announced officially that Jews were forbidden from selling their property in Syria—as a means of preventing Jewish capital from being smuggled abroad.[24]

Three years later, in January 1952, Yosef Hadas—then an official in the research department of Israel's Ministry of Foreign Affairs, and later on, the Ministry's director-general—summarized the economic sanctions placed on the Jews of Syria immediately preceding the State of Israel's establishment:

After the riots at the end of 1947 [the Aleppo pogrom], many Jews succeeded in liquidating their businesses and transferring the money abroad, mainly to Lebanon, Italy, the US, and Mexico. In early 1948, the Syrian government issued a regulatory order, which did not require parliamentary approval, which forbade Jews from selling their property to members of other nationalities, but did not restrict its transfer from Jew to Jew. The authorities' goal in issuing the order was to prevent possible smuggling of Jewish assets abroad, and lay the groundwork in the event of a decision to confiscate Jewish property. The practice among Syrian Jews living abroad was to grant power of attorney to a relative still living in Syria for the purposes of managing their property, collecting revenue, or rent. The Syrian authorities are ignoring these transactions. Regarding Jewish deposits in Syrian banks, the government has instructed bank managers not to allow transfers from Jewish accounts until permission is granted by the authorities.[25]

THE JEWS OF SYRIA CALL FOR HELP FROM ISRAEL AND THE WORLD

Over the coming years, conditions for Syria's Jews were also influenced directly by the internal political situation, given the fact that in the late 1940s and early 1950s Syria suffered significant political upheaval. The shocks were expressed by a series of four military coups d'etat over a two-and-a-half year period, between March 1949 and December 1951.

The first revolt was headed by Syria's Military Chief of Staff General Husni Za'im and resulted from a crisis that came in the wake of the Arab defeat in the war against Israel. Za'im took over the presidency, government, and parliament and promised to eliminate corruption, initiate reform, and development. Secretly, Za'im tried to make contact with the Israeli leadership, indicated his willingness to make peace and solve the central problems in Arab-Israeli relations, chiefly the refugee problem.[26] Given this fact, it is not surprising that Za'im also tried to ease matters for the Syrian Jews. But Za'im was no hero; he did not repeal restrictions on Jews, either because he never got around to it or because, despite it all, he wanted to keep Syria's Jews as hostages of a sort against Israel.

In early May 1949, Eliyahu Cohen reported that until Za'im's rise to power, the situation in Aleppo was at its worst. "Jews passing in the street are usually beaten, and in one specific case, they assaulted a great scholar [the Chief Rabbi of Aleppo], Rabbi Moshe Mizrahi. Jews could not sell property or houses, bank accounts were confiscated, drivers licenses revoked, and all freedom of movement taken away from them." According to Cohen, the Jewish community poor lived off packages received from the United States, and "from selling things to one another." But in April 1949, immediately after the Za'im coup d'etat, matters improved significantly. "On the last day of Passover, Za'im gave the order granting freedom of movement to Jews; the order to report to the police [placed on Jews arrested and released in

1948] was cancelled, drivers licenses were returned, and overall, Jews were given some leeway; now they are almost never beaten in the street."[27]

New immigrants reaching Israel from Syria via Beirut in early May said that as of the Za'im coup d'etat conditions for the Jews of Damascus had improved slightly. "Most merchants sold off their shops and inventory, very few reopened their businesses, but the local residents' attitude reeks of poison, hatred, and destruction, despite government assurances of fair treatment." The new immigrants employed the services of border smugglers, who often gouged them of hundreds and thousands of Syrian pounds above and beyond the agreed upon price. They also reported that the Jews of Aleppo were not granted total freedom of movement; it was sometimes given, sometimes taken away, sometimes granted freely, and sometimes given only to those who could prove they had business to attend to in Beirut.[28]

Even after Za'im was overthrown and executed in a coup d'etat headed by Colonel Sami Hinawi on August 14, 1949, the Jewish situation stayed the same, as reported by an informed source to Israel Defense Force intelligence officers: "The Syrian government knows about Jewish illegal immigration to Israel via Lebanon and in general does not interfere. Jews sell their possessions and property and move to Lebanon en route to Israel. The government generally turns a blind eye to these activities."[29]

But the vicissitudes of politics rapidly began affecting conditions for Jews. A week before the fall of the Za'im government, Jews were again attacked in Aleppo and Damascus, in two simultaneous events on Friday night, August 5. In Damascus, three bombs hurled by Arabs killed thirteen Jews, including eight children, and wounded twenty-six others.[30]

An anonymous letter, received in mid-August by the Magen David congregation of Aleppo Jews in Brooklyn, read:

Last Friday, the holy Sabbath eve, invaders entered the Great Synagogue when the entire community, schoolchildren included, were engaged in prayer, and four vicious thugs threw five large bombs—two did not explode—wounding sixty adults and children, and killing eleven, much to our distress; eight children died unfortunately, two adults and one elderly person. The wounded are in terrible condition, God speed them to a complete recovery, should it be His will.

In light of this, we wish to consult with the leaders of your community,and request that the United States government pressure the authorities here to grant us the rights given to other Syrian citizens, meaning to move freely from our city to wherever we want, to repeal the seizure of our assets and real estate, etc. This is the only remedy for those remaining here. The new Syrian regime and [Za'im's] new revolution came about only because of United States and French support, and the United States undoubtedly has the power to put pressure, with all its might, on our government to release us from all this. According to our government's laws, every citizen has the right to choose where he wants to live, and international law preserves the rights of all nations, in every city.

> Our request is that you review situation as it stands, as our lives are in terrible
> danger, and may God help you in bringing about our speedy redemption. God
> helps the righteous, and you hold the power to request mercy for us, you must
> not ignore us, pray for us and God will repay you for your kindness. In short:
> we are truly like hostages, with no way of coming or going, without money
> or property, in great danger of the mob! The authors [of this letter] write to
> you in great fear, and with bitter tears.

Magen David's Rabbi Ya'akov Katzin handed the letter over to Israel's
Minister of Foreign Affairs Moshe Sharett requesting that he help the Jewish
community of Aleppo.[31]

Sharett's response is not documented, but existing documents indicate that
those involved with immigration to Israel did not change their policies and
were not convinced of the immediacy of the threat. The Jews of Aleppo
continued to leave Syria for Beirut and trickle into Israel without any special guidance or help from the Israeli government. The new immigrants,
therefore, lost more of their property as they were forced to pay cold, hard
cash for their illegal exit from Syria. Sometimes, what little property left was
also stolen, as in this heart-wrenching letter of complaint sent by Ha'im Amija
to the Jewish Agency in July 1950:

> I am a new immigrant from Syria, I left Aleppo on July 27, 1949, and when I
> arrived in Lebanon, I was approached by two people—Aslan Antebi and
> Shlomo Jamus—who told me I could pay them a fee to travel from Lebanon
> to here [Israel], and that the best way to Israel was on a fast fishing boat, and
> I agreed. We left the city, and weren't more than two kilometers out to sea
> when someone informed on us to the Lebanese police, who captured us, and
> the reason they informed on me to the Lebanese police was because there were
> two rival gangs. . . .
> The informants knew that I had gold coins, so they informed so that some
> of the money would be confiscated. Afterwards, they caught me and took all
> my money, and jailed me for two months. The money was: 360 gold pounds
> [in cash], 20 gold pounds in jewelry, in all 380. . . . I ask for the Jewish
> Agency's assistance because I am indigent, please help me for merciful God's
> sake. Help me with money, or housing, or light work, as I am weak and ill,
> give me a shop of some sort. I have a family and children, and so I ask that
> the housing project be near the city.

Moshe Carmil, then head of the Mossad le-Aliya Bet, responded in brief
to the Jewish Agency Aliya Department: "With great sorrow, we have read
the letter sent by Amija Haim. The people who handled this man's immigration were private 'handlers' of Jewish immigration, and the letter's contents come as no surprise to us."[32] The question is, did most immigrants have
another option but the expensive, risky services of private smugglers? The
answer is, apparently, none.

THE SHISHAKLI REGIME REVIVES AND REVITALIZES PERSECUTION

On December 19, 1949, the tables turned again. In the third coup d'etat in nine months, Colonel Adib al-Shishakli took control of Syria, mainly in opposition to Hinawi's intention to unify Syria and Iraq. Shishakli was Deputy Chief of Staff and until December 1951, had preferred to control Syria from behind the scenes, leaving the president, government and parliament in place. Shishakli's attitude toward Israel and the Jews may be encapsulated in one fact: During Israel's War of Independence, he served in Fawzi Kaukji's Palestinian "Rescue Brigade."[33] Any hope in improving the lot of Syria's Jews was now lost.

A series of reports from the early 1950s show that repressive measures against the Jews were quickly reinstated, and the situation steadily worsened. In March 1950, Moshe Sasson of Israel's Ministry of Foreign Affairs wrote a memo to Foreign Minister Moshe Sharett, prior to a Knesset debate on the Syrian Jewish situation:

"Syria's house of representatives did not pass a law stripping Syrian Jews of their citizens rights, but since the UN Partition Plan was announced, an increasing number of administrative orders have placed various restrictions on Jews that essentially impinge on their citizens rights. Some of those orders are still in effect." Sasson itemized these restrictions; they included rejecting Jews from civil service, forbidding Jews from entering Syria or exiting for Lebanon, a ban of property sales, confiscation of bank accounts, and seizure of the Alliance school in Damascus to house Arab refugees from Israel. On the other hand, wrote Sasson, camps holding so-called suspect Jews were closed down, and the Jewish prisoners released.[34]

At that same time exactly, the Mossad le-Aliya Bet received a direct report from Damascus on the status of Jewish assets in Syria.

All real estate, lands and buildings located in Syria, and belonging to Jews, mortgaged or in probate, or with any indication that the beneficiaries are Jews—cannot, under administrative order, be sold, registration changed, converted to cash, or ownership transferred. All monies resulting from debt redemption are deposited in official banks and frozen, with no possibility of transferring assets.

All Jewish assets entrusted to debt collection agencies for the purposes of payment after trial [meaning, assets deposited on behalf of Jews who won lawsuits], have been confiscated. All sums owed by the government to Jewish individuals, excluding pensions and severance pay, were confiscated. All confiscated property may be released upon payment of fees owed to the administration according to various tax regulations.[35]

It soon became clear that this report—harsh though it was—still did not fully reflect the reality of the situation. In late May 1950, a new immigrant from Syria, A. H. Davidof, arrived in Israel. Jewish Agency staff members rushed to hear details on the Jewish community there. Davidof said that conditions for the Jews of Damascus were "very bad. The Jews have been seized by fear, and they attempting to flee in all directions." Matters were slightly better in Aleppo, due to more developed trade and the city's proximity to the Turkish border. "In any case," Davidof continued, "most of Aleppo's wealthy Jews have left Syria, for Turkey or Italy." Damascus's Jews were attempting flight through Lebanon, but the restrictions imposed by the Syrian government had stopped all but fifty families from exiting the country legally. Due to strife between Damascus and Beirut, Lebanon now forbade passage to Syrian Jews seeking to enter its borders. There were cases of Jews captured on the Syrian side of the border who had their passports taken away and were then refused passage to Lebanon. The result was 400 to 500 Jews stuck in Damascus, "who intended to leave Syria, sold all their property, and are now suffering from starvation."[36]

A summary report of Syrian immigration to Israel appears in an unsigned document received by the Mossad le-Aliya Bet in September 1950:

> Many obstacles stand in the way of Syrian Jews wishing to leave the country. Jews wishing to leave Syria for Lebanon must receive a special exit visa, for which they deposit a 500 Syrian pound guarantee with the government, to be paid back only upon their return to the country. Jews leaving Syria for Lebanon must also present signatures of two recognized guarantors. Syrian Jewish immigration to Israel was apparently legal, in general [the meaning is unclear, but from the context it appears this should read "illegal"]. After many attempts, Jews holding foreign citizenship were recently allowed to leave Syria for any destination, excluding Israel, of course.
>
> The cost of illegal Jewish immigration to Israel from Syria reaches up to 1,200 Syrian pounds. Transporting Jews to Israel is done with the aid of Druse and Lebanese Christian smugglers. Jews wishing to come to Israel must first move to Lebanon and are then smuggled via the sea in motor boats, to Ziv [Achziv north to Haifa]. About 30 people can be taken in one boat, in a 12-hour journey (which generally starts at 9:00 in the morning). Today, only a small number of immigrants arrive in this manner, assisted by immigration organizers located in Beirut.[37]

THE SYRIAN PROPOSAL TO CONFISCATE JEWISH PROPERTY

In the course of 1951, the Syrian government headed by Shishakli began discussing the possibility of confiscating property belonging to Jewish citizens. The proposal was first raised in a memorandum sent in late March from Damascus to the Arab League secretariat in Cairo. The memo considered compensatory action following laws passed by Israel regarding abandoned property belonging to Palestinians who had fled Israel; those laws essentially transferred ownership to the Israeli government.

Several days later, in early April, the Arab League's legal committee made a decision with a dual meaning. On one hand, it determined that Israel's actions on the matter of abandoned property were illegal. It also declared that as there was a state of war between Israel and the Arab countries, it was possible to rescind the citizenship of Jews living in the Arab world, categorize them as "enemies," and hand over their properties to a trustee. On the other hand, the committee ruled, any act of compensation to the Palestinians would tacitly recognize the State of Israel, as it would constitute a reaction to Israel's actions—a state the Arab countries refused to recognize.[38]

Apparently, the Arab League's response confused Damascus. In any case, Syria was occupied, once again, by violent struggle against Israel, mainly over Israel's efforts to drain the Hula valley swamps,[39] as well as its own internal power struggles. This reached a head on November 29, 1951, when Shishakli decided the time had come to openly take control of the government. He fired the president, disbanded the parliament, nullified all political parties, and established a dictatorship; in July 1953, Shishakli was elected president of Syria.[40]

On December 9, 1951, less than ten days after Shishakli's second coup d'etat, Syrian newspaper *al-Ayam* reported renewed efforts by the government to violate Jewish property. According to the report, Syria's Ministry of Justice was "preparing a special law regarding the Jews of Syria and their assets." The nature of the law was not detailed, but it was clearly not going to make conditions for Jews any easier, if only give the fact that the Ministry of Justice had asked the Ministry of Foreign Affairs "for a copy of the Israeli law regarding Arab property in Israel, and a copy of the Arab League's decision on the matter."

Moshe Sasson responded quickly to the report in January 1952 with a characteristically in-depth analysis that was categorized as Top Secret and distributed among senior officials at Israel's Ministry of Foreign Affairs. Sasson wrote:

"After the freeze of Jewish property in Iraq, Syria has begun displaying interest and initiating actions towards confiscating Jewish property in Arab countries. Early on, as Damascus was just beginning to consider this, Syria's policy-makers thought of freezing Jewish property in Arab countries as an act of compensation, taken against Israel, which took control of abandoned Arab property." Sasson noted that in August 1951, the Arab League's legal department presented a legal opinion on Syria's proposal, which "limited Syria's possibility of action no little." Apparently, Syria will not rest quietly, and will try to raise the issue again, mainly through the Syrian Ministry of Justice.

"There is no wonder that Syria initiated and is the driving force behind this action. The Syrian national temperament and the country's internal situation have done their part. Syria's upheavals require the government to take drastic, demonstrative measures from time to time, to turn public opinion away from the country's difficult internal situation. Therefore—Syria's military needed a skirmish over the Hula valley [in 1951] in order to focus mass public discontent against Israel, "unite the Syrian nation at a moment of crisis, raise high the Syrian military banner that guards the homeland, and call for national support of the military."

> Upon Shishakli's most recent *coup d'état*, we feared the Syrians might need to revive their old ploy and engage us in a border conflict. It seems to me that Syria's preparations for seizing Jewish property, from a diplomatic standpoint, should also be viewed in this light. We would not be surprised if, at a moment of crisis, Syria decided to announce a freeze on Jewish assets within the country.
>
> In accordance with the opinion of the Arab Leagues' legal advisor, the Syrian government may take compensatory actions only as regards Jews who have migrated from Syria and become Israeli citizens, or those who have declared their wish to gain this citizenship at any price. Only after rescinding the citizenship of the Jews still living in Syria, may they be viewed as citizens of an enemy country, and on these grounds, their property frozen.
>
> I would assume that Syria's Ministry of Justice is now searching for a way to freeze property belonging to Jews still in Syria, without the need for extraordinary actions (declaring them enemies, putting them in detention camps, etc). In the event the legal means are found, they may announce a freeze on all Jewish assets in Syria, whether the owners are in the country, have emigrated to Israel, or to other countries. It seems to me that we must prepare for this eventuality, as if it takes place, it will set a precedent and serve as an example for other Arab countries.[41] [Words underlined in the original].

TORTURE, SEIZURE, AND LOSING SOURCES OF INCOME

Between late November 1953 and early January 1954, Yosef Hadas compiled two reports on conditions for the Jews of Syria. In the first, Hadas noted that, "By all accounts, their economic situation is not bad, but their personal suffering is unbearable. They live in constant terror, and from day to day grow more afraid. Risking their lives, a few individuals have fled to Lebanon, and from there to Israel."

The Jews of Aleppo were worst off: "With nightfall, they dare not leave their homes. Very often, stones are thrown at their houses, the synagogues (during prayer), and windows are broken. Accompanying them, as they pass in the street, are cries of '*Yahud*' [Jew] along with vile curses issued from the mouths of every Arab. Dozens are in prison on false charges. They are tortured with unimaginable cruelty. . . . In one case, a man was blinded as a result of torture. They do not pass over even women and children."

The authorities had to be more careful with the Jews of Damascus, said Hadas, because of the presence of foreign legations in the city, and the Jewish community's capability of forging ties with foreign countries. Despite this, the Jewish community lived in "terrible fear, not daring to leave their quarter, unless there was absolutely no other choice."[42]

The report filed by Hadas two months later relied on interviews with new immigrants to Israel from Syria, who painted a harsh picture of plots and ever-increasing economic hardship. Hadas said there were 4,000 Jews living in Syria, most (2,500 to 3,000) in Damascus, the others (1,000 to 1,500) in Aleppo, and a few in Kamishli. Over two-thirds of Syria's Jews left between December 1947 and May 1948, and after that—during the months of Za'im's regime.

"Many Syrian Jews were merchants who benefited from the trust of wealthy property-owners," Hadas continued.

> Among the Jews of Aleppo were many wealthy families (such as Nehmad, Sha'yu, Bidda, Hazan, Chamma, and Jammal). In contrast, most of the Jews of Damascus were middle-class (small shop-owners) or poor. The Jews of Kamishli—Kurds and Iraqis—farmed, or to be more exact, leased large tracts of land and gave them over to tenant farmers. A year and a half ago, controls were placed on them, limiting their activities in the region.

Hadas reviewed the economic regulations placed on Syria's Jews prior to the establishment of the State of Israel and noted that "Husni Za'im was more liberal, and during his period, many Jews managed to liquidate their assets in Syria." He then turned to present day matters:

> After the Hula valley confrontation (April–May 1951), the government of Syria ordered tenants of buildings belonging to Syrian Jews living abroad to pay their rent to the government and not to the owners' legal representatives. Following the recent Shishakli *coup d'état* (in late November 1951), the authorities ordered the Ministry of Justice to prepare a law for confiscation of Jewish property in Syria. In early January of this year, the authorities closed the Jewish-owned Bank Zakhla in Damascus and appointed a committee to settle accounts and examine its sources of income.
>
> Syria's masses, who have long regarded the Jews as a manipulative foreign element, nourish their hatred and await the day of vengeance. Many have already imagined the Jewish houses, shops and women that will be theirs at the first opportunity. In late November 1947, there was a mass outburst against the Jews of Aleppo, and the authorities did nothing to prevent the vandalism, looting and arson.
>
> Most of the educated classes (nationalist students, etc.), view Jews as Zionists and therefore hate them. As for the middle-class—they are the ones who aspired to remove Jews from the jobs, in order to inherit them, and in doing so, eliminate their talented competition in the job market. Only the feudalistic, large property-owners took a broader view of Jewish businesses. They had tears in their eyes as they parted from the Jews leaving Syria. Many Syrian businesses were damaged by the departure of Syrian Jews, who managed them with great talent and loyalty.

Now, the Jews of Syria live under the most difficult conditions, and arriving new immigrants to Israel describe the situation as hopeless. There is little work, and most live off savings. The Arab children of Aleppo attack Jews in the street, throw stones, break windows, etc. Most of the Jews remaining in Syria are of limited means. The poor are supported by the Joint Distribution Committee and by private donations from relatives and friends abroad. As for the rich, most have left Syria, some are stuck in Lebanon where they live in unparalleled luxury."[43]

That same month, Yosef Golan of the World Jewish Congress also wrote a report on the Jews of Syria. Golan said that Syria's Jewish community live, first and foremost, off the illegal sale of property, along with assistance from the Joint Distribution Committee, other charitable organizations, and donations from Syrian Jews living in Mexico, Argentina, western Europe, and the United States. Some of the money from abroad was used for paying bribes to government officials, police officers, as well as the policemen stationed in the Jewish quarter. Golan added that Damascus's Jewish merchants were forced to close down their shops and waive their rights to their use (as the merchants did not own the shops), without any compensation. Since 1948, he said, Jews were required to abandon one-third of the stores located in the city's textile market and one half the stores in the gold market (the names of these open markets do not necessarily reflect the activities therein).[44]

THE FREEZE OF SYRIAN JEWISH PROPERTY

Among the files of the Jewish Agency and Israel's Ministry of Foreign Affairs there is no direct mention of a freeze on property belonging to the Jews of Syria, and in any case, there are no estimates of the volume of property. But Rabbi Avraham Hamara, the last chief rabbi of the Jewish community of Syria before coming to Israel in 1992, says the government froze property belonging to Jews fleeing illegally from Syria, from the 1940s and up until 1992, when President Hafez al-Assad allowed Jews free passage to emigrate from Syria (to all destinations excluding Israel). Control of the confiscated properties was transferred to the so-called Palestinian Committee For Management of Assets Belonging to Jews who Fled—an entity whose first members were Palestinian refugees from the War of Independence, with close ties to the Syrian government. To this day, according to Hamara, the committee manages the affairs of private properties confiscated from Jews and receives income on the rent but is not entitled to sell those properties. "There are a lot of assets," Hamara says. "Almost all of the Jewish quarter of Damascus and property in Aleppo and Kamishli."[45]

There is a reference to a special department handling Jewish property, without mentioning its connection to the Palestinian refugees, in a World Jewish Congress report filed in January 1954; Golan called it the Division for Management of Jewish Property. In November 1953, meanwhile, Ya'akov

Rabbi Avraham Hamara, the last chief rabbi of
Syria (photograph by Yossi Zeliger)

Rofe reported on the Jewish community in Aleppo, which numbered 2,000.
Most, Rofe said, lived off donations sent by Aleppo's immigrant community in the United States. Some dealt in trades such as tailoring, shoemaking,
storekeeping, and light commerce. "The security situation is quiet, aside from
isolated incidents, here and there, where one family member leaves the country and persecution begins," added Rofe. The following is the reference to
frozen assets:

> In late August 1953, the police turned to people living in buildings controlled
> by the Custodian of Abandoned Property [emphasis added], and handed them
> an announcement in writing telling them to vacate their places of residence
> by the end of September 1953, and hand the keys over to the police. This
> action added to the fear in their hearts, and rumors abound that they will be
> transferred to an encampment, put in a walled military camp, a closed ghetto,
> etc. The situation changed after the police changed its intentions, returned
> to those people and canceled all orders.

It is worth noting that Ezra Chammah—quoted at the beginning of this
chapter—said the family house in Aleppo was seized by the government even

before the deaths of his grandmother and uncle in the late 1950s, so there apparently was a freeze on Jewish property in Syria.

In his report, Rofe told of how the Jews of Aleppo were forced to leave behind their property when they fled Syria.

> In general, the Jews lived in constant fear and there are a large number interested in coming to Israel. There is the possibility of free passage to Damascus, where there are people (Rabbi Shaul Naftali) known to have connections to Arabs working for the railway; in return for 150 Syrian pounds per person, they transport them to Beirut. But lack of money prevents many from taking these steps, and the fact is that every Jew with the financial means leaves the house, as is, closes the door on furniture, and the like, goes off as if to work, without even a suitcase in hand, out of fear that someone will sense they are leaving. Those without the means needed to make the journey, sit and wait for salvation.[46]

Moreover, the World Jewish Congress—the most reliable source of information on every Jewish community in the world—determined definitively that "After the establishment of the State of Israel, several anti-Jewish laws were passed in Syria, which prohibited the sale of Jewish property and froze Jewish bank accounts. A great deal of property was confiscated by the Syrian authorities and was thereafter transferred to Palestinian ownership."[47]

Chapter 10

"For God's Sake, Please Help Us"

The Jews of Syria Between Persecution and Relief

After sporadic reports on the fate of Syrian Jewry and their property from 1953, there is blackout on information about the community spanning almost two years. Documentation preserved at the Jewish Agency and Israel's Foreign Ministry archives offers no explanation for the silence, and at the same time there is no reason to assume that these specific documents were lost. During this time Colonel Adib al-Shishakli's regime fell in a military takeover in February 1954, and parliamentary rule was reinstated—but not political stability. Governments changed hands at a rapid pace, and left-wing forces, chiefly the Ba'ath party, began playing a central role in Syrian politics.[1] Whatever the reason for the missing documents, reports began flooding in again in 1956, mainly via Istanbul, where the Jewish Agency Aliya Department had a permanent presence.

THE MID-1950s—THE JEWISH SITUATION IN SYRIA TAKES A TURN FOR THE WORSE

In January 1956, the head of the Jewish Agency office in Istanbul, Itzhak Passal, reported to the head of Aliya department, Shlomo Zalman Shragai, that ten Jewish families from Syria, numbering eighteen persons, had arrived in the Turkish city of Iskenderun. These were Iranian citizens living in Syria ordered to leave the country within twenty-four hours. "The aforementioned left all their property there and are now making efforts to get it back, as they are foreign nationals," Passal reported. "They told me that in recent days, identity cards were collected from all Jews and were returned only after the documents were stamped with a red line."

In passing, Passal made a connection between the worsening situation for Syrian Jews and increased tensions on the Syrian-Israeli border, which reached a breaking point with an IDF attack on Syrian outposts on the eastern Sea of Galilee in mid-December 1956.[2] After this military operation, Passal said, Jews were forbidden from listening to Israeli radio stations and the Jewish community and its institutions were forced to contribute to the Syrian national defense fund. "The rabbis of Aleppo, Rabbi Raphael Lagnado and Rabbi Ezra Antebi, asked them [the deportees] to issue a cry for help to save the Jews of Syria, because they do not know what tomorrow holds for them," added Passal.[3]

Over the coming months, Passal reported on deteriorating conditions for the Syrian Jews. In March 1956 he wrote: "The authorities are ready to concentrate the Jews in ghettos, and have even started doing so in one Syrian city. The community, and its rabbis, are shouting, crying out for help to let them leave the country, which is possible after paying 500 Syrian pounds for a passport, plus a 500 Syrian pound bribe to avoid the draft. Naturally, very few have the means to pay such sums for every family member."[4]

The situation was particularly grim for the Jews of Kamishli. In March 1956, an anonymous letter from Kamishli reached the Alliance school in Beirut. It read: "We wish to inform you that we are 1,000 souls in this city in great danger because our homes and shops have been marked, and we are forbidden from walking outside at night. We dare not go out, even in daylight, as they attack us at every turn. No one pays attention to our pleas. Our lives are like a prison; we have no possibility of earning a living. For God's sake, please help us somehow. Bring our case before a large international organization, like the United Nations, the Red Cross, and maybe they will bring us some help. Likewise, notify the U.S. government. We are in great danger, with nowhere to turn, except to you. Please, save us!"[5]

By October 1956, Jews could not obtain passports, even for money. Rumors were rife of horrors perpetrated on Jews, including suspicions that a "campaign of death" was in the works. When David Pichato left Aleppo on his way to Israel via Turkey, Jewish community leader Rabbi Antebi told him, "You are, in fact, the last who will leave." In Kamishli, the authorities forbade Jews from tending their farmlands, and in doing so, blocked their source of income. New immigrants to Israel related that conditions for Kamishli's 2,000 Jews were worst as, "the income dwindling, their houses marked, Jewish schools closed, and every local Jew issued a red identity card." In Damascus, Jews suffered from violence and libelous attack, such as the claim that Jews were trying to buy arms. "Each time someone manages to cross over into Lebanon, the authorities take revenge on that person's relatives and neighbors, preventing any further action or initiative."[6]

Later on, it transpired that Syrian Jews could receive passports, but that this involved a high fee, and a waiting period of up to a year and a half. "However," Passal reported to Shragai in April 1957, "there are many cases where people are asked to pay the required fees when they lack the means, and the community is unwilling to participate in funding this sort of expense." Passal suggested that Shragai allocate Jewish Agency funding for this purpose, stressing the tragic family circumstances that sometimes accompanied the lack of funds. "We have an actual case where the mother and children have been in Israel for several years now, while the father and daughter were apprehended, and are presently situated in Aleppo. They have a sister-in-law here [in Istanbul], whose Israeli husband works for us, and various sums of money have been transferred several times by the family. They now lack $200 to receive passports." Passal asked Shragai's permission to loan the family the balance, but Shragai's response to this and many other suggestions made in the letter, has not been preserved.[7]

SYRIAN JEWS AND THE UNITED ARAB REPUBLIC

Years passed, but conditions for Syria's Jews did not change. During those years, the left wing Ba'ath party gained strength, and power was concentrated in the hands of military commanders supporting the party. In February 1958, the Syrian Ba'ath party maneuvered Egyptian President Ghamal Abd el-Nasser into agreeing to a unification of Syria and Egypt, and the United Arab Republic (UAR) came into being. Nasser was president of this united state, in charge of foreign affairs, defense, education, and industry. At first, Damascus was charged with finance and the economy and many other internal affairs, but Cairo quickly gained control of these areas as well.[8]

The formation of the UAR did not improve matters for Syria's Jews, and from certain aspects, only made things worse. In September 1961, Edmond Muller, head of the Red Cross mission to Cairo in the early 1960s, reported Abd al-Hammid al-Saraj's actions against the Jews of Syria. Al-Saraj was Syria's strongman in the days of the UAR—the Prime Minister, Minister of the Interior, and commander of the security services in Damascus. He established a special department to handle Jewish affairs and ordered that funds transferred by international organizations to aid to the Jewish community be seized and given over to Palestinian refugees living in Syria.

In March 1958, Baruch Duvdevani, one of the Jewish Agency Aliya Department heads, visited Iran and was given a report on the Jews of Syria by Arref Rahmani, former principal of Damascus' Alliance school. In Rahmani's assessment, there were currently 3,000 Jews in Aleppo, 2,000 in Damascus, 1,300 in Kamishli and the surrounding villages, plus 50 Jews in Dayr al-Zawr in eastern Syria. "Recently, 50 Jewish families in Aleppo requested permission to exit Syria, and similar requests were submitted by 40 families in

Damascus. The applicants were told they could receive exit visas if they renounced their citizenship, waived all rights to real estate, and transferred ownership to Palestinian refugees. To date, not one has received an exit visa," Rahmani related. He estimated that 1,000 Jews in Aleppo, 1,000 in Damascus, and 900 in Kamishli wished to emigrate from the land of their birth, most for Israel.[9]

Just as the overall situation had not changed, so the painful personal stories remained the same. As Shaya Meir Masri wrote in a letter to the Jewish Agency, asking for aid to take his family from Aleppo to Israel:

> We work with the Kurds here, and recently our material situation has deteriorated badly, because of debts the Kurds owe us, and the impossibility of collecting our money from them. Our family comprises nine people, and because of the difficulties, and heavy expenses, especially of late, we are now in a situation where we find it hard to make a living. We therefore have decided to leave this place, and come to you, with the whole family, to work at any sort of job.
>
> I imagine you know that if we wish to leave, we are required to pay 'a donation' [in lieu of army service] of 1,000 pounds, additional expenses on tax and documents for which we must pay an additional 1,000 pounds, and we will need another 500 pounds for other expenses. We want to assure you that we haven't even one pound, and can therefore not meet these expenses (you can confirm the truth of our statements with whomever you like).
>
> We heard that you can help us, in cooperation with our brothers from Aleppo. We ask that you do us this great favor and help us, as we cannot ask for help from our acquaintances here, as all are difficult financial situations, and are unable to give us any sort of assistance. Our family has sons and daughters of employable age. They will work any job in order to earn money, something they cannot do here. We hope to receive an answer from you as soon as possible, and hope you will not disappoint us, and God help you in all that you do. Rest assured, if we were not in dire straits, we would not write to ask your help.

Masri was one of those who later received Jewish Agency assistance, in the summer of 1958, and managed to leave Aleppo.[10]

THE JEWISH AGENCY HELPS THE JEWS OF ALEPPO COME TO ISRAEL

The Jewish Agency was far from insensitive to the sufferings of the Jews of Aleppo. In May 1958, Istanbul-based emissaries Haim Shadmi and Y. Fa'el decided to hand the matter of Aleppo Jewish immigration to Ya'akov Shamosh. According to Shamosh, all of Aleppo's Jews wanted to leave Syria, and 90% wanted to move to Israel; thirty percent, he added, "are indigent, lacking everything." The emissaries decided not to deal with the matter of Kamishli's Jews, even though they themselves described their situation as "hopeless and mired in hatred and fear." The reason: spiriting individuals out of Kamishli was impossible; the community needed to be moved *en masse,* but "it is necessary to wait for the results and developments of matters in Aleppo, which all agree is the most burning issue, requiring an immediate solution."[11]

In the second half of 1958, Jews from Aleppo began arriving in Israel via Turkey. The only thing stopping the entire community from migrating was money. As previously mentioned, the Syrian authorities demanded payment for passports and army exemptions; in addition, there were travel expenses to be funded. Army exemption fees were 1,000 Syrian pounds, ($500 to $700 at that time) for every Jewish male over the age of forty-one, while males aged thirteen to forty-one were required to pay 2,000 Syrian pounds. A passport cost 250 Syrian pounds, other documents cost an additional 150 Syrian pounds, and an identical sum was needed for bribes. After decades of persecution, the Jews of Aleppo were already bereft of all their assets and could not afford all this by themselves. The Jewish Agency tried to assist them with funding, which was not very much, supplemented by funds raised from Aleppo Jews living in Iskenderun and some funds raised in Aleppo itself. In this way, Jews managed to leave the city, bit by bit, and by November 1958, the Jewish Agency confirmed it had funded the immigration of forty-four families from Aleppo.[12]

The complete migration list for 1958 reveals that the average cost per immigrant was 832 Syrian pounds, or $238 at that time. The list includes 393 names, with the estimated cost of their immigration—including bribes and other expenses—totaling $92,599. Simple arithmetic proves that the cost of bringing 5,000 Jews out of Syria was $1.2 million. The Jewish Agency refused to pay for passports, out of consideration, as Shragai wrote, that "if we give money to the needy—and it is not always possible to know who is needy and who isn't—then everyone will ask us for money for passports, and this will cost about another half million dollars." The Jewish Agency simply could not afford these expenses.

Matters improved in late September, when Shragai received from the Aleppo Jewish community (probably via Istanbul) "a list of all the city's [Jewish] residents considered for immigration, and the economic situation of each and every one. It appears there are 373 families, or 1,800 persons, of which 121 or 604 persons are in bad shape, and 7 families or 39 persons in very bad shape. Clearly we will finance passports only for them, and then only in part, not 100%, aside from exceptional cases whose situation is very bad, but they are only a very small minority." Even assuming a full subsidy, according to the aforementioned calculations, expenses came to only $153,000, which the Jewish Agency could afford.

In and of itself, the list is a rare document, which details the professions and economic situation of hundreds of Aleppo's Jews at that point in time. From the document, it is clear that wealthy and middle-class Jews continued to live in Jamilieh, with the lower-middle class and poor living in the Asita neighborhood. Ordinary professions included tailors, greengrocers, fabric and shirt vendors, butchers, and the like. There were also those who made their livings in less conventional fashions: "fortune-tellers," "clothes pressers," an *arak* liquor store worker, a woman who "circulated among weddings"—it is unclear whether she was a beggar or an entertainer of some sort—laundresses, cafe help, and one doctor.

A relatively large number of Jews "lived off income" and were classified as middle-class, well-off, or even very well-off; these were apparently own-ers of profit-yielding assets. There were also several wealthy families, and serious businessowners: the Chammah family (introduced in Chapter 9), which dealt in textile; silver- and goldsmiths Salim Masri, Ezra Masri, and others; Yosef Abadi and Nissim Bigio who "work with the Arabs"; Shaya Masri, Jamil Berjo, and others who "work with the Kurds"; textile merchants like Zaki Kira, Aslan Lagnado, Salim Shami, and the Amkiya family; customs agents Tawfiq Antebi, Albert Istanbuly, and David Senior; Naftali Halfon, who sold medicine; money changers Avraham and Ya'akov Cohen; Haim Mizrahi, who owned a paper factory; Hillel Tawil, who owned a cardboard factory; Avraham Lagnado, partner in a biscuit bakery; and the Salim Kandy family, who owned a henna factory (Aharon Salim Kandy was the only well-off Jew who expressed an desire to go to Israel).[13]

At the same time, there still remained the problem of the Jews of Kamishli. The Jewish Agency tried to help in November 1958, as Duvdevani reported to Shragai:

There are 1,800 to 1,900 Jews in this town, sunk in a Diaspora of slavery and misery that is hard to describe. All attempt made to contact these Jews have, to date, come to nothing, despite [our] emissaries' constant efforts. The situ-ation at present is: several families, up to 26 in number, arrived in Aleppo on their own initiative and effort. We are now trying to transfer them to Turkey, as we transfer the Aleppo Jews themselves.

Recently, a businessman from Aleppo made contact with Mr. Shamosh of Iskenderun to encourage other Jews to continue going this way [meaning, leaving Kamishli for Aleppo, then on to Turkey]. According to recent reports received via Mr. Shamosh, it appears the Governor of the Kamishli Region is allowing Jews to depart for Aleppo, something that was forbidden till now. The problem is how to gain the Kamishli Jews' trust, get them to agree to leave for Aleppo, and make them feel sure that from Aleppo they will go on to Israel. We have given this responsibility to a man from Aleppo, who has set out to visit them there.

We are also trying to work with Lufthansa [airline] of Germany in this way: There is a large German factory near Kamishli where, rumor has it, several Kamishli Jews work. The [local] manager of Lufthansa of Germany will visit the factory and make contact with these Jews, to motivate them to go to Aleppo. Clearly, Lufthansa will not do this out of charity and if this succeeds—

we will have to fly the people out of Aleppo to Istanbul on the company's planes, increasing costs considerably.[14]

As the next chapter will show, Lebanon's Jews were flown to Israel with Lufthansa's assistance, but this channel was apparently not utilized in the case of the Jews of Kamishli.

A COMPREHENSIVE 1959 REPORT ON THE JEWS OF KAMISHLI AND DAMASCUS

A comprehensive report on the Jewish community of Damascus, classified Top Secret, reached the Jewish Agency in October 1959, from a source unnamed in the document. At that time, the source said, the community numbered 400 families or 3,000 persons: 700 children under the age of fifteen; 500 young singles; the remainder being married couples and the elderly. The source mentioned the arrest of a number of Jews from Aleppo, Hims, and Damascus, due to their involvement with illegal immigration. Several admitted to the charges after being cruelly tortured, others managed not to crack, and were later released. The source hinted that young Jews might be the victims of the community leadership, which, he said, opposed emigration from Syria, and even maintained constant contact with the authorities on the subject. Matters had reached a point where the *mukhtar* (head of the Jewish quarter), Farrah Romano, regularly carried a gun, and fearing for his life, did not leave his house at night. His sisters, "old maids" of forty and fifty, "provide intelligence against Jews to the Security [service] and their brother."

Economic conditions for the Damascus Jewish community remained difficult. Every month 2,000 to 3,000 Syrian pounds were distributed among the needy—contributions from former community members in the United States. Syrian security agents and officers, who came each Thursday to the offices of the Jewish community, supervised distribution. An additional 60,000 Syrian pounds in contributions from the United States arrived in the spring of 1959, when the Syrian authorities ordered the community to pay a 615 Syrian pounds levy for the draft deferment of every Jewish male whose age made him eligible for military conscription, including those already deferred long ago.

Regarding employment in the community, the report said:

Most young men and women work in brass and copper engraving, or sewing nightgowns and pajamas supplied by tailor shops. They work inside the Jewish quarter, at home, or in designated studios for metalwork. The quarter also has stores with basic supplies, grocers, greengrocers, booksellers, etc. About ten Jews own stores, businesses, etc. outside the quarter, in the big open markets. They try to live peacefully with their Arab neighbors, and ignore all sorts of insults, humiliations and attacks. The Muslims do not boycott [these] Jews, [but] buy from and sell to them.

Seventeen Jews are peddlers, wandering the villages, selling them cloth and buying farm products. These Jews set out for the villages only after being outfitted with a special permit, issued by the Ministry of the Interior—the Department of General Defense. The permit is issued only after bribes are paid to *mukhtar* Farrah Romano and the General Defense officials. The permits are valid for 15 days, and permit holders must renew them, otherwise they are liable to be arrested. During the Sinai Campaign, the authorities stopped granting permits for two months, and these Jews were left without work. After that, Jewish community committee member Tushe Langnado and the *mukhtar*, requested the General Defense renew the permits. (Farrah Romano received 25 Syrian pounds on every permit issued and he personally hands the permits to their owners).

About ten Jews deal in buying used goods from Damascus' various quarters, and no restrictions are placed on their freedom of movement. About three Jews wander the various markets and streets, shining shoes. Three or four young Jewish women work in a bone factory located in the Hamidiya open market. They have worked a long time in this profession, and continue to do so; they would otherwise stay in the [Jewish] quarter, as they fear for their safety.

Additionally, three Jewish doctors and two Jewish lawyers practiced in Damascus, and all had clients from every ethnic and religious group.

This report also stressed the serious threat to the Jews of Kamishli, "most of whom are without work, with downcast eyes." The authorities forbade them from leaving the town for their fields, and in town they were subject to incessant attacks from their Muslim neighbors. "There are several ill persons in almost every Jewish family, illnesses caused by malnutrition such as anemia, tuberculosis and more; and there is no possibility of medical treatment, or sufficient food." At that time, there were only five or six wealthy Jewish families in Kamishli, "and every family is patron to a number of poor families, providing them with essential food products, but this assistance is less than minimal." One of those wealthy Jews, Itzhak Yehudia, was murdered in August 1959 at a coffeehouse meeting with a Muslim who owed him 600 Syrian pounds.

At the end of the report, the informant said:

All residents of Damascus' Jewish quarter wish to immigrate to Israel in any way. Morale in the quarter is very low, due to the recent incidents of . . . apostasy [three Jewish women had converted either to Islam or Christianity the year before], and plots by the authorities. About 50 families with Syrian citizenship have submitted requests to emigrate from Syria, renounce their citizenship and their property. But five or six months ago, the authorities blocked their trips, on the recommendation of the Jewish community leadership in Damascus. Some had already sold their shops and furniture, and are now consuming their savings, and their situation is getting close to dangerous.[15]

A FEW KAMISHLI JEWS LEAVE SYRIA

The status of Syrian Jewry was discussed at two meetings in December 1959, called by Baruch Duvdevani, senior official at the Jewish Agency Aliya Department. The first dealt with the Kamishli community, the second with the Jews of Syria and Lebanon overall. At the first meeting, attended by representatives of Kamishli Jewish immigrants to Israel, Duvdevani rejected the claim that the Jewish Agency was ignoring Kamishli. Haim Shedmi, the emissary in Istanbul, reviewed the matter at length and, among other things, noted that Syria's borders closed whenever Farrah Romano of Damascus intervened. It was Romano who "notified the authorities not to allow the young people leave Syrian boundaries, as if they reached Israel, they would be drafted into the ranks of the IDF." Shadmi said he met Romano's daughter, who immigrated to Israel over her father's protests, as he did not want to be left alone. Romano himself knew, Shadmi added, "if he ever wanted to come to [downtown] Israel, he said openly that what awaited him was a gallows on Tel Aviv's Allenby Street."

Shadmi reported on contacts he had with a Syrian Muslim who was willing to smuggle Jews out of Kamishli for money. "Today, the Jews of Kamishli receive a great deal of support from us and may approach the authorities to request passports. And if the deal with the 'goy' [gentile] goes according to plan, we will get exit visas from Kamishli, and then we will celebrate the great event together."[16] In fact, nothing ever came of this plan.

The next day, eleven members of the Israeli Syrian and Lebanese Immigrants Organization came to Duvdevani's office. In this discussion, Shadmi expressed optimism regarding the possible migration of Syrian Jews, as UAR vice president, General Abd al-Hakim Ammar of Egypt, had give the order to organize all of Damascus's government ministries. "This will doubtless make the Jews' exit easier," said Shadmi; the minutes of the meeting fail to explain the connection. Shadmi further said that "Most of the new immigrants bring worthless items with them, including house and kitchenware which can be purchased at the cheapest of prices." The organization delegates' response was that these were impoverished immigrants, "who essentially have nothing except this meager baggage."[17]

In mid-1960, the Syrian authorities suddenly began issuing exit visas to the Jews of Kamishli. By October 1969, visas had been granted to twenty-three families, and Shadmi was deliberating two questions: What was the meaning of Damascus's sudden goodwill, and should illegal immigration of the city's Jews continue? Shadmi wrote to his fellow Aliya Department official Yehuda Dominitz:

> There are two scenarios regarding Syria, especially Kamishli. One is that the Kamishli authorities decided to grant exit visas out of pity for the Jews, because of their difficult situation. The second is the local authorities sensed the

young people were running away, apparently had no way to detaining them, and were therefore losing money—the poll tax—and so, felt it better to issue the permits. I will not go into analyzing the twos scenarios at present, but clearly the first one is unlikely, that compassion would grow among the Arabs.

And now the question posed is whether to continue with illegal immigration, which could endanger passage for those holding exit visas. But on the other hand, I do not know if we can completely stop the latter, as I am not sure the persons currently at our service will want to continue in the future. My opinion is that we must continue both activities simultaneously, and it seems to me that illegal immigration will be easier, and the absence of locals less noticeable, in the presence of legal immigration.[18]

This proposal was apparently accepted.

Legal immigration also cost money, of course, with the Jewish Agency still covering the balance of payment. That month, Yom-Tov Cohen, who organized immigrant affairs in Kamishli, submitted a report detailing the costs involved in obtaining exit permits for the first twenty-three families. Ya'akov Shamosh, of the Jewish Agency in Iskenderun, transferred $10,000 to Cohen, the equivalent of 36,125 Syrian pounds. Aid to the families totaled 28,290 Syrian pounds, an average 1,230 Syrian pounds ($340) per family, mainly to pay levy on draft deferment.[19]

Sometimes the need arose for larger funding, which the Jewish Agency refrained from providing, apparently because of limited resources. In December 1960, Shamosh asked Shadmi to assist the Mahluf family, who were being asked to pay a 1,000 Syrian pound bribe, which it could not afford as the authorities were also asking for 20,000 Syrian pounds in property taxes on houses the family owned. The Jewish Agency in Jerusalem responded that it did not understand the request. If the family owned houses, why not sell them to pay off the tax and the bribe; if they could not sell them, "we cannot support such heavy costs, for if we begin taking on these expenses, who knows where it will lead." In other words, this would create a precedent that others would try to manipulate to their advantage.[20]

It seems that financial problems caused most Kamishli Jews, including the Mahluf family, to "get stuck" even after receiving their exit permits, for in July 1962, the community issued another request for assistance. Meanwhile, dramatic shifts were taking place on Syria's political scene: A military coup in 1961 led to Syria's withdrawal from the UAR; another revolution in March of 1962 toppled the civilian government, which was replaced by a series of unstable, leftist regimes.[21] A letter sent by the Jews of Kamishli and signed by the community leaders, along with twenty families (including the Mahluf family), contained a request similar to the Mahlufs—assistance from the Jewish Agency with tax payments:

We, the members of the Jewish community of Kamishli, young and old, appeal to you and ask that you review the request made in this letter, that you view favorably and mercifully our situation, made difficult because of heavy taxes levied on us. As you know, we cannot leave Kamishli's boundaries. Secondly, we are all unemployed, no one will employ us, and we have no income aside from your monthly assistance [from the Joint Distribution Committee], allocated to each person in foreign currency [dollars]. We have now received a message from Mr. Yom-Tov Cohen, saying that even the assistance you were giving us, to save us, has been canceled. This announcement shocked us deeply, and caused both young and old to weep.

We have lost all hope of ever being freed, and now see ourselves as indentured and rejected from all sides. You certainly will not agree to this fate. You are merciful people who will certainly take pity on this miserable community, in a situation that gets worse from day to day. Truth be told, no one else can do this but you. We therefore appeal to you and request that you reverse your decision that prevents us from receiving assistance.

Once again, we appeal to you and ask that you review the request to continue giving us assistance to pay poll taxes and various fees owed to the government, and by doing so, you will save us from indenture, as the Bible says: "He who saves the life of one Jew, it is as if he has saved the entire world."

The letter was transferred to Shadmi, who had already returned to Israel. He answered that the Jewish Agency could not cover tax payments, and "as regards poll tax, etc.—at every opportunity we have announced that people of Kamishli will be the first to receive our assistance in leaving. Shadmi also noted that he knew nothing of the notion that funding from the Joint Distribution Committee might be cut.[22]

ESCAPE FROM SYRIA ON THE EVE OF THE SIX DAY WAR

Immigration from Syria continued to trickle into Israel, assisted by Syrian smugglers. Some, like Thabet Kurdi of Aleppo, became regular smugglers of Syrian Jews. Kurdi had connections with smugglers in Turkey and security servicemen in Aleppo. He charged 250 Syrian pounds for each person smuggled, although "he did give breaks to people of limited means, and charged them less." The runaways had to leave all their property behind, taking not even a suitcase, so that they would appear to be casual travelers. At the most, each took an envelope or matchbox, inside where was some jewelry. Kurdi and his team bribed the Syrian customs officials, drove through customs, then walked five or six hours to the border with Turkey, where they were warmly received. In Iskenderun, the immigrants were handed over to Ya'akov Shamosh, who housed them—under false identities—in a local hotel. After a few hours rest, they were transported to Istanbul, then continued on to Israel.

On the other hand, there were less successful attempts, especially with smugglers who did not coordinate matters with the Jewish Agency staff and who smuggled new immigrants to Israel on dates when, for various reasons, the Jewish Agency had specifically requested that emissaries prevent this from happening. Sometimes the Turkish authorities arrested the smugglers operating on the Turkish side of the border. At the same time, Syria was noticing the ongoing disappearance of Kamishli's Jews; in 1962 there were only 530 left in town. Shamosh reported that "The situation is bad overall, they are under constant surveillance by the local authorities, who take attendance every day." There were also 280 Jews from Kamishli in Aleppo; the Jewish Agency staff in Istanbul intended to bring out eighty, openly and legally, and smuggle the rest.[23]

In March 1963, Syrian underwent another military coup d'etat, this time spearheaded by officers associated with the left-wing Ba'ath party. After a few months of internal struggle, General Amin al-Haffez took control of the country and instituted socialist policies that included nationalizing factories and banks, and allocating farmlands taken from landowners to farmers. Between February and April 1964, protests waged by merchants and landowners were repressed cruelly, and a new constitution declared Syria "A True People's Democratic Republic," in other words: A communist-style dictatorship.[24]

As always, dictatorship meant the Jewish situation in Syria would get worse. In May 1964, a delegation of Syrian immigrants met with the head of the World Jewish Congress's Israeli branch, Arie Tartakover, to report on the situation in Syria. According to the delegation, there were 5,000 to 6,000 Jews in Syria, most in Damascus and Aleppo. They were forbidden from any sort of work, only 5% still dealt in trade and selling; the community subsisted on support from the Joint. "Anti-Jewish riots are a most common nightmare in Syria, especially over the recent revolutionary period. The last was two months ago, one man was killed, and several others wounded, and a great deal of Jewish property was destroyed," they claimed.

The delegation emphasized that there was no chance the situation would improve, as Syria's Jews essentially lived in a ghetto, surrounded by hatred and disrespect. The only hope was to get them out. But, at that time, there was no possibility for legal Jewish migration. Two years earlier, under pressure from the other Arab countries, legal Jewish migration in return for paying a levy on draft deferment was canceled. Since then, there had been only a trickle of legal migration to Israel, limited to young persons only, and involving heavy expenses. Delegation members were convinced that outside pressure from Great Britain, for instance, Yugoslavia or West Germany, might pressure Syria into reviving legal immigration. If and when a permit of this sort was issued, it would require agreements with Greece and Italy for absorbing the immigrants on their way to Israel. Turkey, they noted, had decided to forbid entry to people without citizenship—and there was no question that Syria's Jews would lose their citizenship the moment they left Syria.

Tarktakover reported on the meeting to Dr. Nahum Goldman, president of the Jewish Agency and chairman of the World Jewish Congress, and

Alexander Easterman, diplomatic secretary for the Jewish Congress in London. He noted that there was a need to find source of funding Jewish emigration out of Syria and immigration to Israel, but was not particularly worried about that point. Tartakover estimated that the Joint and the Jewish Agency could manage the cost, if the World Jewish Congress succeeded in changing Syria's policy. In his opinion, this was a practical plan, worthy of the Jewish Congress's undivided attention[25]—but there is no proof that something was actually done.

PERSECUTION AND ATTACK FOLLOWING THE SIX DAY WAR

The Six Day War only made matters worse for Jews in Syria—insofar as it was possible. The extreme faction of the Ba'ath party ruled Syria at that point, headed by General Sallah J'did, and Minister of Defense Hafez Al-Assad (who took control in November 1970). The regime's position on Israel in 1967 was hard-line; it raised tensions along the border and effectively dragged Egypt into a war it had no interest in then.[26] This military conflict, and ensuing defeat of the Arab countries, cost the Jews dearly all over the Middle East—and Syria was no exception.

When, during the Six Day War, IDF forces conquered the city of Qunaytriah in the Golan Heights, they gained access to many Syrian documents. One, from September 1965, describe how Jewish property was nationalized to fund Syrian intelligence activity along the border with Israel. According to the same document, released as early as July 1967 by the IDF Spokesman's Office, revenues on nationalized Jewish assets totaled $5,180 (apparently per month—the document does not specify), and represented 88% of the Syrian intelligence budget for the Golan Heights.[27]

What happened to Syria's Jews during the war, and in its immediate aftermath, was described in a 1970 Israeli Ministry of Education pamphlet. It should be kept in mind that its purpose was as propaganda but nonetheless appears based on actual fact:

> When the Six Day War broke out, many Jews in Aleppo and Damascus were arrested, while other members of the community lived in fear and distress. The Jews of Kamishli and Aleppo were down to their last crust of bread. Arab Palestinian refugees were moved into the Jewish quarter intentionally, prey on their fears, threaten them, taunt them, throw stones, and humiliate them in public. The Jewish cemetery in Damascus has been destroyed and a road paved over it. The Jews of Kamishli have a curfew, allegedly for "security" reasons, and freedom of movement has been taken away entirely from this small community.
>
> Other decrees reinstated at this time include not giving Jews telephones. Their drivers' licenses are not renewed after their expiration date, so that within a short time no Jew will be permitted to drive. As the last academic year was

starting, all Jewish schools in Syria were shut down. Prior to that, in July of last year [1969], Jewish teachers were banished from the Jewish schools, and Muslim teachers brought in instead, to prevent Jewish studies in these schools.

Reviewing these decrees, reinstated as of July last year, one gets the impression that things are not so bad. Doubtless, for Jews in several other Arab countries such as Egypt, Iraq and even Libya—the situation is dramatically worse than in Syria. But this is not because Syria is soft on Jews, quite the opposite; conditions for the Jews of Syria are among the worst in the Arab world. But their situation was difficult even before the Six Day War, and the Damascus authorities could do little over the past year to compound the misery that, in any case, runs rampant within the Syrian Jewish community. . . .

The economic situation for Syrian Jews is critical. As far as is known, there are no wealthy Jews among them. This is a merchant community, for the most part, dealing mainly in light commerce and peddling. There are also a few craftsmen, such as silver- and goldsmiths, and a few self-employed professionals. But Jews are not accepted to work in either civil or public service. Many other professions are also denied them.

Moreover, there is a boycott of Jewish stores. Documents captured by the IDF in the Golan Heights reveal an order, given by the Syrian Military Chief of Staff, forbidding the Syrian army, police other security forces, and their families, from shopping at Jewish stores, or conducting any transactions with Jews. Attached to this order was a detailed listing of Jewish shops. Economic conditions for Jews are bad all over Syria, and they require assistance from their American relatives. Things are worse in Aleppo and Kamishli, where the Jews are actually suffering from starvation. . . .

Syrian Jews live in ghetto conditions, already familiar to us from the dark days of our history.[28] They are closed up in their quarter, limited in terms of livelihood, stripped of basic civil liberties, subject to constant terror, oppression and repression. The Syrian people did not initiate these anti-Jewish measures, their source is the government, which bears direct responsibility for Jewish oppression.[29]

The same pamphlet presents an eyewitness account from a young man, 20 years old, who managed to escape Syria and come to Israel. The man, who remained anonymous, said:

After the [Six Day] war, many Jewish workers were laid-off, myself included, leaving them with no income. At first, the Jewish community aided their needy brothers with money collected from Jewish donations, but when the government got its hands on the Jewish funds, there was no point to collecting more money for this purpose. Economic conditions are very bad for Jews. Many are literally starving to death. I don't know how they can survive without income, and without community assistance. . . .

The Syrian government distributes weapons to the mob, and from time to time they run riot in the Jewish quarters, threaten Jewish lives, taking anything they can. To avoid outside interference, the Syrian government publishes false reports on the supposedly good conditions for Jews. When Red Cross staff members visited Damascus to clarify the Jewish situation, they were accompanied by Syrian officers on their visits to Jewish homes, so that the Jews would say only what the authorities were interested in having them say.

Conditions for the Jews of Kamishli and Aleppo are worse than in Damascus. In Kamishli, a curfew has been placed several times, lasting several weeks. The Jews could not buy food and were forced to ask their neighbors, in secret, to buy them food so they would not starve to death. Phylacteries and other holy relics belonging to the Kamishli Jews were collected by a malicious government official, and as the Jews watched, were burned in the town square.[30]

These stories bring to mind the book burnings and *Kristallnacht* of Nazi Germany.

American journalist William Tuohy of the *Los Angeles Times*, reported in August 1969 that the Jews of Syria were forbidden from either selling property or giving it as a gift. "If they manage, one way or another, to get out of the country, ownership will be transferred to the authorities," he emphasized. Although Tuohy quoted Jews who said their lives were not so bad (and it is unclear whether Tuohy was allowed to speak freely to his interviewees, out of the presence of government officials), he ended his article with a quote from a Syrian citizen: "I would not like to be a Jew in Syria today."[31]

Another piece written mainly for propaganda purposes is David Sitton's book *The Sephardic Communities Today*. Nevertheless, the stories presented are apparently based in fact. Sitton tells of a Syrian-Jewish merchant, Zaki Katzav, murdered in his home in the summer of 1973 by Syrian security officers, and a Jewish girl raped twice by policemen—the second time in front of her father. In 1973, a number of Aleppo Jews were arrested after their sons successfully escaped Syria for Israel.[32] Professor Harold M. Troper of the University of Toronto says that in March 1974, four young Jewish women were raped and murdered near the Syrian-Lebanese border. The authorities claimed the women were trying to flee the country and fell victim to their smugglers. Later on, two of the smugglers and two respectable Damascus Jews were arrested; they were tortured and forced to confess their part in the robbery, rape, and murder.[33]

Another account, the date of which is unknown, says the Jews of Syria did not suffer from poverty and starvation, but asks, "was man born only to eat and sleep?" According to the witness, the community was watched closely, and any purchase or sale of property required a permit from the security services. If a Jewish child was absent from school, detectives were sent immediately to the child's home to clarify what had happened and, consequently, every knock on the door inspired terror. Restrictions on movement remained in effect; the government allowed only a few Jews to leave the country on short trips to appease international criticism regarding its treatment of the Jews. Those allowed passage were required to put up large guarantees, and their families were kept hostage to ensure their return. Identity cards and passports held by Jews were stamped with the word "Jew," at first in red letters, and later in smaller blue ones.[34] They could not work in government and could not trade with government controlled agencies. Because of the system of centralized socialism, this meant trade with Syria's largest economic entities was off-limits to Jews.[35]

GRADUAL IMPROVEMENT UNDER ASSAD

In the mid-1970s, restrictions on travel for Jews relaxed slightly, and they were allowed temporary stays outside the country, after putting up a guarantee and leaving at least one family member behind. Other Jews risked illegal immigration to Lebanon or Turkey, en route to Israel. During these years, Toronto's Jewish—with its high concentration of Syrian Jews—organized in support of illegal immigration. A small group of activists, headed by Judy Feld-Carr, raised money and found ways to smuggle Jews out of Syria without paying for smugglers or exit visas. Most potential immigrants, who did not have relatives outside Syria to pay for their passage, were helped by someone known only as "Mrs. Judy." Concurrently, a small group of heroic Jews

Farangi Synagogue, Damascus, 1994 (photograph by ABPix)

put their personal safety on the line to work in Damascus and Aleppo, receiving funds from Toronto and ensuring they reached the proper recipient.[36]

The shift in conditions for the Jews of Syria was gradual and took twenty years. Rabbi Avraham Hamara, the last chief rabbi of Syria, says that in the early 1970s, President Assad allowed a limited number of Jews to exit the country for commercial or medical reasons, though entire families were not allowed to leave. "Maybe he wanted to hold us hostage," Hamara says today. In 1977, Assad met with then U.S. president Jimmy Carter. As a gesture, he allowed fourteen young Jewish women to leave Syria in order to marry members of the Syrian Jewish community in Brooklyn. Since then, over 300 Jewish women left Syrian under the same regulation. A major change occurred in 1992, when Assad agreed to allow Jews to leave Syria permanently, so long as they did not go to Israel. Over 4,000 Jews took advantage of this regulation.

There were two reasons for the change, Troper believes. First, just as the USSR had opened its gates in the early 1980s—clearing the way to unrestricted Jewish immigration—so, a decade later, Syria was interested in improving relations with West. This was especially true after the fall of the Eastern Bloc, to which Syria had been tied on the financial, diplomatic, and military levels for 30 years. Secondly, Syria did not wish to remain outside the peace process, which began after the 1991 Gulf War; granting exit visas to Jews was a sort of gesture to Israel and eliminated one obstacle in the way of Damascus's joining the process. Troper concludes: "This tortured remnant needed no additional inducement to pack its bags and leave, bringing down the final curtain on the millennium-old Syrian Jewish community."[37]

Not all left. As of this writing, there are still seventy Jews left in Damascus and one family in Kamishli. Some stayed because of business, others—as Rabbi Hamara puts it—"out of sheer stupidity." During the initial months of migration, taking property was forbidden in principle, as Syrian law did not allow the transfer of capital outside the country. However, Hamara says, almost everyone managed to do so, as the authorities turned a blind eye and enabled Jews to leave with the money received for their property. Hamara himself left a spacious house behind in Damascus ("I bought it a year earlier for $120,000, because we had no idea we were going to be allowed to leave. It's a large, beautiful house in a good neighborhood, with a pool in the yard"), along with his books and papers. "During the first two years, I traveled back and forth between New York and Damascus, to make sure everything was all right and because I thought I might return. When I immigrated to Israel in 1994, my brother-in-law tried to sell the house, but was told [by the Syrian authorities] that it was forbidden because the rabbi's house is like a synagogue, and cannot be sold," the rabbi says, smiling at the Syrians' patent untruth.

The Rambam Jewish school in Damascus, which
currently houses a government-run school, 1994
(photograph by ABPix)

As mentioned in the preceding chapter, private property belonging to
Jewish individuals who fled Syria is managed by a joint Palestinian-Syrian
committee that collects rent. Most of Damsacus's Jews lived within 10 to
15 minutes walking distance from the major open markets, in houses whose
modest facades belied their opulent interiors. In the past, they housed Palestinian refugees, but since the wave of Palestinian migration in 1992, they
stand shut and abandoned. To this day, the Jewish community owns the
community property, excluding the Alliance school, which since 1948 has
served as a Palestinian school. Some of the community's buildings are rented
out and the rent money deposited in the community chest. During the
1980s, these funds, together with donations from abroad, paid to refurbish
twenty-two synagogues in Damascus and the Great Synagogue of Aleppo.
Syria's land registry is very organized, Hamara adds, and every Jew who owns
a piece of real estate knows that, come the day, the precise records are there
to prove it.[38]

Chapter 11

"The Community Was Reduced to Ruin"

The Jews of Lebanon: Between Prosperity and Total Annihilation

The Jewish community of Lebanon—Beirut, to be more precise—was a sort of branch office for the Syrian Jewish community, both because this community's roots were in the neighboring country and because the two communities were strongly tied. Beirut's development as a port city, which transformed it into one of the central trade and financial centers of the Mediterranean, attracted Syrian Jews from as early on as the Ottoman Empire. During the mid-1900s, Beirut had 50,000 residents, of which 5,000 were Jews. Between the two world wars there were 6,000 Jews in Lebanon, half of them in Beirut. After the State of Israel was established, many Syrian Jews emigrated to Lebanon from Syria, raising the number of Jews in Lebanon to 9,000 in 1958. The most common professions for the Jews of Beirut were trade, brokering, and money changing.[1]

The good conditions under which the Jews of Lebanon lived may possibly be attributed to the fact that the entire country is a composition of different religions that, until the 1970s, was kept in a delicate balance. After World War I, when Great Britain captured Lebanon from the Ottoman Turks, control of Lebanon and Syria was mandated to the French. In August 1920, France created "Greater Lebanon" by annexing the Muslim regions in Tripoli, the Bekaa Valley, Sidon, and Tyre to the mainly Christian enclaves of Mount Lebanon.

In 1943, the heads of Lebanon's ethnic groups agreed to an unwritten national treaty, dividing the center of power between the major groups: Marronite Christians, Sunni Muslims, Shi'ite Muslims, and Druse. Despite several crises, this structure stayed in place until civil war broke out in 1975.

Ohel Ya'acov Synagogue, Aley, Lebanon, 1982
(photograph by Micha Bar-Am)

This was due mainly to demographic changes that reduced the amount of power held by Christians and increased the power held by Muslims (who were also reinforced by the presence of the PLO in Lebanon). The civil war, where both Israel and Syria interceded, continued intermittently until 1991, when Syria effectively managed to gain control of Lebanon.[2]

THE JEWS OF LEBANON AFTER THE ESTABLISHMENT OF THE STATE OF ISRAEL

In June 1948, the Jewish Agency estimated there were 7,000 Jews living in Beirut. According to a report prepared at that time by A. Abas, most Lebanese Jews, like their Syrian brethren, were traders, government officials, and "over the past two decades" Jewish lawyers and doctors had appeared on the scene.[3] Apparently, this data was correct regarding the Jews of Syria; as mentioned previously, the Jews of Lebanon dealt mainly in trade and related services.

The establishment of the State of Israel had little effect on the Jews of Lebanon, who continued their lives untroubled, even while battles raged between the Israeli and Lebanese armies and Israeli forces conquered fourteen villages in south Lebanon.[4] In July 1949, the Mossad le-Aliya Bet gathered eye-witness accounts from two Lebanese new immigrants, Ya'akov Molho and Avraham Beraha, who said Beirut's Jewish population had risen markedly, from between 4,000 and 5,000 two years earlier, to between 8,000 and 10,000 that year. "The situation of Beirut's wealthy Jews is very good," the pair continued. "Business is booming. There are Jewish doctors and Jewish lawyers. There is an official Jewish community, headed by Ya'akov Safra [father of well-known bankers Edmond, Moise and Joseph Safra], a banker from Aleppo, aged 60–65. The head of the Jewish committee in Beirut is Dr. Attiya . . . the rich Jews do not want to come to Israel. They have not suffered particularly. During the war with Israel, the Arabs took only 50,000 pounds from them, which is not a large amount for them."[5]

In June 1950, Zvi Yarkoni of the Mossad le-Aliya Bet wrote: "The situation in Lebanon is good, and Jews are not treated badly. As opposed to Syria, the government of Lebanon allows assets to be transferred abroad, excluding gold. Aside from the poorer classes that wish to come to Israel, those Jews remaining have no desire to leave Lebanon. The wealthy Lebanese Jews invest most of their money in buying buildings in Beirut, and are not interested in Israel, even though some of them own tracts of land and houses in Haifa." Lebanon even allowed the Syrian Jews free passage through its territory on their way to Israel, until Damascus began confiscating passports belonging to Jews, and Beirut announced it could not accept persons without documents.[6]

THINGS CHANGE—THE CIVIL WAR OF 1958

During those years, the most comprehensive report on Lebanon's Jews was issued in 1958 by Yosef Sedaka, a Lebanese-born Haifa merchant with good contacts among Beirut's economic elite. Sedaka was sent by IDF intelligence to Lebanon; the files on him in the Israeli Foreign Ministry archives do not mention his primary mission, and his name and identifying characteristics have been blocked out. Upon his return from Lebanon, he was interviewed by Jewish Agency officials, and told them:

Among Beirut's 8,000 Jews (almost all are concentrated in Lebanon's capital, and there are only 100 living in Sidon), there are approximately 400 who are ready to come to Israel. The only obstacle is the 200 Lebanese pound per person cost of illegal immigration.[7] These people are of the lowest social level in the Beirut Jewish community. At present, they live off donations of around 15–20 Lebanese pounds per week, allocated to them by the Jewish *mukhtar*, the contact person between them and the Community Council. They are also given free medical service (two doctors provided by the Community Council), and sometimes helped with housing. The children of the indigent study at schools on scholarships provided by the Community Council. . . .

Regarding the Jewish middle-class and well-to-do of Beirut, their immigration to Israel is prevented on one hand by the as yet still unsolved question of transferring assets,[8] and on the other hand, by rumors of lack of worthwhile capital investment opportunities in Israel.[9] They prefer emigration to Europe, and 1,000 Jews did emigrate last year from Beirut and Syria (as a large number of Jews in Beirut are Syrian, for example most of the Community Council members are from Damascus), to Italy, Belgium, Switzerland, and others.

Members of this class have no trouble arranging for passports and leaving Lebanon for Europe. Difficulties are overcome by leaving "hush money" in the appropriate places. "Arranging" a passport costs 400–500 Lebanese pounds. There are also 300 "foreign" Jews in Beirut, in other words, they hold Persian, Spanish, French and other passports. These passport-holders may leave the country, but [the authorities] make it very difficult for them to come back to Beirut.

The economic situation in Lebanon is very difficult, and Jews suffer from it as much as their Muslim and Christian neighbors. There is a great supply of product, but no turnover and no orders. As an example, Yosef Sedaka mentions the high commercial interest rates currently given in Beirut, of between 25% and 35%. Jewish businesses are not persecuted but nonetheless, most Jewish merchants have taken Arab partners, against any eventuality. Further evidence was the low amount of traffic in the Port of Beirut. This apparently results from the Syrian "boycott." They recently opened the Port of Latakia on the [northern] Syrian coast, to serve as an import and export point instead of Beirut in Lebanon.[10]

Despite worsening conditions for Lebanon's Jews, the overwhelming majority were still not interested in leaving the country, and handling of their affairs was also set aside. This is apparently the reason why, for a four-year period, the documentation makes no mention of the Lebanese community. Only in July 1958, at the height of the first civil war in Lebanon—which broke out after the internal balance of power was disturbed after Iraq's pro-Western royalist regime was toppled—did Israel again show interest in the Jews of Lebanon. This interest should also be viewed in light of Israel's indirect assistance of Lebanese president Kamil Sham'un, whose regime was saved with the intervention of U.S. military forces.[11] That same month, Haim Shadmi, the Jewish Agency emissary in Istanbul, reported to Baruch Duvdevani, a senior official at the Aliya department: "The situation in Lebanon is such that more and more Jews are ready to leave Lebanon for Israel. The situation for Jews in Lebanon is generally good, but there are certain families (25) whose circumstances are hard, and they have no way of getting to Istanbul. Each family requires 200–300 Syrian pounds in assistance."

A month later, Shadmi reported to Aliya department head Shlomo Zalman Shargay, that "individual families have recently begun arriving from Lebanon. They told me that many families are ready to leave, but they lack the means to buy airline tickets to Istanbul." Shadmi made an arrangement with German airline Lufthansa, which flew the immigrants from Beirut to Istanbul, after which El-Al flew them to Israel's Lod airport.[12] One interesting point is that Shadmi does not mention government interference, only the potential immigrants' limited financial resources. This may be due to Israel's links with the Sham'un regime, although there is no direct proof.

THE JEWISH EXODUS FROM LEBANON IN THE LATE 1950s

The Jewish Agency rushed in to help, as Duvdevani reported in November 1958:

> We have begun taking Jews out of Lebanon using the Lufthansa company. The price of the flight to Istanbul is [up to] $63 per person, according to age, as with every airline. We hope to receive a 10%–15% discount on every ticket, which would be returned to us as a donation. Generally, the people pay their fares, and we subsidize only the trips of those cannot pay their own way at all. For instance, 40-something Jews were sentenced to death because of their association with the Falange [former president Sham'un's Christian party that had both Jewish sympathizers and activists], and we are saving them. Of course, they are not paying for themselves, and we are obligated to pay for their trip. . . .
>
> In most cases, Lebanon's wealthy Jews do not go. The middle class families do, while the poor families wait for our funding. The Jewish immigration committee in Lebanon is made up of three very respected Jews who are members of the Community Council, such as Dr. Attiya, Yosef Kovo and Albert Abdullah Alya. The latter is our acting representative, and he decides who deserves our funding, and who does not.
>
> Lebanon's Jewish community is ruined after the strikes [accompanying the civil war], as a paradox occurred here that characterizes the Jewish situation in the Diaspora overall: During the [Muslim] Arab strikes, Jews were also required to strike so as not to be suspected of disloyalty. Yet, during the Falange counter-action, they were also required to strike. Of course, all this reduced the community to deep financial ruin. There are 8,000 Jews in Lebanon, of which half are Lebanese and half are Syrian. Most live in the city of Beirut, and some in Sidon, where there are 100 families numbering 550 persons.[13]

In September, Shadmi told his Israeli headquarters he needed $1,500, "to cover the cost of issuing passports, such as police B.R.B. [bribes], formal arrangements, and sometimes giving financial assistance to the poorest families to buy clothing. The local community helps out anyone wishing to leave for Israel, but the community's current financial state is bad, and they have asked for our assistance."[14]

A year later, in December 1959, Shadmi was able to report to the Israeli representatives of the Lebanese and Syrian immigrations that since beginning to handle the Lebanese Jewish matter, 1,000 persons had gone to Israel, many of them young people. At the same time, 4,000 Syrian Jews still remained in Lebanon and their "situation was very difficult. Their status is unclear as they have no documents, and no possibility of getting a passport to leave Lebanon." The Jewish Agency reached an agreement with the government of France, according to which France would issue travel documents for these individuals, but opposition from the Lebanese authorities shot the plan down. Later on, Beirut itself agreed to issue its own travel documents, and 150 Syrian Jews managed to leave in this way, before the Lebanese government changed its position. These difficulties were expressed by the fact that in 1959, only 239 Jews left Lebanon for Israel—only one quarter of the previous year's amount.[15]

In 1959, the Jewish Agency staff noted that Jews migrating from Lebanon preferred destinations other than Israel. In fact, this was first hinted at by Jordanian paper *Falasteen*, which wrote—in an anti-Semitic vein—that, "Reports from Beirut say that 32 Jewish business-owners are liquidating their businesses and assets in Beirut before emigrating to Brazil. From the beginning of this year, over 400 Jewish Lebanese merchants, and Syrian Jewish merchants residing in Lebanon, have gone to Brazil. Because they are required to liquidate their businesses, the Jews sell off their shops at cheap prices, and sometimes even waive their rights to key-money. These Jews are concentrated in a village, established with Zionist capital from Sao Paulo, in order to [increase] the number of Jews in Brazil, and their ability to take over trade there."[16]

The Latin American division at Israel's Ministry of Foreign Affairs asked the Israeli embassy in Rio de Janeiro to look into the matter, and in late October Alexander Dotan, the embassy's temporary *chargé d'affaires,* sent back a detailed report. He said most of the Jews arriving in Brazil were assisted by the international Jewish organizations, including the Jewish Agency (although this seems unlikely), the Joint Distribution Committee, and Hebrew Immigrant Aid Society (HIAS). Dotan reported that, as of late 1958, eighty-four Jews had arrived in Brazil from Lebanon including Syrian Jews who were mainly from Aleppo. Additionally, at that time the HIAS center in Paris was handling 300 requests from Lebanese and Syrian Jews wishing to migrate to Brazil.

Dotan continued:

> Travel expenses for the Lebanese, Syrian and Egyptian Jews is funded mainly by HIAS. . . . HIAS houses immigrants in Rio for up to three weeks in a hotel, and helps with job searches. Assistance in arranging for work, housing,

professional training, loans for rehabilitation and education is shared by HIAS, the Joint Distribution Committee and the local [Jewish] social service institutions. . . . Aside from social welfare cases, there is generally no problem in arranging for jobs, for those willing and able to work. Things are hard for those who want to get rich quick, but lack the capabilities, at least in their first years here. The Egyptians, for example, managed to settle in fairly well as clerks, and industry and trade "professionals," because in contrast to professionals found here in Brazil, any quick-witted person with a minimal education can sell himself as a "expert." I was told, for example, that after the Joint brought a number of Egyptian Jews to work at a Sao Paolo car factory, as clerks, warehouse managers, and foremen, the factory asked them to find another 200 'experts' at any price. On the other hand, assimilation is difficult for the Lebanese and Syrian Jews who know only Arabic, and for the most part, can't find work except as peddlers, or in small businesses.[17]

The files do not indicate how matters were handled afterwards.

THE 1960s—DESTRUCTION OF THE LEBANESE JEWISH COMMUNITY

Jewish emigration from Lebanon continued throughout the 1960s. In 1969, the Lebanese paper *al-Sa'id* summarized what had happened over the previous decade, as quoted by David Sitton:

Although the Jews of Lebanon enjoy the full benefit of Lebanese citizenship, with all the rights it grants, although they deal in trade and industry, in banking and finance, in complete freedom without impediment, and although the authorities grant them special protection in their residential areas during any public demonstrations in Lebanon—despite all this, the Jews have begun liquidating their affairs, selling their property and withdrawing their capital from the economy in preparation for their emigration. The reasons for Jewish emigration from Lebanon is not rooted in any immediate danger, but due to unfounded fears of impending anti-Jewish riots.

Jewish migration from Lebanon, which accelerating in 1964, reached major proportions only after the June 1967 war.[18] The Jew first prepares a passport. Afterwards he makes sure to liquidate his affairs, and gradually sell his property. He does this to ensure against significant material loss, and to safeguard against attack by his enraged neighbors. Before leaving, Jews who are not Lebanese citizens sign a declaration stating that they promise never to return to Lebanon. The Lebanese authorities enter their name on a blacklist, and their right to re-enter Lebanon is taken away.

For many years already, Jewish merchants have felt the [effect of the] boycott enacted by their neighbors, as a hostile reaction to the State of Israel. Under these conditions, and in preparation for leaving Lebanon, the Jews decided to freeze commercial activities. Given this background, it is easy to explain the wave of bankruptcies flooding Lebanon in recent years. The main cause of this is the withdrawal of Jewish capital from the economy.

In 1969, no more than 3,000 Jews remain in Lebanon, out of 15,000 Jews once holding Lebanese citizenship; and 200 out of 500 families either without any citizenship, or Syrian and Iraqi citizens. Informed sources say that by the end of next year [1970] no more than a few hundred Jews will remain in Lebanon. Most of the commercial companies once owned by Jews have become companies with shares held by Lebanese, that is to say Christians or Muslims, as the Jews turn them into public companies, and sell shares to their neighbors. The Jews of Lebanon are 'happier' than their brothers in Syria and Iraq, whose governments forbid them from leaving those countries.[19]

Only twenty Jewish families remained in Lebanon by 1997, almost all in Beirut. The World Jewish Congress reported that, "Because of the current political situation, Jews are unable to openly practice Judaism. There is a committee in Beirut which represents the community." The WJC further noted that "In contrast to their co-religionists in other Arab countries, Lebanese Jews were almost always free to emigrate and some were permitted to liquidate their property prior to emigration and expatriate the proceeds."[20]

Chapter 12

"Our Account with the Arab World"

Israeli Policy and Attitudes of Immigrants from Arab Countries Toward the Question of Property

The only time the government of Israel made any sort of policy regarding property belonging to Jews from Arab countries was in March 1951. How the decision was made, immediately after Jewish assets were frozen in Iraq, has already been described in Chapter 3. The declaration that determined Israeli policy, made to Israel's Knesset by then-Minister of Foreign Affairs Moshe Sharett, bears repeating:

> By freezing the property of scores of Jews coming to Israel . . . the government of Iraq has opened an account between itself and the State of Israel. There is an account between us and the Arab world, and it is the amount of compensation owed to the Arabs who left the State of Israel's territory and abandoned their property, following the war of aggression of the Arab world against our country. The act perpetrated now by the government of Iraq regarding the property of Jews, who did not break Iraqi law, disturb its status, or undermine its security, [now] forces us to link the two accounts. Therefore, the government [of Israel] has decided notify the appropriate UN institutions, and I state this in the plural, that the value of Jewish property frozen in Iraq will be taken into account by us, in [calculating] the compensation we undertake to pay those Arabs who abandoned their property in Israel.

KNESSET DEBATES ON PROPERTY BELONGING TO JEWS FROM ARAB COUNTRIES

For twenty-four years, the Knesset was never asked to attend to the matter, until late 1974, when member of Knesset Mordechai Ben-Porat proposed that "exercising the rights of Jews from Arab countries" be put on the daily agenda. The plenum discussed the issue in January 1975 and decided to hand the matter over to the Foreign Relations and Security Committee for further discussion. The committee got around to the subject in November 1975, and issued the following decision:

1. For centuries, Jews lived in Arab countries. In most [countries], Jews were cruelly persecuted and considered low class. With their longings for the land of their forefathers, and because of persecution of the Jewish community that escalated with the Arab war against Israel, most Jews left the Arab countries, and the overwhelming majority came to Israel. The Jews who escaped were not able to take out their property. This property was stolen, confiscated, frozen or nationalized.

2. The bloody attacks waged by Arab gangs against the Jewish settlement in the Land of Israel, prior to the establishment of the State [of Israel], and the invasion of Arab armies into the State of Israel's territory, immediately upon its establishment on 15.4.48, caused Israel's Arab residents to flee to Arab countries. This process was abetted by the Arab leaders who called on the Arab population to leave Israel, despite Israel's appeal to this population to stay and live in peace with its Jewish residents.[1]

3. The flight of Israel's Arab residents to the Arab countries, and the exodus of a comparable number of Jews from Arab countries to Israel expressed, in essence, a population exchange, examples of which this century has seen take place in a number of places around the world. While the State of Israel rehabilitated and absorbed the Jews arriving from Arab countries without means, both socially and economically, the Arab countries did not do everything in their power to absorb, as citizens with equal rights, the Arabs arriving from Israel.

4. The Arab countries must pay the Jews who left them, proper compensation on stolen assets and property, as well as on the severe oppression which caused them great suffering. They must also return cultural and religious items left behind to the Jewish community.

5. Israel, for its part, announced that within the framework of a peace agreement, it is willing to compensate the Arab population who left the State. Discussions on compensation will take into account the rights of Jews who were forced to leave Arab countries, and abandon their property.

6. The Committee calls on the nations of the world and the international organizations to help Jewish from Arab countries exercise their rights.[2]

The Knesset approved the decision made by the Foreign Relations and Security Committee. The plenum dealt again with the matter in July 1987, following submissions to the daily agenda made by Knesset members Benjamin Ben-Eliezer and Eliahu Ben-Elissar. Ben-Eliezer, who was born in Iraq, said: "I was a boy of twelve who left his home and his family behind in Iraq. Following paths unknown, in suffering and pain, I finally reached the Land of Israel. About a year later, my parents followed with nothing in hand, having left behind all their property and our family property. My family lived in a shantytown [in Israel] for almost two years; my late father began rebuilding his family here. In suffering and pain he succeeded in establishing and rehabilitating our family, but to my regret, did not live to see the fruits of his labor."

Ben-Eliezer described how Arabian Jews were forced to flee the lands of their birth, leaving behind their personal and community property, adding: "This century has known many refugees. The term 'refugee' has become synonymous with a reality we must all identify with. This phenomenon has crossed borders, nations and cultures; in many cases this reality has led to surprising revelations of goodwill on the part of individuals, societies, states and nations. In this case alone—the matter in general of Jewish refugees who came to Israel, and specifically Jews from the Arab world—is the subject denied."

In his response, then Deputy Prime Minister and Minister of Foreign Affairs Shimon Peres reiterated the operative Israeli policy: "The problem of Jewish property in Arab countries was raised, and will be raised, in talks between us and the Arab countries. . . . At the same time, the State is collecting information on the fate of this property and its location, in hope that we may bring up the subject in the future, when we reach peace negotiations with the other Arab countries." With Peres's approval, it was decided that the Knesset plenum would debate the matter in October 1987, concurrent to the third international congress of the World Organization of Jews from Arab Countries (WOJAC).

Ben-Eliezer introduced that debate and clearly defined the link between the problem of Jewish property in Arab countries and the question of compensation for Palestinian refugees. "Every time the matter of diplomatic arrangements in the region comes up," Ben-Eliezer said, "the world only remembers the problems of the Palestinian refugees. The fact that hundreds of thousands of Jews from Arab countries were absorbed by the State of Israel—in contrast to Palestinian refugees who were not absorbed by Arab countries because the Arab world, mainly the Palestinian Liberation Organization, turned them into political tools and hostages—does not erase the problem of these Jews, and the denial of their rights."

Once again, Peres answered by repeating Israel's standing policy.

Many families living today in Israel were forced to leave behind their personal property in Arab countries, along with vast community property, property which has not only material worth, but are also repositories of history, culture and invaluable emotion. These facts were evident to all of Israel's previous governments, and continue evident before the present government, of course. . . . We ask that these people, who lived for generations in Arab countries, and whose property was stolen, be compensated for theft and loss of property. . . . At the appropriate occasion of talks, which I believe will happen, we will make our demand to return property that belonged to Jews, or at least receive proper compensation in return. In our agreements with the Arab countries, we will emphasize the advantage of arranging the cases of Jews from Arab countries.

The debate included an almost unanimous Knesset decision, stating, among other things:

> Most Jewish immigrants to Israel came with almost nothing, having left behind in their countries of origin, large amounts of assets, great culture and wealth. Even today, although their integration into the daily life of the State is *faits accomplis,* the Knesset has determined that the Arab countries must compensate them for property stolen, confiscated, frozen or nationalized, for the severe oppression that was their lot, and return to the communities all cultural and religious assets. Israel, for its part, announces that within the framework arrangement for peace, it will be willing to compensate the Arab population that left the State. Discussions of compensation will take into account the rights of Jews forced to leave the Arab countries, and abandon their property.[3]

The idea of attaching Palestinian and Jewish property was hatched not in Jerusalem, but rather in Damascus. In January 1951, two months prior to Sharett's Knesset address, Syria's Ministry of Foreign Affairs submitted a proposal to the Arab League General Secretariat, requesting a discussion of reprisals against Israel, due to its appropriation of abandoned Palestinian property. The General Secretariat handed the Syrian proposal over to its legal department, which issued an opinion only in December 1951. Briefly put, the opinion stated that confiscating Jewish assets in Arab countries could be interpreted indirectly as recognizing the State of Israel's right to exist, something the Arab countries denied vehemently. The legal department suggested the Arab countries revoke the citizenship of their Jewish inhabitants and reclassify them as citizens of the enemy—in this way, the Arab League accepted the Iraqi position, Iraq having implemented precisely this policy two years earlier.

Egypt's attorney general, Wahid Rafat, reached a similar conclusion a few months later. In his opinion, international law in principle allowed the Arab countries to freeze only the property belonging to their Jewish citizens, not the property of foreign nationals living within their borders. Rafat warned: "Touching assets belonging to Jews who are not Israeli citizens [and therefore might be considered 'enemies'] is cause for international intervention on the part of foreign governments, who will protect the property [rights] of their Jewish citizens."

But Rafat also emphasized that touching property belonging to Egyptian Jews violated the constitution, which ensured equality among citizens. Passage of a special law for this purpose, "certainly would be unacceptable for many, who see the Jews of Egypt as people well-integrated into the daily life of the State, with no proof that they have betrayed Egypt, their homeland, to date."[4] It should be noted that these words were written before the revolution of 1952, after which Nasser and his regime might have felt themselves exempt—officially, not morally—from these instructions.

CLAIMS REGISTRATION FOR NEW IMMIGRANTS FROM ARAB COUNTRIES

The only practical expression of Israeli attention to the problem of property belonging to new immigrants from Arab countries was claims registration, which began in the early 1950s, in the case of Iraq. As noted in Chapter 3, the Bureau for External Claims began registering claims in November 1949, though response was low. Therefore, in July 1950, the bureau published an announcement in the newspapers, calling on all immigrants from Arab countries to come forth and document their claims, as "the government can protect the rights of all citizens in any negotiations [with Arab countries] only if it has full details on property in its possession. Property owners who do not notify [the authorities] may not benefit from any agreement signed by the government, and it will have no recourse but to withdraw its support of those [unregistered] claims on property." But the announcement had no real effect. In February 1956, before the expulsion of the Jews from Egypt, Israel's foreign currency division at the Ministry of Finance (which was in charge of the claims registration), had 5,262 claims amounting to $13,373,584, divided as follows:

Egypt: 176 claims—$2,171,196

Saudi Arabia: 18 claims—$4,260

Iraq: 3,040 claims—$48,796,014

Yemen: 43 claims—$191,502

Syria: 150 claims—$2,507,532

Trans-Jordan: 48 claims—$9,826,780

Parts of the Land of Israel not under Israeli control: 1,587 claims—$38,677,701

Absentee Arab property: 118 claims—$698,576[5]

This list, the latest and most complete of the files open to the public, requires some explanation. First, it is unclear why there are claims relating to "parts of the Land of Israel not under Israeli control." The intention apparently relates to property left behind or destroyed in Jewish settlements conquered by Arab armies. The same is true of Trans-Jordan; it must be assumed that the claims relate to property belonging to residents of the Old City of Jerusalem's Jewish quarter. Second, it is hard to understand what "absentee Arab property" is doing on this list, unless this relates to Palestinians with property in Arab countries who could not access it, for one reason or another, after Israel's War of Independence. Certainly, they were not

Israeli citizens, otherwise they would not have been classified as "absentee Arabs."

Another important note regards the relationship between the number of claims and the number of new immigrants to Israel from Arab countries, certainly as regards new immigrants from the four countries dealt with in this book. In 1948–1952, 11,917 Jews immigrated to Israel from Egypt, 125,305 from Iraq, and 3,257 from Syria and Lebanon. Of these, 21% of the families had six or more members, with an average number of four family members.[6]

Every claim represents one family. Given this, we may calculate the following: more than 31,000 families immigrated to Israel from Iraq, but only 3,040 claims were filed. Therefore, it may be assumed that the value of property belonging to the new immigrants was ten times the amount registered, or close to $500 million. Almost 3,000 families emigrated from Egypt, but only 176 claims were filed, making the estimated value of property 17 times higher than registered, or $37 million. There were 800 families that immigrated from Syria and Lebanon, and 232 claims were filed; the same calculations reveal claims of over $10 million. The estimated value of claims for all four countries is $574 million in 1956 terms, or $3.15 billion in today's terms. Once again it must be emphasized: The calculations do not take into account property belonging to the legions of Egyptian Jews deported after the Sinai Campaign.

In September 1969, the Israeli government decided to reopen claims registration for immigrants from Iraq, Egypt, Syria and Yemen. The responsibility for claims registration was given to a special department created within the Ministry of Justice, which was asked to coordinate all claims already registered by the various immigrant organizations and institutions. Similarly, the division was to cite the orders under which Jewish assets were confiscated in those countries, organize evidence of Jewish persecution, and register personal and community claims regarding property damage and physical harm. "The time will come when this material, organized by the division, will be used as a basis for these claims against these specific countries, and international entities," the decision mandated. Then legal counsel on Arab law at the Ministry of Justice, Professor Ya'akov Meron, was put in charge of the division, which he still heads today.[7]

The division's claims registry is not among the files open to the public, but at least one document indicates that the matter was handled very slowly, if at all. In October 1970, the World Sephardi Federation (WSF) turned to the members of Knesset, saying that "to date, the work has not been done," and requesting that claims registration be stepped up. Here too, there is no indication that things began moving after the appeal. According to Mordechai Ben-Porat (who, after ending his term as a Mossad le-Aliya Bet emissary in Iraq, entered politics, serving both as Knesset member and government minister), "They began registration, but it wasn't serious; they did not invest money in the project, and did not ask the immigrant associations for assistance."[8]

Another thirty years passed before the claims registration initiative was again raised. In mid-1999, The American Sephardic Jewish Federation (ASJF), a branch of the WSF began distributing a claims registration questionnaire among Sephardic immigrant communities in Israel and the world, to register private houses, local synagogues, and workplaces. The project was initiated by Bobby Brown, advisor on Diaspora affairs to then-Prime Minister Benjamin Netanyahu. In introducing the questionnaire, ASJF president Leon Levy said: "Clearly no one believes the Arab countries will compensate their Jews, but that is not our prime objective. We must have a counter-claim to Palestinian claims, to serve Israel in negotiating a permanent [peace] settlement."[9]

In the cover letter to the questionnaire, Amram Attias, chairman of the ASJF's committee of Jews from Arab countries, writes: "We must not forget that as part of the final negotiation process between the Israel and the Arab countries there will be an Arab claim on abandoned property. We must demand that the Israeli representatives involved in the process present our claims, against the Arab claims." Questionnaire recipients were asked to give details not only regarding personal property, but on any community property they knew of—synagogues, schools, hospitals, soup kitchens, ritual baths—as well as their neighborhoods. As of this writing, in April 2001, results of this survey have not yet been published.

WOJAC ACTIVITIES

The Jewish immigrants from Arab countries did not directly ask the Israeli government to act in restoring their property. Most of the activity on their behalf is carried out by the World Organization of Jews from Arab Countries (WOJAC). Founded in 1975 by a group of Israeli and other immigrant associations for Jews from Arab countries, WOJAC was headed by Mordechai Ben-Porat and Swiss-Jewish millionaire Leon Tamman. The timing of WOJAC's establishment after the 1973 Yom Kippur War, and at the height of negotiations over interim agreements with Egypt and Syria, was not coincidental. The founders were sure a doorway to Middle East peace was opening and that property claims by Jews from Arab countries would be raised as part of negotiations. WOJAC is registered as a non-profit organization in Israel, has 300 members (43 on the board of directors), one full-time staff member, two part-time staff members, 35 volunteers, and 11 branches around the world.

Ben-Porat says WOJAC's primary goal was to save the small Jewish communities left in Iraq, Syria, and Yemen. The matter of property belonging to those who had already left the Arab countries, he claims, was secondary. As WOJAC chairman and businessman Oved Ben-Ezer explains: "WOJAC's central role was political and civic—to raise public awareness about the legitimate rights of Jews from Arab countries—not register material claims."

WOJAC's main contention is that what happened since the founding of the State of Israel was a de facto exchange of populations between Israel and the Arab countries. WOJAC data shows that 600,000 Palestinians left Israel, and 800,000 Jews left the Arab countries, of which 600,000 settled in Israel. But while Israel absorbed its new arrivals, the Arab countries did almost nothing to help the Palestinian refugees. WOJAC contends that while the world should not ignore Palestinian distress, it must remember that an equal number of Jews also suffered—at least in material terms.

WOJAC's main public relations tools were three international congresses: Paris in 1975, London in 1983, and Washington in 1987. Participants included politicians, public figures, and academics from many countries. WOJAC has also organized many local congresses, and its representatives have participated in international forums and diplomatic platforms; WOJAC sends speakers to Jewish and non-Jewish audiences, maintains press contacts, organizes exhibitions, publishes booklets and research in several languages. This activity has brought about several major achievements, including the aforementioned Knesset debate. The U.S. Congress has also expressed its support for WOJAC's campaign for Jewish liberation from Arab countries, and in December 1987 called for the Arab governments, Syria in particular, to cease holding Jews hostage. Leading Israeli public figures, chiefly Shimon Peres and Benjamin Netanyahu, have expressed public support for WOJAC's central objectives.

An important public relations coup was scored in October 1987, when two leading American legislators held a public trial, which ended with the adoption of WOJAC principles. The tribunal was headed by former UN Ambassador and U.S. Supreme Court Justice Arthur J. Goldberg together with Professor Irwin Kotler of Harvard Law School. The two heard testimony, some quite shocking, given by Jews from Arab countries. At the end, it was decided that a population exchange had indeed taken place between Israel and the Arab countries. Jewish immigrants from Arab countries were integrated into Israeli society, whereas Arab countries put Palestinians in refugee camps. The Palestinian refugees were handled largely by the United Nations Relief and Works Association (UNRWA), which had spent $2.9 billion to this end by 1986; Israel had funded the absorption of Jewish refugees from Arab countries by itself.

The tribunal determined that Jews from Arab countries were refugees whose assets were confiscated in contravention of international law, and in most cases, whose basic civil rights were taken away. Goldberg and Kotler called on the Arab countries to recognize the rights of Jewish refugees and the international community to assist in granting them compensation, along with compensation to Palestinian refugees. They also recommended the establishment of an international claims committee within the framework of any future peace agreement, to deal with claims from refugees all over the Middle East, both Jews and Arabs. The conclusion was that continued silence on the part of Israel, and the Jewish people, regarding the claims of Jews from Arab countries, was intolerable.[10] We will soon see that silence on this matter is the cornerstone of Israel's policy. Surprisingly, WOJAC believes this policy is enlightened and correct.

WOJAC ON THE VERGE OF COLLAPSE

Ironically, WOJAC's last international congress took place thirteen years before these lines were written, and now, at the height of the Middle East peace process, the organization has all but disappeared. The reason is very simple: lack of funding. For most of its existence, WOJAC was funded by Leon Tamman who, according to Ben-Ozer, "gave millions and funded the international congresses." Since Tamman's death in 1995, WOJAC does not solicit private donors officially, "in order not to be dependent on one

Oved Ben-Ozer, co-chairman of the World Organization of Jews from Arab Countries (WOJAC) (photograph by Yossi Zeliger)

individual," and instead depends on the Israeli government and the Jewish Agency.

One diplomatic source in Jerusalem offers a different view of WOJAC. "This organization does nothing. They exist only to exist. The entire budget goes to rent, travel and salaries, nothing is spent on any real activity. There are no receipts, no paperwork. In 1998, Israel's State Comptroller came down hard on the Ministry of Foreign Affairs for supporting WOJAC, and for this reason, support was withdrawn."

Indeed the State Comptroller, former justice Eliezer Goldberg, wrote in his May 1999 report:

> The Comptroller has revealed that for over 20 years, the public affairs budget for the Ministry [of Foreign Affairs] has included an allocation to WOJAC, given to the organization without being discussed by an allocations committee. ... The [WOJAC] budget proposal submitted to the Ministry for its 1997 allocation included activities such as: recording data on property claims by Jews from Arab countries, research and publication, educational activity abroad. But recent reports obtained by [the public affairs division] in reviewing the organization's 1996 balance sheet do not include these activities, only costs for keeping an office, secretary and manager. The Ministry's 1997 allocation to the organization was NIS 85,000.
>
> In May of that same year, Ministry representatives visited the organization to examine closely the extent of its work. Ministry reports show an organization whose activity is very slow. Ministry representatives recommend not increasing the organization's allocation, and examining its contribution to the Ministry's field of responsibility. In 1998, the Ministry allocated NIS 92,000, the same sum as the previous year, adjusted for inflation. In our findings, the Ministry did not examine what use the organization made with the allocated funds, or to what extent the allocation contributes to promotional activities. In its response [to the State Comptroller] the Ministry announced that, after reexamination, it found the organization's activity was important, and would continue its budget support."

In response, Ben-Ozer says the problem is that no one is willing to fund WOJAC.

> In the past two or three years, both the government of Israel and the Jewish Agency have said that claims must be registered. We submitted a budget proposal: newspaper ads, pollsters, direct appeals to synagogues and clubs. We asked for $1 million for a three year period, stressed that the current generation was dying out, and this was our last chance to register claims. The Jewish Agency said it had no sources of funding for us, and Avraham Burg, who was the Jewish Agency chairman at that time, said he would speak to the World Jewish Congress—but nothing came of it. Afterwards, the government came asking for the claims registry, and we asked how were we to fund it with an annual budget of NIS 100,000 [$25,000] and a half-time office secretary; one newspaper ad alone costs NIS 10,000.

We said, the World Jewish Congress has experience because of its handling of the Holocaust victims' assets, so let's use that experience in handling Jewish property in Arab countries. We asked Zalman Shoval, then Israel's ambassador to the US [and Ben-Ozer's business partner], to meet with WJC president Edgar Bronfman, and WJC secretary-general Israel Singer. Singer told Shoval that the WJC did have experience, but would require funding. We again pressured the Ministry of Foreign Affairs to ask the WJC to take on the matter of Arab countries, or fund WOJAC. We received no reply.

WJC executive-director Ilan Steinberg says in response:

The WJC is firm in its commitment to raising the question of Jewish assets in Arab countries, although it is clear to us that this is a political question, beyond being a moral question. Some claim the issue should not be raised, as it will cause the Palestinians to bring up their own claims; the fact is that they have already brought up their claim. Because of the matter's extreme sensitivity, it will be handled in coordination with Israel's government and other relevant organizations, such as WOJAC and the WSF. We are ready to cooperate in all areas, including funding, though I did not say we would provide full funding.

In Steinberg's opinion, there are similarities between the problem of Jewish assets in Arab countries, and the Holocaust victims' assets—an issue the WJC has dealt with intensively since 1995.

The similarity is that Jewish property was stolen and not returned, and due to political considerations, the necessary efforts were not made. But of course, there is a great difference: the Arabs are not Nazis, the Arab countries did harm the Jewish communities and robbed them of their possessions, but made no attempt to wipe out Judasim. As in the case of Holocaust assets, the survivors play a leading role, we expect the same of the relevant organizations representing Jews from Arab countries. We have already announced that we represent the moral and political demands, and initial efforts are already underway to raise awareness of the matter among Jews from Arab countries, along with preliminary research.

In response to the question, does he believe that Jews from Arab countries were prejudiced against, relative to European immigrants, on the matter of property, Ben-Ozer says with emotion and even some anger:

What complete nonsense. They burned the Jews of Europe, not a trace was left; how can it compare? How can someone make a claim like this? A man received 500 marks—a broken man, sitting in a room or half a room—to buy a sweater or better food from the grocery store; am I that petty?! In 1950-1951, there were two great waves of immigration to Israel—Romania and Iraq. The Romanians were shattered by Nazi and Communist persecution, while within a short period of time the Iraqis created a bourgeoisie; before that they were either wealthy or paupers. Iraqi immigrants were doctors, engineers, accountants, assessment officials—within a year or two they controlled the system. True, they lived in shantytowns, and times were hard. True, these immigrants came without property, but their cultural and intellectual faculties were intact. They were not a broken people like the Europeans.

Of the State Comptroller's report, Ben-Ozer says: "If you ask for a NIS 400,000 [$100,000] budget, and you're given only NIS 85,000—of course you're not going to be able to do much. As far as I'm concerned, let them say 'No' and shut us down. I hope that this year [2000] we will receive our budget; to date, we haven't received anything. We all volunteer and do it for the good of the State; if the State doesn't want that—shut us down, for goodness sake." In April 2001, WOJAC was still active.

Another complaint raised by WOJAC insiders is the role played by Raphael Fallah, a Jewish merchant of Lybian extraction, living in Rome, and with extensive ties to the Arab world. As of this writing, Fallah is co-chairman of WOJAC, in parallel to his role as advisor to Palestinian Authority chairman Yasser Arafat on Jewish investment in the occupied territories. "His interests do not match those of the State of Israel," sources in Jerusalem say. "He wishes to transfer Jewish property not to Israel, but to other destinations. A man like that can—unintentionally and naively—harm the interests of those Jewish property owners, and most likely, also harm Israel's interests."

Ben-Ozer rejects this critique as well.

Fallah is one of WOJAC's founders, together with Tamman from day one. Years before Israel kissed Arafat's cheek, he held the same opinions as [controversial Israeli left-wing politician and journalist] Uri Avneri—talk with the PLO, establish a Palestinian state—but with one difference: He actually had ties to the Arab world and Arafat. One bright day, Fallah became the darling of the Israeli establishment, transferring messages to and fro, received by the Prime Minister and Minister of Defense. Now, when he arrives in Israel, he's received by the Prime Minister's Office within 24 hours.

And what about Fallah's calling card, stating his occupation as Arafat's advisor?

He's everyone's advisor—mine, yours, Arafat's and Ehud Barak's. He has no assignment from Arafat; Arafat hands out titles to everyone, he'll give you one too.

Last year [in 1999], WOJAC was in very dire straits. We hadn't paid our secretary for six months, and we had a NIS 100,000 [$25,000] deficit. We called a WOJAC board meeting, attended by the founders, and decided to close the business. Heskel M. Haddad, a well-known ophthalmologist from New York, said he was prepared to maintain the New York office and cover the Israeli deficit. But Haddad's opinions are far right, which do not always complement Israeli government policy, and we did not want him to speak for the international organization, and embarrass the Israeli government. Then Fallah came and said: "You have no right to close WOJAC; if you shut it down in Tel Aviv, I'll keep operating in Rome." He promised to cover the deficit, allocating $150,000 out of pocket to operating the organization, and holding an international WOJAC congress to decide on the organization's future and method of operation. Fallah said: "I don't want anything in return, just to be the chairman abroad, alongside the Israeli chairman,"—that's me—and the offer was accepted. He has more rights than any other WOJAC activist, including the Israeli ones.[11]

THE ABSENCE OF AN ISRAELI POLICY ON ARABIAN-JEWISH ASSETS

Superseding all organizational and personal questions is the question of actual Israeli policy towards assets belonging to Jews from Arab countries. The answer is unequivocal and clear: The policy is that there no policy. Says one deeply involved source:

Israel has no policy on the matter, and in my opinion, this is not due to negligence. But if there was at least a guiding hand, someone to say: "This matter is politically inconvenient,"—fine. The problem is, they don't even say that, and there's no one in the Israeli government whose job it is to deal with the matter. Let me be clear about this: we have a problem with Palestinian claims, and that's the reason for, on one hand, collecting information on Jewish property in Arab countries—just in case, perhaps to be used in negotiations with them—yet on the other hand, they don't want to bring up [Jewish] claims.

The Ministry of Foreign Affairs conducted a tiny sample study of Jewish claims, and it was very hard to arrive at an estimated valuation. But according to that sampling, the ratio of claims is 22:1 in the Palestinians' favor. In February 1999, the Palestinians presented a $670 billion compensations claim before the European Union Commission, regarding assets, use of those assets and emotional distress. For Israel, the higher the amount, the better, because it increases the chances that no one will take the claim seriously. But there's no question that there is a problem, because they speak very rationally about a minimum $13 billion in [abandoned] property, in 1948 terms.[12]

The question of calculating assets—Palestinian and Jewish—for the purpose of compensation is a complex legal matter. Should claims be made according to values at the time of the confiscation/freezing/robbery, or the date when the claim was filed? Naturally, differences could be enormous; what was once an agricultural field could have become an oil field, miserable hovels might have given way to luxury high-rises. The approach accepted by the international community is "as is," or calculating property according to its value at the time it was taken from the owners. This approach was also adopted regarding Holocaust victims' assets, in cases where the stolen

"Declaration of property and claims in the Arab states," submitted by a Jew formerly from Iraq to the Israeli government, January 1953 (Author's Collection)

2254/30/52

E

CONFIDENTIAL

British Embassy,

BAGDAD.

10th December, 1952.

Dear Secretariat,

E Q110/4/1

As you know, one of the biggest obstacles to economic and social progress in this country is the problem of the inefficiency of the Iraqi administration.

2.   A particular aspect of this has recently been giving us direct cause for concern, since during the last six months there has been a noticeable deterioration in the handling of the salary and accounts of the British officials employed by the Iraq Government. This has resulted in numerous delays in the payment of monthly salaries, and in some cases failure to pay allowances which were due.

3.   The first result of the new Government's decision to purge its Ministries has been the dismissal from the Iraq Ministry of Finance of the seven remaining Jewish clerks. One of these used to handle the British officials affairs, and although he was anything but efficient, he had at least a knowledge of accounting procedure.

4.   The Iraqis have now left themselves, in all their departments, with hardly any trained accountants. Is there any possibility of arranging short courses of six to nine months duration in government accounting for some of the Moslem Iraqi officials who have recently been given Accounts jobs in the Ministries? If so, I think we might be able to persuade the Iraq Government to send one or two at a time under the Development Board's Scheme for financing training abroad.

Yours sincerely

Robert Belgrave

(T.R.D. Belgrave)

Middle East Secretariat,
     Foreign Office,
          S.W.1.

Letter from the British Embassy in Baghdad to the Foreign Office in London, describing some of the difficulties facing the Iraqi government following the wave of mass Jewish immigration, December 1952 (Public Record Office)

Commercial Secretariat,
British Embassy,
Bagdad.

April 13, 1955.

Dear Department,

Please refer to F.O. tel. no. 393 of March 7 on the subject of frozen Jewish assets.

2. We have been in touch with the American Embassy and have tried to get estimates by round-about means, this Embassy working through the three British banks here and the American Embassy gathering information from the Jewish Rabbi and from certain Jewish citizens who are on the immigration lists for the United States.

3. As was to be expected the estimates from the different sources vary considerably. After discussion with the American Embassy, the combined estimates are as follows:

(a) Bank assets — From I.D. 600,000 to I.D. 1,100,000.

(b) Immovable properties - (i) From I.D. 4 million to I.D. 5 million, at 1951 values (bank estimates)

(ii) From I.D. 12 million to I.D. 15 million (statements of Jewish citizens)

(c) Movable properties - (i) From I.D. 1 million to I.D. 2 million (bank estimates)

(ii) From I.D. 3 million to I.D. 6 million (statements of Jewish citizens.)

To summarise, the conservative estimate of the total value of Jewish property held is something between I.D. 5,600,000 and I.D. 8,100,000, while the higher range, according to statements made by interested parties, is from I.D. 15,600,000 to I.D. 22,100,000.

4. There is I.D. 89,000 blocked in the Ottoman Bank while the British Bank of the Middle East has I.D. 31,616 in suspense and has also paid over I.D. 51,520 to the Custodian-General. The Eastern Bank has paid in cash, bonds and value of goods some I.D. 1 million to the Custodian General. The Eastern Bank and the Ottoman Bank both estimated the value of frozen Jewish property

/in 1951

Levant Department,
Foreign Office, S.W.1

Report by the British Embassy in Baghdad on the remaining Jewish property in Iraq, April 1955 (Public Record Office)

- 2 -

in 1951 as about I.D.5 million, and they consider that it has doubled or trebled in value since then.

5. Further background information which may be of interest to you is that recently the question of a Japanese Peace Treaty came up in the Iraq Parliament, and it was shelved pending further investigations into the question of monies owing by Japanese firms to Jewish agents formerly resident in Iraq. These monies, which consist mainly of commission on goods sold, are estimated as between I.D.400,000 and I.D.1,300,000.

6. The office of the Custodian-General of Jewish Property is not a very efficient organisation, and they never answer letters or enquiries addressed to them by the Embassy, nor do they appear to be administering the properties under their control in a very correct manner. For instance some years ago the Iraqi Bookshop was sold to the Ministry of Education for about I.D.700 when the total value of the property was much in excess of this. (The Publishers Association of Great Britain itself had an unpaid bill from the Bookshop for some £800 worth of books delivered). It is also alleged that friends of the Custodian-General's organisation can purchase property at far below its current market value, with the result that any attempt at a careful appreciation of the value of Jewish property is defeated.

Yours ever,

(R. W. Munro)
First Secretary (Commercial)

Report by the British Embassy (continued)

property itself could not be returned, mainly real estate that was destroyed, or converted to other functions.

To date, only one independent study has been conducted on Palestinian refugee property. The survey was conducted in the late 1940s by John Brantcastle, former chief assessment officer for the British Mandatory Government in Palestine, on behalf of the UN Conciliation Commission on Palestine. Brantcastle's initial estimate of the value of assets, according to its value in November 1947, was £100 million—close to $3 billion today. Later on, Brantcastle raised his estimate by 20% and included compensation on unutilized building rights.[13] However, it is very likely that Israeli-Palestinian negotiations on refugee compensation will factor in many other calculations, and Israel prefers not to get involved too early in the game.

Israeli policy was expressed in practical terms after the signing of the peace agreement with Egypt. As described in Chapter 8, one clause in the agreement mentioned the establishment of a joint claims committee. But the committee was never formed, mainly because Israel allowed the matter to be forgotten. Jerusalem feared that Cairo might file claims on Israel's use of the Abu Roddes oil fields in Sinai, prior to their return in 1975. But primarily, Israel did not want to open the Pandora's box equating Jewish and Palestinian assets. Twenty-one years have passed since the agreement was signed, and almost no one remembers this clause exists.[14]

WOJAC's leadership supports this approach. Says Ben-Ozer: "The State of Israel never assisted WOJAC, as we would doubtless come up short in

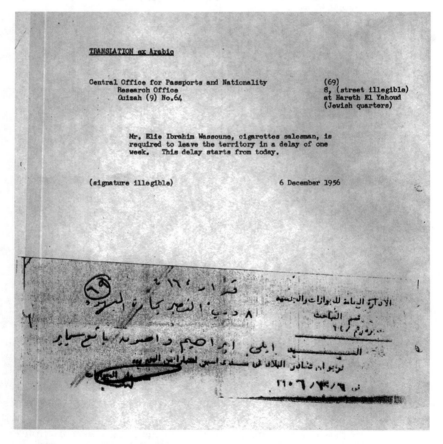

Expulsion order issued to Elie Ibrahim Wassoune, Egyptian Jew, December 1956 (Central Zionist Archives)

relation to the Palestinians. The State intentionally forgot the Arabian Jews and their assets, because of the Palestinians, and was right in doing so." Ben-Ozer and Ben-Porat believe the solution is to establish a vast international fund to compensate both Palestinians and Jews. "The fund would be set up, let's say, by the industrialized countries, the Arab countries, Israel and the Jewish organizations, and would compensate all sides," says Ben-Porat, outlining a possible framework.

Both Ben-Ozer and Ben-Porat emphasize that their intention is not to equalize accounts, by subtracting the value of Jewish assets from that of the Palestinians. "Of course we opposed equalizing accounts," says Ben-Ozer, "because who authorized me to give up their property? If the State of Israel would equalize accounts—property owners could file a claim against the State. I personally think the Israeli government is correct in not raising the subject, but why shouldn't I get my own property?" Does that mean Ben-Ozer thinks that individual interests are more important than overall interests, or those of the State? "Sometimes yes," he says. "I don't believe individuals should waive their rights to property. I would assume the State of Israel will deal with community property as representative of the majority of Jewish people, but I doubt it can waive property rights for one or another individuals. After all, there are many Jews with claims who are not Israeli citizens."[15]

Up until July 2000, the Israeli government avoided making any public statement regarding its position on the matter of property belonging to Jews from Arab countries. The subject suddenly came to public attention because of U.S. President Bill Clinton, in an interview with Israel Broadcasting Authority's Channel One, several days after the failed Middle East Peace Summit at Camp David between then Prime Minister Ehud Barak and Palestinian Authority Chairman Yasser Arafat. Clinton said:

> There is, I think, some interest, interestingly enough, on both sides, in also having a fund which compensates Israelis who were made refugees by the war which occurred after the birth of the State of Israel. Israel is full of people, Jewish people, who lived in predominantly Arab countries who came to Israel because they were made refugees in their own lands.
>
> That's another piece of good news I think I can reveal out of the summit. The Palestinians said they thought those people should be eligible for compensation. So we'll have to set up a fund and we will contribute . . . and I asked the Europeans and the Japanese to contribute as well. And there will be other costs associated with this. So it will not be inexpensive.

Only after this statement did Israel finally make its position known. The Office of the Prime Minister said: "Israel supports the establishment a framework to allocate compensation to persons who suffered as a result of the 1948 war, that would also grant compensation to Jews from Arab countries." Minister for Social and Diaspora Affairs Rabbi Michael Melchior, who had

JEP 3/126.

SWISS DEPOSITS

ABOUHAROUN Isaac H.		330.
ARWAS Elie Michel	7, Ambrose Ave., Golders Green, London, N.W.11	300.
ABOAF Nadia Helen (Mrs.)	227, Rue de la Convention, Paris, 15ᵉ.	100.
AQUILINA Albina (Mrs.)	6400, Sherbrooke St., West, Apt. 20 N.D.G., Montreal, Canada.	100.
ABADI Ibram	30, The Drive, Golders Green, London N.W.11.	300.
ABOUHAROUN Jack	166, Grasmere Ave., Wembley, Middlesex.	300.
ALDWINCKLE D.J.	c/o Personnel Records, British Council, 41 Davies St., W.1.	90.
AGIUS Willy Alfred	The Shell Company of Aden Ltd., P.O.Box 1236, Aden	300.
ABOUHAROUN Mayer	52, Imperial Drive, North Harrow, Middlesex.	2,964.
ABADI Jack	30, The Drive, Golders Green, London, N.W.11.	300.
ARWAS Joseph Michael	34D, Vernon Road, Edgbaston, Birmingham 16.	300.
AUSTIN Therese (Mrs)	49 Grove Road, Sutton, Surrey	200.
ABRAMOVITCH Marcelle (Mrs.)	5, Harrington Gardens, S.W.7.	2,000.
ANZARUT Leon	6, Knoll Rise, Orpington, Kent.	200.
ABOULAFIA Marie (Mrs.)	c/o J. S. Sassoon, Piazza Diaz No. 1, Milan.	100.
ABADI David	14, Montpelier Rise, London, N.W.11.	100.
ADERETH Jacques Elie	Shikun Hé No. 108/2, Beer Sheba, Israel	300.
ABOUHARUN Isaac	c/o Cia United Shoe Machinery Do Brasil, Caixa Postal No. 953 Sao Paulo, Brazil.	300.
ARWAS Reine Elie (Mrs.)	7, Ambrose Ave., Golders Green, London, N.W.11.	300.
ALEXANDRIA BRITISH BENEVOLENT ASSN.	(c/o J. Bellamy, The Lint and Seed (Marketing Board, Private Bag, Pamba (House, Garden Avenue, Dar-el-Salaam.	49.
ALLEN H.E.	6, Rue des Martyrs, Paris 9ᵉ.	200.
BEHAR Farida (Mrs.)	29, Rue Ml. de Lattre de Tassigny, Rueil Malmaison (S&O) France.	100.
BOHGOSSIAN Eugenie Jenny (Mrs.)	6, Crescent Grove, London S.W.4.	100.
BORG Raymond	7, Sandra Grove, Moorabbin, Melbourne, Australia.	200.
BRIFFA Lewis	(Flat 2, Caledonia Mansions, Qui-si-Sana (Sliema, Malta.	265.
BORG MICHEL A.G.	278, Franklin Road, Kings Porton, Birmingham 30.	300.
BONNICI Edgar	47, Abercorn Crescent, South Harrow, Middlesex.	300.
BIGIO Lillie (Mrs.)	Hotel City, 5, Caroline Bessveres, Lausanne, Switzerland.	100.

List of funds deposited in the Swiss Embassy in Cairo by British citizens prior to their exit from Egypt, 1956. About half of the names in this page are Jewish (Public Record Office)

11.

January 28, 1959.

ASSETS OF OVER £E 1 MILLION

(1) SEQUESTRATED

(All figures in £E..)

1.	Anglo-Egyptian Oilfields	45,887,000	
	Shell Petroleum Co.	1,753,442	
	Shell Co. of Egypt	7,874,000	
	Shell Chemicals		
	Distributing Co of Egypt	158,000	55,672,442
2.	Joseph SMOUHA and family		14,313,674
3.	David Ades & Son		1,469,457
	(It has been reported by the Swiss, but not by the Egyptians, that this firm has now been Egyptianised.)		

Total	71,455,573
Balance of Seq. Assets	61,946,752
GRAND TOTAL	133,402,325

(2) EGYPTIANISED

1.	Myddleton Investment Co. (Eastern Co. S.A.E.) Including Dividends		17,200,314
2.	British Banks:-		
	(I) Barclays Bank, D.C.O.	2,322,087	
	(II) Ottoman Bank	2,129,392	
	(III) Ionian Bank	176,070	4,627,549
3.	Tunnel Portland Cement Co. (Helwan Portland Cement Co.) Cumberland Holdings Limited		4,202,348
4.	Bradford Dyers Association Limited (Beida Dyers S.A.E.)		3,218,046
5.	Peel & Co. Limited		2,059,699
6.	British schools (8 plus British Council Institutes Alexandria and Cairo)		1,798,904
7.	Cable and Wireless Limited (Eastern Telegraph Co. Marconi Radio Telegraph Co.)		1,629,621
8.	Egyptian Phosphate Co. Limited		1,348,236
9.	Calico Printers Association (Société Egyptienne des Industries Textiles)		1,060,475
10.	60 British Insurance Firms, (including (Prudential Insurance Co. £E.1,939,703.)		4,291,699

This does not include Tractor and Engineering Co. and Sinai Mining Co. Ltd. who have concluded a "side-deal".

Total	41,436,891
Balance of Eg. Assets	3,931,521
GRAND TOTAL	45,368,412

List of British claims in Egypt for assets over 1 million Egyptian pounds, 1957. The Smouha family was the biggest private claimant (Public Record Office)

231

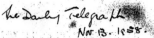

The Daily Telegraph
Nov 13. 1958.

House of Lords

EGYPT REFUGEE FAMILY HAS £10-£20m. CLAIM

Minister Opposes Peers' Demand For British Compensation

BY OUR OWN REPRESENTATIVE

WESTMINSTER, Wednesday.

One British family expelled from Egypt after the Suez incident has put in claims for its assets seized by Col. Nasser totalling between £10 million and £20 million.

Viscount Hailsham, Lord President of the Council, making this disclosure in the House of Lords to-day, gave no clue as to its identity beyond saying that 16 claimants formed part of a single family unit.

"That is about £1 million each. This single unit has already received £80,000 out of the loans scheme, and will be entitled to receive another £80,000 out of the extension recently announced."

Lord LLOYD, in opening a debate on the refugees from Egypt, had urged that the time had come for the Government to recognise the claim of the dispossessed Britons to compensation.

Lord HAILSHAM turned to him and pointed out that this question had no necessary relationship to hardship. "What is it that he is asking us to do?" he demanded.

EXCEPTIONAL CASE
Public Money Involved

"Is it that we should spend between £10 million and £20 million of public money, free of tax, on a single family? I do not utter a breath of criticism against this family that has done so well in the world. But is it asked that we should spend public money on this scale?

That was an exceptional case. But not one person claiming £5,000 or over had received less than £2,700 under the scheme announced a year ago. Those with claims for £20,000 or over had received £8,000."

The MARQUESS of SALISBURY, from a seat below the gangway, intervened to ask: "Are you suggesting that these people are making a false claim?"

"If I do not intend to suggest or imply that in any way," Lord HAILSHAM replied. "These claims are made on assets at present in Egypt which cannot be verified." Public money cannot be paid out in full on a claim of that kind.

£7,000 PAYMENT
Generous Treatment

He told of another couple whose total capital in Egypt was registered at £10,000 and who had received £1,883 in grants and maintenance and £4,000 in loans in two years. Under the extension of the loans scheme recently announced this couple would receive in all about £7,000.

"I do not think any other class of refugees in our history has been more generously treated. By the time this extension is in force we will have dispensed upwards of £10 million on 7,000 people. £3 million in resettlement, £4 million on the original loans scheme, and £3 million more on the extension."

It had been suggested that the Government did not recognise any obligation to the claimants. What it had refused to do was to undertake in advance to compensate claimants for losses not yet fully ascertained.

The Government refused to accept the view that if an expedition had among its objects the protection of British lives and property, that automatically put on the British Government the obligation to compensate out of the taxpayer's money anyone who could show that their property was not in fact protected.

OBLIGATION LIMIT
Making Losses Good

"With all respect to Lord Salisbury, nor do we accept the general proposition that every time British policy, directly or indirectly, as a result of violence or lawlessness by a foreign Power, leads to loss on the part of British subjects, there automatically arises a financial obligation on the British taxpayer to make these losses good."

Lord KILLEARN, former Ambassador to Cairo, bitterly commented: "Do you contend that to the end of time you are going to shelter behind Nasser on this?" Lord HAILSHAM replied that that was the exact opposite of what he had said.

Lord SALISBURY recalled the Foreign Secretary's statement at the time of the landings that one of the objects was to "protect British lives and interests." He did not consider that ex gratia loans were an implementation of that declaration.

He could not understand why the Government did not appreciate the difference between ex-gratia loans

Cyprus statements P.20;
Statement on O.H.M.S.
Labels P.19.

and absolute personal property. It was not fair to claimants to have to pin their hopes on a settlement with Nasser.

The motion asked the Government to discard the basis of ex-gratia loans and accept the principle of compensation. He hoped the Government would accept it, but if it would not he would have to go into the Lobby in support of the motion. In this matter he felt that his own honour and that of the House and the country were engaged.

BIG COMPANIES
Socialist Dilemmas

Viscount ALEXANDER OF HILLSBOROUGH, Leader of the Opposition, said their intention had been to vote for the motion to express dissatisfaction with the Government's niggardliness. But if it meant accepting the principle of full compensation for big and wealthy companies they could not.

The Earl of HOME, Leader of the House, interpreted Lord Salisbury's views on this as being that large companies should be included.

Lord SALISBURY replied that it would be no more than accepting the principle of compensation. Its application would be a matter for future discussion, but if the principle were not accepted they would still be keeping these people on charity.

DIVISION PRESSED
26-23 Vote Defeat

A confused situation developed when Lord LLOYD insisted on putting his motion to the vote as an expression of dissatisfaction with the Government's handling of this matter.

Lord HOME pointed out that the motion, which "drew the attention of the Government to the continuing distress of British nationals expelled from Egypt," did not contain any of the words Lord Lloyd or Lord Salisbury had used about the general principle of compensation.

Urging Lord Lloyd not to press for a vote to-night, he said: "We would like to think about their proposition, and they should think of the full implications of the motion, which makes clear none of these things.

"I am quite willing with my colleagues to look at the scheme and see whether it can be stretched to embrace them." He could not advise the House to accept these general propositions without much greater thought."

To this Lord LLOYD replied that this was "a matter of honour for ourselves and our country."

A division was then called, and the motion was defeated by 26 votes to 23, many peers on both sides of the House abstaining.

Lord Jeffreys, Lord Killearn, Lord Derwent, Lord Gifford, Lord Grenfell, Viscount Colville of Culross, Viscount Massereene and Ferrard, Lord Hampton and the Earl of Woolton also spoke.

Daily Telegraph report about Smouha's claim, November 1958. The family's name, not disclosed in this report, was published a few weeks later (Author's Collection) t2

(2) The lands in the United Arab Republic of any United Kingdom nationals appearing on the following list:—

Kafr El Dawar Region
1. Arman Victor Nahman.
2. Raymond Elie Nessim Ades.
3. Temouni Raymond Elie Nessim Ades.
4. Max Rolo Jack Rublin.
5. Paul Jack Victor Rolo Jack.
6. Jacqueline Rolo Max.
7. Sasson Isabel and Coy.

Abu El Matamir Region
1. Adolph Yacoub.
2. Oland and Zammit.
3. Salomon Sawares.
4. Irama Zammit daughter of Oland.
5. Jean Sanid.
6. Rene Saumit Oland.
7. Richard and Finan Garcian.
8. Fotine Hector.
9. Michel George Ben Gaud.
10. Leopold James Ben Charles.
11. Antoun Bayboun Ben Jean.
12. Mary Joseph Emmanuel.
13. Ellet Elma Avar wife of Armando.
14. Ellet Anaketripiides.
15. Edward Ben George Keram.
16. Eliofen Bosco.
17. Slin Gabriel Tewfik Karam.
18. Gabriel Tewfik Karam.
19. George Gabriel Karam.
20. Restor Peracos.

Etia El Baroud Region
1. Robel String John.

Dessouk Region
1. Yanni Christopaki.
2. Emil Ades.

Kafr El Cheikh Region
1. Jack Chalom Tobi.
2. Georgette Tobi.
3. Nelli Fares Nemr.
4. Emil Fares Nemr.
5. Jacqueline Astrok.
6. Geora Fiorah Harout.

Seberbai Region
1. Mahmoud Mohamed El Meshad.
2. Aram and Max Rollo.

Dekernes Region
1. Paulette Khalil Saab.
2. Fortune Aribol.

Sherbin Region
Paulette Khalil Aziz.
Carver Brothers.

Mansurah Region
1. Robert Macledin.
2. Carver Brothers and Company.

Fakous Region
1. Nelli Fares Nemr.
2. Caroline Smith.
3. Lewis Simon Sednaoui.
4. Commandant of British Forces.
5. Harold Boubagiar son of Joseph.
6. British Marine and Air Force Association.
7. William Narengo.
8. Leao Levi.
9. Mathon Oil Co.
10. English Oil Co.
11. English Oilfields Co.
12. Evan Throp.
13. Josephine daughter of Kwar.
14. Francis Bergeba.
15. Caramelle Gouti Kerdana.
16. Lewis Kamelleri Bargoun.
17. Cook & Son.

Zagazig Region
1. Felix Antonu Youssef Micallef.

Damanhour Region
1. Ellet Kharikelia widow of Redokaneki daughter of Bandelet Salvago.

El Manshiet Region
1. Antom Carlena.
2. William Narengo.
3. Hena Read.
4. Johny Quilina.

Qualiubia Region
1. Emanuel Eil.
2. Osman Khalil.
3. Estate of Nessim Ades.

Gizeh Region
1. Captain Demitri Claidon and Mrs. Doren Claidon and Gerald Charles.
2. Captain Melawla.
3. Moussa Green.
4. Jack and Elie Green.
5. Samuel Sortoga.
6. Yanni Makokiano.

Fayoum West Region
1. Alfred Karmy.

13

List of nationalized property in Egypt that would not be returned under the Anglo-Egyptian compensation agreement of March 1959, as it appeared in the agreement (Public Record Office)

British Legation,
Damascus.

No. 4
(19/1/48)

9th January 1948

22 JAN 1948

Sir,

      I have the honour to report that since the decision of the General Assembly of the United Nations in favour of the partition of Palestine there has been a clearly marked tendency on the part of the Syrian press to incite the public against Jews living in Syria.

2.   The recent outbreak of cholera was, in a number of Syrian newspapers, ascribed to intentional pollution of water supplies by Jews; it has been suggested that no visas for Syria should be granted to Jews of any nationality; Jewish merchants and commercial concerns have been accused of failing to contribute to the fund for the liberation of Palestine, and publicity has been given to the dismissal of certain Jewish Government employees. Attached is a translation of an article from a Damascus newspaper of January 7th typical of many which have appeared during the last month.

3.   Up to the present time no incidents affecting Jewish life or property have resulted from this press campaign (the destruction of Jewish property in Aleppo reported in Damascus telegram No. 537 of the 1st December was not the result of any statement contained in the press). Further serious Jewish acts of terrorism against the Arabs of Palestine might however result in demonstrators in Syria, egged on by the press, attacking Jews and Jewish property.

      I have the honour to be,
      with the highest respect, Sir,
      Your most obedient, humble Servant,

The Right Honourable C.R. Attlee,
      C.H., M.P.,
Foreign Office, S.W.1.

Report from the British Legation in Damascus to Prime Minister Clement Attlee on anti-Jewish propaganda in Syria, January 1948 (Public Record Office) been in charge of the return of property to Holocaust victims, made it clear there would be no talk of offsetting Jewish against Palestinian claims but rather, that every person must be compensated individually.

The Knesset's Parliamentary Inquiry Committee for the Location and Restitution of Assets of Holocaust Victims, headed by Abraham Hirchson, discussed the matter in late July 2000. Ben-Porat appeared before the committee, as did Rabbi Avraham Hamara, the last chief rabbi of Syria, and Daniel Nevo, coordinator of refugee affairs at Israel's Ministry of Foreign Affairs. Ben-Porat reiterated WOJAC's claim regarding non-registration of property and enumerated the obstacles in its way. Nevo explained that WOJAC's funding had been cut following publication of the State Comptroller's report.

At the discussion's conclusion, Hirschson said: "I am not willing to live with the current state of affairs, but I also do not want to hear about equalization with Palestinian property, only about the establishment of a compensation fund for Jewish property." Hirschson announced that he would lend a hand to the World Jewish Congress's fight for justice and stressed the need for a central claims registry where he could put to use his experience gained in the fight to return property belonging to Holocaust victims. He further said that the issue would remain on the committee's agenda in the coming months.[16]

Despite these events, as of this writing in April 2001, the question of property belonging to Jews from Arab countries is still not on the agenda for either the Israeli-Palestinian or Israeli-Syrian negotiations. But among the many difficult decisions lying ahead, Israel's leaders will have to decide whether to leave compensations claims up to the individual—meaning only the wealthy will have any chance of reclaiming even a part of their assets or compensation in lieu of those assets—or risk raising the claims filed by refugees. Taking this risk would mean some sort of justice for anyone forced to leave their home, against their will, carrying only one suitcase in hand.

Notes

INTRODUCTION

1. Bernard Lewis, *Semites and Anti-Semites* (New York: W.W Norton 1999). See additional sources at Chapter 2, note 25.

2. Regarding the case cited in Chapter 8 of *Bigio vs. Coca-Cola*, see: case no. 98–9058, United States Court of Appeals for the Second Circuit on appeal for the United States District Court for the Southern District of New York. The reference is to the opinion submitted by the International Association of Jewish Lawyers and Jurists, American Section, and the Allard K. Lowenstein International Human Rights Law Clinic at Yale University. Coca-Cola contended that measures taken by the Egyptian government in confiscating Jewish property were legal, but the claim was raised disingenuously and did not take into account a long list of evidence provided by the Bigio family.

3. *Findings of the Tribunal Related to the Claims of Jews from Arab Lands* (World Organization of Jews from Arab Countries, 1987), 5.

4. See Ya'akov Meron, "The Deportation of Jews From Arab Countries and the Palestinan Approach Towards It," *Medina Mimshal ve-Yahasim Beinleumiyim*, no. 36 (Jerusalem: The Hebrew University, Summer 1992, Hebrew): 27–56.

CHAPTER 1

1. Interview with source that wished to remain anonymous, October 1999.

2. Avi Beker (ed.-in-chief), *Jewish Communities of the World* (Jerusalem: Institute of the World Jewish Congress, 1996), 197–198.

3. Hayyim J. Cohen, *The Jews of the Middle East, 1860–1972* (New York: John Wiley and Sons; Jerusalem: Israel Universities Press, 1973), 89–91.

238 Notes

4. Nissim Kazzaz, *The Jews in Iraq in the Twentieth Century* (Jerusalem: Ben-Zvi Institute and the Hebrew University, 1991, Hebrew), 95.

5. Ibid., 75–79; Cohen, 90–91.

6. Ya'akov Shimoni, *Political Dictionary of the Arab World* (New York: Macmillan, 1987), 224–225.

7. Kazzaz, 81–86, 110–111; Moshe Gat, *A Jewish Community in Crisis* (Jerusalem: Zalman Shazar Center for Jewish Studies, 1989, Hebrew), 16.

8. Yigal Lucin, *The Pillar of Fire* (Jerusalem: Shikmona, 1982, Hebrew), 303.

9. Gat, 17–23; Central Zionist Archives (CZA), file C2/1658.

10. Tikva Darvish, *The Jews in the Economy of Iraq* (Ramat Gan: Bar-Ilan University, 1987, Hebrew), 20, 44, 61–69.

11. Hagannah Archives (HA), file 14/29; Israel State Archives (ISA), file fo 2563/8.

12. ISA, file fo 1963/5.

13. Moshe Devori, *Amara: Town Amidst Palms* (Ramat Gan: Nasi, 1999, Hebrew), 95–102.

14. Ezra Lagnado, *The Jews of Mosul* (Tirat Carmel: Institute for Mosul Jewry Studies, 1981, Hebrew), 321–339.

15. Mordechai Ben-Porat, *To Baghdad and Back* (Or Yehuda: Sifriyat Ma'ariv, 1996, Hebrew), 223–224; Interview with Oved Ben-Ozer, March 2000.

16. HA, file 14/29; ISA, files fo 2563/8 and 2387/4I.

17. ISA, files fo 2563/8 and 2387/4I.

18. HA, file 14/437; ISA, file fo 2563/8.

19. HA, file 14/30; Gat, 128.

20. HA, file 14/389.

21. ISA, file fo 1963/1.

22. Gat, 26–29.

23. HA, file 14/437; ISA, files fo 2563/8 and fo 2387/4I.

24. CZA, file S20/359I.

25. HA, file 14/29; ISA, file fo 2563/8.

26. Gat, 31–33.

27. ISA, file fo 2563/8; CZA, files S20/539II and C2/1658; Kazzaz, 111.

28. Kazzaz, 322–326.

29. HA, file 14/27.

30. ISA, file fo 2563/10.

31. HA, file 14/393. It is not certain that the memorandum was sent by authorized community representatives, but the very act of forwarding was a courageous one.

32. Esther Meir, *Zionism and the Jews of Iraq, 1941–1950* (Tel Aviv: Tel Aviv University and Am Oved, 1993, Hebrew), 181–183.

33. CZA, file S20/539II; ISA, file fo 2563/8.

34. Gat, 29.

35. CZA, file S20/539II; ISA, file fo 2563/8.

36. Avner Shashua, *Baghdad Times* (Tel Aviv: Author's publication, 1999, Hebrew), 101–106.

37. Gat, 43–44; ISA, file fo 2387/4I.

38. Gat, 51–52.

39. HA, file 14/29.

CHAPTER 2

1. Meir, 217–221.

2. Gat, 22–24.

3. Ibid., 35–37.

4. Ibid., 43–55.

5. Shlomo Hillel, *Operation Babylon* (Tel Aviv: Yediot Aharonot and Ministry of Defense Publishing, 1985, Hebrew), 263–264.

6. Ben-Porat, 69–70. For the original telegram see: HA, file 14/393.

7. The sentence in parentheses is, to a certain extent, proof of the difficult situation presented earlier in the chapter.

8. HA, file 14/393.

9. The reason was alluded to as early as September 1949 by Iraq's acting Minster of Foreign Affairs, Yussuf al-Kilani, who, when asked why his government so vehemently opposed Jewish illegal migration, said: "We are happy to be rid of them, but they take with them gold and other valuable amounting to millions of dinar. We therefore capture the runaways in order to deter them." Quote taken from Dafna Zimhoni, "The Iraqi Government and Mass Immigration of Jews to Israel," *Pe'amin*, no. 39 (1989, Hebrew): 64–102.

10. Meir, 229–231; Gat, 58–65.

11. Ben-Porat, 230.

12. HA, file 14/393.

13. Gat, 126; ISA, file fo 2563/6I.

14. ISA, file fo 2397/14a.

15. Gat, 127–128; ISA, files fo 2564/20 and 2387/4I. Ben-Porat claims that by March 1950, he had already suggested an exchange of property between Palestinian refugees and Jews from Iraq, but that his proposal was rejected by the Mossad le-Aliya Bet on orders given by the Ministry of Finance (Ben-Porat, 225).

16. Interview with Ben-Porat; Hillel, 274–275; Kazzaz, 293; ISA, files fo 2588/16 and fo 2563/8; CZA, file S20/359II; Ben-Porat, 100.

17. Hillel, 313; Gat, 98–100.

18. Ben-Porat, 100.

19. Ibid.

20. CZA, file S20/470.

21. The complete names are not given, by request of the source providing the author with the forms.

22. Bureau for External Claims form, circa December 25, 1954.

23. CZA, file fo S20/582.

24. ISA, file fo 2563/2.

25. Zimhoni, 84.

26. The similarity to anti-Semitic propaganda seen in Europe is no coincidence. Adolf Hitler wrote in *Mein Kampf*, regarding the days of World War I in Germany: "The offices were filled with Jews. Nearly every clerk was a Jew and nearly every Jew was a clerk . . . In the year 1916–1917 nearly the whole production was under control of Jewish finance . . . the Jew robbed the whole nation and pressed it beneath his domination." Quoted by William L. Shirer, *The Rise and Fall of the Third Reich* (New York: Simon and Schuster, 1960). Noted Middle East scholar Professor Bernard Lewis devoted an entire essay to refuting the claim that Arabs are not anti-

Semites, and perhaps cannot be anti-Semites because of their own origin. Bernard
Lewis, *Semites and Anti-Semites* (New York: W.W. Norton and Company, 1999).
The Protocols of the Elders of Zion—arguably the most blatant anti-Semitic tract aside
from Nazi literature—is still a best seller in the Arab world, although it has long been
recognized as a fake; see: Hadassa Ben-Itto, *The Lie that Wouldn't Die* (Tel Aviv:
Dvir, 1998, Hebrew), 332–339. The Stephen Roth Institute for the Study of Contemporary Anti-Semitism and Racism at Tel-Aviv University publishes an annual
report on anti-Semitism in the Arab world, as part of its overall research into anti-
Semitism worldwide; see, for example: Dina Porat and Roni Stauber (eds.), *Anti-
Semitism Worldwide, 1998–1999* (Tel Aviv: Tel Aviv University Press, 2000), 16–
30, 223–236. Particularly harsh anti-Semitic statements, centered around Holocaust
denial, were made in January 2000 by *Tishrin*, the Syrian government daily, in reference to the difficulties in negotiations between Israel and Syria; see, for example:
Globes, February 1, 2000. Moreover, in March 2000, the Grand Mufti of Jerusalem
Akram Sabri claimed that the Jews had greatly exaggerated the extent of the Holocaust in order to gain international support; far fewer than six million were killed in
the Holocaust, he said, adding that it was not his fault that Hitler was anti-Semitic.
"They hate them in lots of places," Sabri said (*Reuters*, March 25, 2000).

27. Kazzaz, 113–116.

28. Esther Meir-Glizenstein, "The Riddle of the Mass Aliya from Iraq—Causes,
Context and Results," *Pe'amim*, no. 71 (Spring 1997, Hebrew): 25–54.

29. K. Gronold, "The Jewish Bankers in Iraq," *Hamizrah HeHadash* 11 (1961,
Hebrew): 163–165.

30. HA, file 14/393; ISA, file fo 2563/6I.

CHAPTER 3

1. Interview with Latif H., November 1999.

2. HA, file 14/389; Kazzaz, 304; Zimhoni, 95–98; Gat, 124–125, 130; Hillel,
321–322; Interview with source who asked to remain anonymous, October 1999.
For the English version of the law see: ISA, file fo 2563/5.

3. HA, file 14/393; ISA, file fo 2563/6I.

4. Gat, 125; Nissim Kazzaz, "The Jews in Iraq during the Rule of General Abd
al-Karim Qasim," *Pe'amim*, no. 71 (Spring 1997, Hebrew): 55–82.

5. ISA, file fo 2563/6I; CZA, file C2/1658.

6. CZA, file S20/540.

7. HA, file 14/389.

8. HA, file 14/zim/73a.

9. HA, file 14/389.

10. Ibid., file 14/zim/73a.

11. ISA, file fo 2563/6I.

12. HA, file 14/389.

13. ISA, file fo 2563/6I.

14. ISA, file fo 2563/5.

15. Forms from the Bureau for External Claims, March 14, 1955.

16. Gat, 131; ISA, file fo 2563/6I; Zakky Shalom, "A Document from the
Archive," *Pe'amim*, no. 71 (Spring 1997, Hebrew): 86–93.

17. HA, file 14/389; Gat, 132.

18. Gat, 133–134.

19. Public Record Office (PRO), files fo 371/115793 and fo 371/115794.

20. During those years, Great Britain's actions were equally insensitive and selfish, but with far more serious consequences, toward those Holocuast survivors whose property was seized during the World War II by the Custodian of Enemy Property. See Itamar Levin, *His Majesty's Enemies: Britain's War Against Holocaust Victims and Survivors* (Westport, CT: Praeger, 2001).

21. PRO, file fo 371/98768.

22. CZA, file S20/583.

23. ISA, file fo 2563/5.

24. PRO, file fo 371/91644.

25. PRO, file fo 371/98733.

26. PRO, file fo 371/98750.

27. Interview with Morris Kanne, February 2000.

CHAPTER 4

1. ISA, files fo 2563/7, fo 3571/23 and fo 2387/5; Interview with source who asked to remain anonymous, October 1999; Interview with Ben-Porat.

2. Kazzaz, "Qasim."

3. PRO, file fo 371/115794.

4. PRO, file fo 371/115767.

5. Ibid.

6. For the list of the released prisoners, see CZA, file S6/10020.

7. Kazzaz, "Qasim."

8. Ibid.

9. CZA, file S6/10020.

10. Shimoni, 228.

11. CZA, file S6/10020.

12. *The Distress of the Jews in the Arab Countries* (Jerusalem: Ministry of Education, 1970, Hebrew), 16.

13. CZA, file S6/10020.

14. Max Sawdayee, *All Waiting to be Hanged* (Tel Aviv: no publisher's name given, 1974), 31, 35–36, 40, 43–51.

15. *The Distress of the Jews*, 16–17, 41–42.

16. Yitzhak Betzalel, *The Vanishing of the Iraqi Jewry* (Tel Aviv: Sifriyat Ma'ariv, 1976, Hebrew), 58–60.

17. Ibid., 65–66.

18. Shimoni, 228.

19. Betzalel, 92–93, 95–101; Interview with source who asked to remain anonymous. October 1999.

20. Betzalel, 93.

21. Ibid., 153–156.

22. *The Distress of the Jews*, 45–48.

23. Sawdayee, 119–131.

24. Ibid., 143–144.

25. Ibid., 148–149.

26. Ibid., 151.

27. Ibid., 172–173.
28. Betzalel, 174–181.
29. Ibid., 193–195.
30. Sawdayee, 174–216.
31. Interview with source who asked to remain anonymous, October 1999.

CHAPTER 5

1. Interview with Levana Zamir, December 1999.
2. Beker, 192–193.
3. Shmuel Ettinger (ed.), *History of the Jews in the Islamic Countries* (Jerusalem: Zalman Shazar Center for Jewish Studies, 1986, Hebrew), vol. 2, 389–399; Cohen, 87–89. A great deal of information on the wealthy Jews in Egypt may be found in articles by Egyptian journalist Samir Raafat, available online at www.egy.com.
4. Michael M. Laskier, *The Jews of Egypt, 1920–1970: In the Midst of Zionism, Anti-Semitism, and the Middle East Conflict* (New York: New York University Press, 1992), 84–89; Michael M. Laskier, "Egyptian Jewry under the Nasser Regime, 1956–70," Middle Eastern Studies 31, no. 3 (July 1995): 573–619.
5. Meron, "Deportation."
6. P.J. Vatikiotis, *The History of Egypt from Muhammad Ali to Sadat* (London: Weinfeld and Nicholson, 1980), 363–364.
7. CZA, file S20/552.
8. Ibid., ibid.; ISA, file 2563/10.
9. Laskier, "Egyptian Jewry"; CZA, file fo S20/552.
10. HA, file 14/11.
11. ISA, file fo 2563/10; CZA, file S20/552.
12. CZA, file S20/552; HA, file 14/11.
13. ISA, file fo 2563/10.
14. Laskier, "Egyptian Jewry"144, 189–190.
15. CZA, file S20/552; ISA, file fo 2563/10.
16. PRO, file fo 371/73648; *International Court of Justice, Yearbook 1949–1950* (The Hague, 1950), 68.
17. HA, file 14/11.
18. CZA, file S20/553.
19. Clearly a contradiction in terms, as it is not reasonable to expect that immigrants would bother taking worthless documents with them or fight for them. It appears Kogan tried—justifiably, from his point of view—to convince the officials with inaccurate as well as accurate claims.
20. ISA, file fo 2563/10.

CHAPTER 6

1. CZA, file S6/7243. About the activities of the World Jewish Congress in the first days of the deportation—see PRO, file fo 371/119/233.
2. Shimoni, 158–165, 467–470; Laskier, "Egyptian Jewry."
3. PRO, file fo 371/119/237; Laskier, "Egyptian Jewry"; *Egypt in September, 1957* (New York: Institute of Jewish Affairs, 1957), 5.

4. PRO, file fo 371/119/236; *Egypt in September, 1957,* 1957, 2.

5. PRO, file fo 371/133992; Vatikiotis, 393–394; *Egypt in September, 1957,* 3.

6. Laskier, "Egyptian Jewry," 256–262; ISA, file fo 2387/9; CZA, files Z6/1584 and S6/6046; PRO, files fo 371/119/236 and fo 371/119265 (Meir's letter is to be found in the last file); Egypt 1957, 4. It may be that Meir exaggerated when she spoke of "hundreds of former Nazis," but there were undoubtedly dozens of Germans with Nazi pasts, employed in the service of Nasser. See Isar Har'el, *The German Scientist Crisis* (Tel Aviv: Sifriyat Ma'ariv 1982) 9–12.

7. CZA, file S6/7243; PRO, file fo 371/119265; *Egypt in September, 1957,* 6.

8. CZA, file S6/6521; PRO, file fo 371/119265. There are conflicting reports on this point. In January 1957, M. Haskel of the Jewish Agency reported that the Jews were permitted to take out 200 Egyptian pounds per couple, plus 100 Egyptian pounds per child, but that emigration costs must be subtracted from this sum. In cash, Jews were permitted to take only 20 Egyptian pounds (it is unclear whether the figure is per person or per couple), and therefore many Jews were forced to buy traveler's checks from American Express and other banks (CZA, file Z6/1281 and S6/6520). Exactly at that same time, another Jewish Agency emissary, D. Asa'el, reported that prior to that time, only 10 Egyptian pounds was permitted per person, and that it was now possible to buy 100 Egyptian pounds in traveler's checks per person (CZA, file S6/6520). In any case, these are clearly very small sums that did not represent even a fraction of the property belonging to middle and upper class Jews. They could not realize the value of their property either because it was frozen, or because they were forced to leave the country within days; therefore, even if it were possible to take out larger amounts matters would not have been easier for the majority of the deportees.

9. CZA, files Z6/1281 and S6/6520; Laskier, "Egyptian Jewry."

10. Joint Archive (JA), shipment Geneva 3, box L-28, file 492.

11. Laskier, 267–270; CZA, file S6/6047; Laskier, "Egyptian Jewry." A lot of documents about the relations with the international organizations regarding the Jewish immigration from Egypt can be found in the following archival sources: CZA, files Z6/1281, Z6/1584, S6/6046, S6/6517, S6/6519, S6/6520, S6/6607, S6/7242 and S6/7243; JA, shipment Geneva 3, box L-28, files 492 and 494.

12. CZA, files S6/6046 and S6/6521.

13. CZA, files S6/6565 and S6/6566.

14. CZA, files Z6/1281 and S6/6520; JA, shipment Geneva 3, box L-28, file 494.

15. JA, ibid., files 496 and 504; Ibid., box L-26, file 459; CZA, file S6/6520.

16. CZA, file S6/6521.

17. CZA, file S6/6046.

18. ISA, file gl 4617/3646.

19. CZA, files S6/6520 and S6/6521; *Egypt in September, 1957,* 4.

CHAPTER 7

1. Interview with source who asked to remain anonymous, January 2000; some details: *The Daily Telegraph,* November 14, 1958 (in PRO, file fo 1004/48) and *The Jewish Chronicle,* September 29, 1961.

2. CZA, files S6/6048 and S6/6049.

3. PRO, file fo 1004/48.

4. Interview with source who asked to remain anonymous, January 2000; *The Daily Telegraph*, November 14, 1958; *The Jewish Chronicle*, September 29, 1961. The following files contain a few details regarding Smouha's claims: PRO, files fo 950/709, fo 950/712, fo 950/716 and fo 950/673.

5. PRO, files fo 1004/48, fo 371/119/236 and fo 950/712.

6. CZA, files S6/6049 and S6/6517; Ronen Bergman, "How many oil barrels equal the Katawi family," *Ha'aretz Weekly Magazine*, December 15, 1995, 46–54, (Hebrew); Samir Raafat, "The House of Cicurel," *al-Ahram Weekly*, December 15, 1994. This article, alongside other articles Raafat wrote about the Katawi, Mosseri and Suares families, are posted on Raafat's web site: www.egy.com.

7. PRO, file fo 950/709.

8. Ibid.

9. PRO, file fo 950/710.

10. PRO, file fo 950/709.

11. PRO, file fo 950/712.

12. PRO, file 950/710.

13. PRO, file 950/712.

14. PRO, files fo 371/119/232, fo 371/119/233, fo 371/119/234, fo 371/119/236, fo 371/119/237, fo 371/119/239, fo 950/714.

15. *Egypt in September, 1957*, 6; JA, shipment Geneva 3, box L-26, file 459; CZA, file Z6/1584.

16. Among the most important files closed to researchers are the following: shipment Geneva 2, box L-26, files 450 (property registration), 452 (letters of credit), 453 (release of frozen assets), 457 (correspondence with the Swiss embassy), 458 (correspondence with the UN High Commission for Refugees), 467 (correspondence with deportees who did not register claims); Shipment Geneva 3, box L-28, files 491 (handling of letters of credit), and 493 (refugees from Egypt); shipment Malben-II, box 129, file 1 (Egypt Jews in Israel who left property behind in Egypt); shipment Geneva 4, box 25/1A, file 9 (claims registration office), box 32/1C, files 2, 3, 5 and 6 (claims registration office).

17. JA, shipment Geneva 3, box L-26, file 459.

18. Interview with Shlomo Cohen-Sidon, September 1999 and documents from his files; ISA, file gl 4617/3646; Bergman, "Katawi"; Inbar Lagstein, "The Egyptian Front," *Shtei Arim*, February 21, 1997, 38–41 (Hebrew).

19. Interview with Cohen-Sidon and his files; ISA, file gl 4617/3646.

20. JA, shipment Geneva 3, box L-28, file 504; Ibid., box L-26, file 459.

21. PRO, file fo 950/673.

22. PRO, file fo 950/716.

23. PRO, files fo 371/138893, fo 371/13888, fo 371/161866.

CHAPTER 8

1. Vatikiotis, 393–397.

2. Bergman, "Katawi"; Yoram Meital, *Jewish Sites in Egypt* (Jerusalem: Yad Yitzhak Ben-Zvi, 1995, Hebrew), 110–118, 124; e-mails from Samir Raafat to this

author, March 2000; Laskier, "Egyptian Jewry"; Interview with Yoram Meital, March 2000. About the Mizrahi's villa, the Castro's palace and the Mosseri's villa, see Raafat's articles in his web site (www.egy.com). Most of Raafat's articles about the Jewish property in Cairo were written before Bergman's, but it seems Bergman was not familiar with them; Raafat's site was launched later.

3. Laskier, "Egyptian Jewry."

4. Ibid., 288–289; Laskier, "Egyptian Jewry"; *The Distress of the Jews*, 8.

5. Interview with Zaki Harari, December 1999.

6. Laskier, 290–293; Betzalel, 63–64; *The Distress of the Jews*, 8–10.

7. William B. Quandt, *Camp David: Peacemaking and Politics* (Washington, D.C: The Brookings Institute, 1986), 223–225, 356–360; Ehud Yaari, Eytan Haber, and Ze'ev Schiff, *The Year of the Dove* (Tel Aviv: Zmora-Bitan-Modan, 1980, Hebrew), 310–313, 318–319; Ezer Weizman, *The Battle for Peace* (Jerusalem: Idanim and Yediot Aharonot, 1981, Hebrew), 322–325.

8. Interview with Cohen-Sidon and documents from his files; Interviews with sources that wished to remain anonymous, October 1999 and January 2000.

9. Bergman, "Katawi."

10. Interview with source that wished to remain anonymous, December 1999. The best description of the community, including its history and current situation, is given by Meital.

11. Ronen Bergman, "Chasing the Nile's Treasures," *Ha'aretz Weekly Magazine*, January 26, 1996, 18–24 (Hebrew); Meital, 85–86, 103–105; Interview with Meital. In March 2000, this writer tried in vain to discuss the state of the Jewish community, and the fate of its property, with Carmen Weinstein. Officially, Carmen's mother Esther Weinstein is the president of Cairo's Jewish community but due to her advanced age, daughter Carmen manages the community affairs. Carmen's official title is director of public relations. Carmen Weinstein tried to avoid meeting with the author and offered various excuses, but she eventually gave in. At the outset of the meeting, she demanded this author promise not to write "anything of a political nature" and claimed that as the interviewee she had the right to determine what would be in the article. Naturally, this demand was unacceptable, and the interview therefore did not take place.

12. Rachel Sarfaty, "The Yedid Bequest: An Unusual Judaica Collection Finds Its Way to the Israel Museum," *The Israel Museum Journal* 27 (1999): 54–57.

13. Interview with source who requested anonymity, March 2000.

14. Meital; Interview with source who requested anonymity, March 2000.

15. Interview with Meital.

16. Interviews with sources who requested anonymity, October 1999 and January 2000; author's notes from his visit to Cairo, March 2000; e-mails from Samir Raafat to the author, March 2000.

17. Bergman, "Katawi."

18. *Business Today*, October 1999, 38.

19. United States Court of Appeals for the Second Circuit, file no. 98–9058; Ronen Bergman, *Raphael Bigio v. Coca-Cola*, *Ha'aretz Weekly Magazine*, July 16, 1999, 37–42 (Hebrew).

20. Interview with Harari.

21. Interview with Zamir.

CHAPTER 9

1. Interview with Ezra Chammah, November 1999.
2. Ettinger, *History of the Jews*, vol. 2, 205–207.
3. Aryeh Cohen, "The Continental 'Ha'apala' of Jews from Syria and Lebanon, 1939–1949" (M.A thesis, Haifa University, 1997, Hebrew), 29–31.
4. Ibid., 97–99.
5. *The Doar-Sakal Families* (Ramat Efal: Yad Tabenkin, 1995, Hebrew), 13.
6. Ibid., 17–18.
7. Ibid., 31–32.
8. Zvi Zohar, "'Ha'apala' and 'Aliya Beit' from Syria in the Forties," *Pe'amim*, no. 66 (Winter 1996, Hebrew): 43–69; *Doar-Sakal Families*, 48.
9. Zohar.
10. Ibid.
11. Interview with Frida Yedid, January 2000.
12. Zohar; "The Continental Ha'apala."
13. Lucin, 497.
14. Interview with Rachel Shushan-Sabbah and Aliza Totah-Sabbah, January 2000.
15. See, in detail, Amnon Shamosh, *Ha-Keter: The Story of the Aleppo Codex* (Jerusalem: Ben-Zvi Institute, 1987, Hebrew).
16. PRO, file fo 371/68803.
17. Shamosh, 144–146.
18. Attributing a "spirit of Nazism" to Syria is based on the fact that in 1941, Syria expressed open admiration and even support for the pro-Nazi revolution that took place that year in Iraq, headed by Rashid Ali al-Khilani. However, pro-Nazism in Syria resulted more from opposition to the French regime, and less from ideological considerations, and was emphasized far less than in Iraq and Egypt. See: Patrick Seale, *The Struggle for Syria* (London: Oxford University Press, 1965), 9.
19. HA, file 14/15; "The Continental Ha'apala," 46–47.
20. ISA, file fo 2563/4.
21. PRO, file fo 371/68803.
22. Ibid.
23. Interview with Shoshana Perez-Hilleli, January 2000.
24. ISA, file fo 2563/4.
25. Ibid.
26. Shimoni, 474–475, 519–520.
27. CZA, file S20/537.
28. HA, file 14/16.
29. Ibid.
30. Ibid.
31. ISA, file fo 2563/4. The general practice within Arab countries, and sometimes outside them, was to trace internal insurrections back to foreign elements, but in most cases these allegations were baseless. This was the case in the Za'im revolt where, as far as is known, neither the United States nor France was involved.
32. HA, file 14/646.
33. Shimoni, 446, 474–475.
34. ISA, file fo 2563/4.
35. HA, file 14/646.

36. CZA, file S20/37.
37. Ibid.
38. ISA, file fo 2563/11.
39. See, in detail, Aryeh Shalev, *Co-operation under the Shadow of Conflict* (Tel Aviv: Ministry of Defense Publishing and Tel Aviv University, 1989, Hebrew), 161–184.
40. Shimoni, 446, 474–475.
41. ISA, file fo 2563/4.
42. ISA, file fo 2387/3.
43. ISA, file fo 2563/4.
44. ISA, file fo 2387/3.
45. Interview with Rabbi Avraham Hamara, February 2000.
46. ISA, files fo 2387/3 and 3571/23.
47. Beker, 208.

CHAPTER 10

1. Shimoni, 446, 475–476; Seale, 307–326. See also Itamar Rabinovich, *Syria under the Ba'ath, 1963–66* (Jerusalem: Israel Universities Press, 1972).
2. *Carta's Atlas of Israel—The First Years: 1948–1961* (Jerusalem: Carta, 1978, Hebrew), 119.
3. CZA, file S6/10123.
4. Ibid.
5. ISA, file fo 2387/3.
6. CZA, file S6/10123.
7. Ibid.
8. Shimoni, 476–477; Rabinovich, 11–18.
9. Laskier, "Egyptian Jewry"; CZA, file S6/10122.
10. CZA, file S6/10122.
11. Ibid.
12. CZA, files S6/10122 and Z6/1383.
13. CZA, file S6/10114.
14. CZA, file Z6/1383.
15. CZA, file S6/10112.
16. Ibid.
17. Ibid.
18. CZA, file S6/10117.
19. Ibid.
20. Ibid.
21. Shimoni, 476–477.
22. CZA, file S6/10117.
23. CZA, file S6/10068. Also in the same file are lists of new immigrants who deposited envelopes and matchboxes filled with jewelry from Syria, with Jewish Agency emissaries in Istanbul to be sent by the Jewish Agency to Israel.
24. Shimoni, 477–478. See, in detail, Rabinovich.
25. CZA, file C2/1713.
26. Shimoni, 73–74, 477–478; Chaim Herzog, *The Arab-Israeli Wars* (Jerusalem: Idabim, 1983, Hebrew), 116–119.

27. *Confiscation of Jewish Property in Syria for the Needs of the Military Intelligence Against Israel* (Israel Defense Forces' Spokesman, 1967).

28. This alludes to the Nazi regime in Germany and the Holocaust, particularly as relates to economic persecution and separation from sources of income. See, for example, Saul Friedlander, *Nazi Germany and the Jews: The Years of Persecution, 1933–1939* (New York: HarperCollins, 1997), 117–137.

29. *The Distress of the Jews,* 11–13.

30. Ibid., 35–36.

31. Ibid., 43–45. The comparison made here is chilling; in November 1938, immediately following *Kristallnacht*, Hermann Goering said (and quoted by Friedlander as the motto of his book): "I would not want to be a Jew in Germany."

32. David Siton, *The Sepharadic Communities in Our Times* (Jerusalem: Committee of the Sepharadic Community, 1982, Hebrew), 50–51.

33. Harold Troper, "Syria, A Special Case", in Malka Shulewitz Hillet (ed.), *The Forgotten Millions: The Modern Jewish Exodus from Arab Lands* (London and New York: Cassell, 1999), 52–79.

34. Again, there is no recourse but to compare this act with that of Nazi Germany, where passports belonging to Jews were stamped with the letter "J."

35. Shulewitz, 221–222.

36. Troper.

37. Interview with Hamara; Troper.

38. Interview with Hamara.

CHAPTER 11

1. Cohen, 99; Ettinger, *History of the Jews*, 207, 219.

2. Shimoni, 175–186.

3. CZA, file S20/538.

4. *The History of the War of Independence* (Tel Aviv: Ma'arahot, 1978, Hebrew), 173–176, 281–282, 321–326; *Carta's Atlas*, 16, 47, 60.

5. HA, file 14/16.

6. CZA, file S20/537.

7. The documentation does not explain why it was necessary to flee Lebanon, as in previous years Lebanese Jews were able to come and go freely. During those years, relations between Israel and Lebanon were stable and were conducted mainly through the cease-fire committee.

8. Here, too, the situation is worse as compared to reports from June 1950, according to which Lebanese Jews took all personal belongings, excluding gold.

9. This was the general situation during the early years of the State of Israel; therefore, these rumors were not without basis. See Nahum T. Gross, *Not By Spirit Alone* (Jerusalem: Yad Izhak Ben-Zvi, 1999, Hebrew), 342–351.

10. ISA, file fo 3571/23.

11. Shimoni, 293–295; Interview with Isar Har'el, June 1987.

12. CZA, file S6/10122.

13. CZA, file Z6/1383.

14. CZA, file S6/10112.

15. CZA, file S6/10114.

16. ISA, file fo 3571/23.

17. CZA, file S6/10112.

18. It should also be noted that Lebanon was the only Arab country bordering Israel that did not take part in the 1967 Six Day War.

19. Siton, 68–71.

20. Beker, 200.

CHAPTER 12

1. In raising this point, the committee touched on one of the most painfully sensitive subjects in Israeli history: the creation of a Palestinian refugee problem. The committee reiterated the official Israeli position, according to which the Arabs and their leaders were responsible for creating the problem. For decades, Israeli historiography was written along those same lines—for example: Gavriel Ben-Dor, "The Effect and Continuation of the Palestinian National Problem," in Eytan Gilboa and Mordechai Naor (eds.), *The Arab Israeli Conflict* (Tel Aviv: Ministry of Defense Publishing, 1987, Hebrew), 166–167. By contrast, the Palestinians insisted that in most cases they had been deported by Israel. An important milestone in presenting a balanced account, including incidents where Hagannah and Israel Defense Forces had ousted Palestinian residents, was Benny Morris, *The Birth of the Palestinian Refugee Problem, 1947–1949* (Cambridge: Cambridge University Press, 1989). Today, the accepted version of events is that some Palestinians left Israel on the encouragement of their own leaders, and leaders of the Arab world, some left on their own initiative while others were indeed deported. See Avraham Sela, "The Palestinian Arabs in the War of 1948," in Moshe Maoz and Benjamin Kedar (eds.) *The Palestinian National Movement: From Confrontation to Reconciliation?* (Tel Aviv: Ministry of Defense Publishing, 1996, Hebrew), 165–173. Also see footnotes there with references to primary research sources.

2. Statement by the Knesset Committee for Foreign and Defense Affairs, November 18, 1975.

3. Knesset Minutes, meetings 349 and 356 of the 11th Knesset.

4. ISA, file fo 2563/10.

5. ISA, file fo 2563/7; CZA, file S20/583.

6. Moshe Lissak, *The Mass Immigration in the Fifties: The Failure of the Melting Pot Policy* (Jerusalem: Bialik Institute, 1999, Hebrew), 9–11.

7. A letter from Haim Zadok to Yitzhak Rabin, September 9, 1974.

8. ISA, file gl 4617/3646; Interview with Ben-Porat.

9. *Ha'aretz* (Hebrew), September 15, 1999.

10. Interviews with Ben-Porat and Ben-Ozer; WOJAC publications.

11. Ibid.; Interview with source who requested anonymity, December 1999; State Comptroller, *Annual Report 49* (Jerusalem, 1999, Hebrew), 194; Interview with Elan Steinberg, March 2000.

12. Interview with source who requested anonymity, December 1999.

13. Ya'akov Meron, "The Expulsion of the Jews from the Arab Countries: The Palestinians' Attitude Towards It and Their Claims," in Shulewitz, 83–125.

14. Interviews with sources who requested anonymity, October 1999 and January 2000.

15. Interviews with Ben-Porat and Ben-Ozer.

16. *Globes*, July 31, 2000 and August 2, 2000.

Bibliography

PRIMARY SOURCES

Archival Sources

American Joint Distribution Committee Archive, Jerusalem (in text references, JA): shipment Geneva 3, box L-26, file 459; shipment Geneva 3, box L-28, files 492, 494, 504.

Central Zionist Archives, Jerusalem (in text references, CZA): file C2/1658, file C2/1713, file S6/6046, file S6/6047, file S6/6048, file S6/6049, file S6/6517, file S6/6519, file S6/6520, file S6/6521, file S6/6565, file S6/6566, file S6/6607, file S6/7242, file S6/7243, file S6/10020, file S6/10068, file S6/10112, file S6/10114, file S6/10117, file S6/10122, file S6/10123, file S20/37, file S20/359I, file S20/359II, file S20/470, file S20/537, file S20/538, file S20/539II, file S20/540, file S20/552, file S20/553, file S20/582, file S20/583, file Z6/1281, file Z6/1381, file 26/1383, 26/1584.

Hagganah Archives, Tel Aviv (in text references, HA): file 14/11, file 14/15, file 14/16, file 14/27, file 14/29, file 14/30, file 14/389, file 14/393, file 14/437, file 14/646, file 14/zim/73a.

Israel State Archives, Jerusalem (in text references, ISA): file fo 1963/1, file fo 1963/5, file fo 2387/3, file fo 2387/4I, file fo 2387/5, file fo 2387/9, file fo 2397/14a, file fo 2563/2, file fo 2563/4, file fo 2563/5, file fo 2563/6I, file fo 2563/7, file fo 2563/8, file fo 2563/10, file fo 2563/11, file fo 2564/20, file fo 2588/16, file fo 3571/23, file gl 4617/3646.

Public Record Office, London (in text references, PRO): file fo 1004/48, file fo 371/119/232, file fo 371/119/233, file fo 371/119/234, file fo 371/119/236, file fo 371/119/237, file fo 371/119/239, file fo 371/13888, file fo 371/68803, file fo 371/73648, file fo 371/91644, file fo 371/98733, file fo 371/98733, file fo 371/98750, file fo 371/98768, file fo 371/115767, file fo 371/115793, file fo 371/115794, file fo 371/119265, file fo 371/ 133992, file fo 371/138893, file fo 371/161866, file fo 950/673, file fo 950/709, file fo 950/710, file fo 950/712, file fo 950/714, file fo 950/ 716.

Interviews

Oved Ben-Ozer, March 2000.
Mordechai Ben-Porat, October 1999.
Ezra Chammah, November 1999.
Shlomo Cohen-Sidon, September 1999.
Rabbi Avraham Hamara, February 2000.
Zaki Harari, December 1999. (Interview by Dalia Tal).
Isar Har'el, June 1987.
Morris Kanne, February 2000.
Latif H., November 1999.
Yoram Meital, March 2000.
Felix Mizrahi, December 1999. (Interview by Dalia Tal).
Shoshana Perez-Hilleli, January 2000. (Interview by Dalia Tal).
Elan Steinberg, March 2000.
Rachel Shushan-Sabbah and Aliza Totah-Sabbah, January 2000. (Interview by Dalia Tal).
Frida Yedid, January 2000. (Interview by Dalia Tal).
Levana Zamir, December 1999. (Interview by Dalia Tal).

SECONDARY SOURCES

Books

Beker, Avi (ed.-in-chief). *Jewish Communities of the World*. Jerusalem: Institute of the World Jewish Congress, 1996.
Ben-Itto, Hadassa. *The Lie that Wouldn't Die*. Tel Aviv: Dvir, 1998, Hebrew.
Ben-Porat, Mordechai. *To Baghdad and Back*. Or Yehuda: Sifriyat Ma'ariv, 1996, Hebrew.
Betzalel, Yitzhak. *The Vanishing of the Iraqi Jewry*. Tel Aviv: Sifriyat Ma'ariv, 1976, Hebrew.
Carta's Atlas of Israel—The First Years: 1948–1961. Jerusalem: Carta, 1978, Hebrew.
Cohen, Hayyim J. *The Jews of the Middle East, 1860–1972*. New York: John Wiley and Sons, Jerusalem: Israel Universities Press, 1973.
Confiscation of Jewish Property in Syria for the Needs of the Military Intelligence Against Israel. Israel Defense Forces' Spokesman, 1967, Hebrew.
Darvish, Tikva. *The Jews in the Economy of Iraq*. Ramat Gan: Bar-Ilan University, 1987, Hebrew.
Devori, Moshe. *Amara: Town Amidst Palms*. Ramat Gan: Nasi, 1999, Hebrew.
The Distress of the Jews in the Arab Countries. Jerusalem: Ministry of Education, 1970, Hebrew.

The Doar-Sakal Families. Ramat Efal: Yad Tabenkin, 1995, Hebrew.
Egypt in September, 1957. New York: Institute of Jewish Affairs, 1957.
Ettinger, Shmuel (ed.). *History of the Jews in the Islamic Countries.* Jerusalem: Zalman Shazar Center for Jewish Studies, 1986, Hebrew.
Findings of the Tribunal Related to the Claims of Jews From Arab Lands. World Organization of Jews from Arab Countries, 1987.
Friedlander, Saul. *Nazi Germany and the Jews: The Years of Persecution, 1933–1939.* New York: HarperCollins, 1997.
Gat, Moshe. *A Jewish Community in Crisis.* Jerusalem: Zalman Shazar Center for Jewish Studies, 1989, Hebrew.
Gross, Nahum T. *Not by Spirit Alone.* Jerusalem: Yad Itzhak Ben-Zvi, 1999, Hebrew.
Har'el, Isar. *The German Scientist Crisis.* Tel Aviv: Sifriyat Ma'ariv, 1982.
Herzog, Chaim. *The Arab-Israeli Wars.* Jerusalem: Idabim, 1983, Hebrew.
Hillel, Shlomo. *Operation Babylon.* Tel Aviv: Yediot Aharonot and Ministry of Defense Publishing, 1985, Hebrew.
The History of The War of Independence. Tel Aviv: Ma'arahot, 1978, Hebrew.
International Court of Justice, Yearbook 1949–1950. The Hague, 1950.
Kazzaz, Nissim. *The Jews in Iraq in the Twentieth Century.* Jerusalem: Ben-Zvi Institute and The Hebrew University, 1991, Hebrew.
Lagnado, Ezra. *The Jews of Mosul.* Tirat Carmel: Institute for Mosul Jewry Studies, 1981, Hebrew.
Laskier, Michael. *The Jews of Egypt, 1920–1970: In the Midst of Zionism, Anti-Semitism, and the Middle East Conflict.* New York: New York University Press, 1992.
Levin, Itamar. *His Majesty's Enemies: Britain's War Against Holocaust Victims and Survivors.* Westport, CT: Praeger, 2001.
Lewis, Bernard. *Semites and Anti-Semites.* New York: W.W Norton, 1999.
Lissak, Moshe. *The Mass Immigration in the Fifties: The Failure of the Melting Pot Policy.* Jerusalem: Bialik Institute, 1999, Hebrew.
Lucin, Yigal. *The Pillar of Fire.* Jerusalem: Shikmona, 1982, Hebrew.
Meir, Esther. *Zionism and the Jews of Iraq, 1941–1950.* Tel Aviv: Tel Aviv University and Am Oved, 1993, Hebrew.
Meital, Yoram. *Jewish Sites in Egypt.* Jerusalem: Yad Izhak Ben-Zvi, 1995, Hebrew.
Porat, Dina and Stauber, Roni (eds.), *Anti-Semitism Worldwide, 1998–99.* Tel Aviv: Tel Aviv University Press, 2000.
Quandt, William B. *Camp David: Peacemaking and Politics.* Washington, D.C: The Brookings Institute, 1986.
Rabinovich, Itamar. *Syria under the Ba'ath, 1963–66.* Jerusalem: Israel Universities Press, 1972.
Sawdayee, Max. *All Waiting to Be Hanged.* Tel Aviv: no publisher's name, 1974.
Seale, Patrick. *The Struggle for Syria.* London: Oxford University Press, 1965.
Shalev, Aryeh. *Co-operation under the Shadow of Conflict.* Tel Aviv: Ministry of Defense Publishing and Tel Aviv University, 1989, Hebrew.
Shamosh, Amnon. *Ha-Keter: The Story of the Aleppo Codex.* Jerusalem: Ben-Zvi Institute, 1987, Hebrew.
Shashua, Avner. *Baghdad Times.* Tel Aviv: Author's publication, 1999, Hebrew.
Shimoni, Ya'akov. *Political Dictionary of the Arab World.* New York: Macmillan, 1987.

Shirer, William L. *The Rise and Fall of the Third Reich*. New York: Simon and Schuster, 1960.

Shulewitz-Hillel, Malka (ed.). *The Forgotten Millions: The Modern Jewish Exodus from Arab Lands*. London and New York: Cassell, 1999.

Siton, David. *The Sepharadic Communities in Our Times*. Jerusalem: Committee of the Sepharadic Community, 1982, Hebrew.

Vatikiotis, P.J. *The History of Egypt from Muhammad Ali to Sadat*. London: Weinfeld and Nicholson, 1980.

Weizman, Ezer. *The Battle for Peace*. Jerusalem: Idanim and Yediot Aharonot, 1981, Hebrew.

Ya'ari, Ehud and Haber, Eytan, and Schiff, Ze'ev. *The Year of the Dove*. Tel Aviv: Zmora-Bitan-Modan, 1980, Hebrew.

Articles and Research

Ben-Dor, Gabriel. "The Effect and Continuation of the Palestinian National Problem." In Eytan Gilboa and Mordechai Naor (eds.), *The Arab Israeli Conflict*. Tel Aviv: Ministry of Defense Publishing, 1987.

Bergman, Ronen. "Chasing the Nile's Treasures." *Ha'aretz Weekly Magazine*, January 26, 1996, 18–24, Hebrew.

——— "How Many Oil Barrels Equal the Katawi Family." *Ha'aretz Weekly Magazine*, December 15, 1995, 46–54, Hebrew.

——— *Raphael Bigio v. Coca-Cola*. *Ha'aretz Weekly Magazine*, July 16, 1999, 37–42, Hebrew.

Cohen, Arye. "The Continental 'Ha'apala' of Jews from Syria and Lebanon, 1939–1949." M.A thesis, Haifa University, 1997, Hebrew.

Gronold, K. "The Jewish Bankers in Iraq." *Hamizrah HeHadash* 11 (1961, Hebrew): 163–165.

Kazzaz, Nissim. "The Jews in Iraq during the Rule of General Abd al-Karim Qasim." *Pe'amim*, no. 71 (Spring 1997): Hebrew, 55–82.

Lagstein, Inbar. "The Egyptian Front." *Shtei Arim*, February 21, 1997, 38–41, Hebrew.

Laskier, Michael. "Egyptian Jewry under the Nasser Regime, 1956–70." *Middle Eastern Studies* 31, no. 3 (July 1995): 573–619.

Meir-Glizenstein, Esther. "The Riddle of the Mass Aliya from Iraq—Causes, Context and Results." *Pe'amim*, no. 71 (Spring 1997, Hebrew): 25–54.

Meron, Ya'akov. "The Deportation of Jews From Arab Countries and the Palestinian Approach Towards It." *Medina Mimshal ve-Yahasim Beinleumiyim*, no. 36. Jerusalem: The Hebrew University, Summer 1992, Hebrew, 27–56.

Raafat, Samir. "The House of Cicurel." *al-Ahram Weekly*, December 15, 1994.

Sarfaty, Rachel. "The Yedid Bequest: An Unusual Judaica Collection Finds Its Way to the Israel Museum." *The Israel Museum Journal* 27 (1999): 54–57.

Shalom, Zaki, "A Document from the Archive." *Pe'amim*, no. 71 (Spring 1997, Hebrew): 86–93.

State Comptroller. *Annual Report 49*. Jerusalem, 1999 (Hebrew).

"The Problem with the Cesil." *Business Today*, October 1999, 38.

United States Court of Appeals for the Second Circuit, file no. 98–9058 (*Bigio v. Coca-Cola*).

Zimhoni, Dafna. "The Iraqi Government and the Mass Immigration of Jews to Israel." *Pe'amim*, no. 39, 1989, Hebrew, 64–102.

Zohar, Zvi. "'Ha'apala' and 'Aliya Bet' from Syria in the Forties." *Pe'amim*, no. 66 (Winter 1996): Hebrew, 43–69.

Media

The Daily Telegraph
Globes (Hebrew)
Ha'aretz (Hebrew)
http://www.egy.com/
The Jewish Chronicle
Reuters

Other Sources

Knesset Minutes, meetings 349 and 356 of the 11th Knesset. Statement by the Knesset Committee for Foreign and Defense Affairs, November 18, 1975.

Index

Egypt, Israel, Iraq, Lebanon, and Syria are not included in the index, as they are the subject of this book, with numerous mentions throughout.

About the Author and Translator

ITAMAR LEVIN is Managing Editor of *Globes—Israel's Business Newspaper.* Since 1995, Levin has been the world's leading journalist in researching and reporting on the issue of Holocaust victims' assets. His previous publications include *The Last Deposit: Swiss Banks and Holocaust Victims' Accounts* (Praeger, 1999) and *His Majesty's Enemies: Britain's War Against Holocaust Victims and Survivors* (Praeger, 2001).

RACHEL NEIMAN is Managing Editor of *Israel's Business Arena* (Globes' English web site).